Reflections of a Country Doctor

First published by Dog Ear Publishing
4010 W. 86th Street, Ste H
Indianapolis, IN 46268
www.dogearpublishing.net

ISBN: 978-160844-199-0

This book is printed on acid-free paper.

Printed in the United States of America

Reflections of a Country Doctor

"The credit belongs to the man who is actually in the arena, whose face is marred by dust and sweat and blood, who strives valiantly, who errs and comes up short again and again, because there is no effort without error or shortcoming, but who knows the great enthusiasms, the great devotions, who spends himself for a worthy cause; who, at the best, knows, in the end, the triumph of high achievement, and who, at the worst, if he fails, at least he fails while daring greatly, so that his place shall never be with those cold and timid souls who knew neither victory nor defeat."

Theodore Roosevelt

"What are the rewards of so laborious a life?'

"They can not be measured, because there is no standard of comparison. To realize that one has devoted himself to the most holy of all callings, that without thought of reward he has alleviated the sufferings of the sick and added to the length and usefulness of human life, is a source of satisfaction money can not buy."

William J. Mayo

Contents

Acknowledgements

For years, I promised patients, colleagues, family and friends that I would write a book about my experiences as a rural family physician. Little did I realize that putting my experiences in medicine into a format that those outside of medicine could easily understand would be such a challenge.

I owe a debt of gratitude to a special group of individuals who read the text and offered editing suggestions along with constructive criticism.

I must thank Bridget Ashcraft for her critical evaluation of the text.

My gratitude toward the staff at Dog Ear Publishing who assisted me in this endeavor.

Finally, a big thank-you to my children, Jennifer, Rebecca, and David, who encouraged me to persevere and who provided valuable input about the content of the book and the cover design.

Author's Note

The stories in this book are true. I have done my best to portray the episodes as accurately as my memory would allow. To protect people's confidentiality, I have changed the names of most of the individuals, the patients, their families, and my colleagues. In a few instances, I changed minor details that might identify certain people or places.

This book is dedicated to my wife, Kay–

Without you none of this would have been possible

Prologue

During the summer before I started the seventh grade I took a course on athletic training and first aid. For me, the experience was earth changing. At the age of 12 I knew I wanted to be a good doctor some day. This idea became not my youthful fantasy but more my lifelong compulsion.

Upon graduating from high school in Billings, Montana, I received a small scholarship that allowed me to enroll at Eastern Montana College, a small local liberal arts school. I worked my way through college and was accepted at the University of Oregon Medical School.

Early in medical school, I decided that I wanted to be a "generalist" physician. With this in mind, I spent a majority of my free time over the next four years, and enhanced my experience and training, by participating in additional activities in obstetrics, newborn intensive care, cardiac and pulmonary intensive care, surgery, orthopedics, and the emergency room.

After completing more training in Spokane, Washington, I joined the National Health Service Corps and was assigned to a small town in Wyoming.

Upon leaving Wyoming, my family and I located to Sidney, Montana where we intended to stay just one year.

I closed my practice 25 years later.

An African proverb says, "It takes an entire village to raise a child." The same can be said of physicians. No one traverses the journey through medical training and private practice by themselves because "*the stars are aligned just right.*" The journey demands a considerable supportive effort from a village of many or perhaps many villages.

This book contains my reflections upon my 26 years as an "old time" generalist family physician in rural America. It is merely a collection of stories that depict some of my experiences over the years. The stories mirror those of many of my generalist colleagues who have experienced "the trenches" of rural primary care. In fact, on occasion, I introduced myself as nothing more than a full time "trenchologist."

My stories span the breadth and depth of the discipline of rural family medicine. Stories range from assisting mothers giving birth to caring for and comforting those at the end of life, from performing surgery to becoming involved in one's community, and from making house calls to providing emergency room care. Some are silly, some are sad, some are funny, and some may make you mad.

I have done my best to present events as accurately as possible. The individuals in the stories and all the people who allowed me the privilege of caring for them became the teachers in my village of many.

Hopefully, when my children and my grandchildren read these stories, they may better understand what dad or granddad did when he was younger. It may help my children understand why the phone always rang, why I missed so many meals at home, and why our family life was so often interrupted by the wants and the needs of others.

I hope you enjoy my journey through the complex, exhilarating, agonizing, enlightening, and fulfilling life of a rural family doc in the trenches.

THE START:

THE NATIONAL HEALTH SERVICE CORPS

"And so, my fellow Americans: ask not what your country can do for you - ask what you can do for your country."

John F. Kennedy

"There is hope in dreams, imagination, and in the courage of those who wish to make those dreams a reality."

Jonas Salk

"The young physician starts life with 20 drugs for each disease, and the old physician ends life with one drug for 20 diseases."

Sir William Osler

Off and Running

The State of Montana helped me finance my medical training at the University of Oregon Medical School through the W.I.C.H.E. (Western Interstate Commission for Higher Education) Program, a program for students from Western states that did not have medical schools. The student's home state governments would pay a significant amount of the tuition for their students to attend particular medical schools in western states. Unlike many other states, Montana did not require their students to repay the money given to the medical schools on their behalf. However, I had always planned on repaying the State of Montana in some way.

About halfway through my internship at the Sacred Heart Hospital in Spokane I decided to forego a residency in family medicine. I had visited multiple Family Practice training programs, and I did not think the training in the residency programs at the time was adequate, an opinion shared by many medical educators at the time. After spending a considerable amount of time with Dr. Ken Granite, the director of the Spokane family practice program, I decided to go into the National Health Service Corps. If I followed a planned program suggested by Dr. Granite, I would still be able to become board certified in family practice via an alternate pathway.

After I signed on with the National Health Service Corps, my wife, Kay, and I toured Montana and visited multiple Health Service Corps sites. Initially, I selected Roundup, Montana where I would be working with a Dr. Cervantes. I made arrangements to start working in Roundup the week after my internship had ended. Unfortunately, I the National Health Service Corps office called me about two weeks before the end of my training program and informed me that the Roundup hospital no longer wanted my services. Interestingly, Dr. Cervantes called me the very same day and asked me when I was going to show up for work. (Obviously, the community was having some internal problems.) I learned later that Dr. Cervantes left Roundup within several weeks.

I was in a panic for about 24 hours. Then, the director of the National Health Service Corps in Denver called me to ask if I would consider going to Wyoming with a physician who was training in California. This physician had lost his NHSC partner for a small town Corps site in Wyoming. The director told me that the physician's name was William R. Berryman, M.D.

Bill Berryman was one of my classmates in medical school; I knew my dilemma was solved. I called Bill that evening in California.

Bill said he was going to Lusk in the southeastern corner of Wyoming.

I asked what was going on in Lusk, Wyoming?

Bill replied, "Not much. There are no freeways."

I said something like, "That sounds good to me. When do we go?

After my internship concluded, Kay, my daughter, Jennifer, and I packed up a U-Haul trailer connected to our Ford Mustang and headed to Wyoming.

We arrived in Lusk, Wyoming about a week before the Berryman clan. The people in Lusk assured us that everything would be ready for us when we arrived, and the two current National Health Service Corps physicians would remain in the community for at least a week or so while we got settled. They promised us that our housing was ready.

Upon our arrival, we found out that the two previous physicians had left town several days before, and neither the physicians nor the hospital had arranged for medical coverage during the transition. Additionally, the community did not secure housing for us. Consequently, my family and I spent our first night in Lusk, Wyoming in a local motel. (It amazed us what people would say and do to get someone to move to a small community.)

The following morning, Kay and I were told we could move into a summer home on a ranch just a few miles north of town. After I got some things arranged in the hospital and in the clinic, we made our way out into the country to our little cottage and arrived in late afternoon. *The place was full of dead mice and moths.* We could handle one only night in this place.

The next morning we moved back into another motel.

About 3 a.m. during our first night in the new motel, there was a knock at our door. I arose and opened the door slightly to find, standing in front of me, an intoxicated man who was complaining of a sore belly. He had gone to the emergency room for help, but the nurse on duty told him that, "The new doctor does not have a phone yet." (Actually, this meant that the motel turned off its phones at midnight.) The nurse, therefore, sent him to my motel room!

I was beyond annoyed. However, I suggested to the man that he return to the hospital, ask the nurse for some antacids, and lie down in the emergency room until it was time for him to go to work. Amazingly, the man did just as I suggested.

Later that same morning, I ventured over to the hospital to lay down a few ground rules for my being "on call".

My family and I spent the remainder of our first week in Lusk in one of the local motels.

Dr. Berryman had relatives in the area that arranged to have a rental home readied for them.

After the Berryman's arrived, we discussed our housing dilemmas. We moved in with the Berrymans.

The people in Lusk thought the West Coast docs had started a commune! We were the talk of the town.

Eventually, Kay and I rented a home on South Diamond Street on the southwest edge of town where we remained for the rest of our time in Lusk.

Teaching and Training

For me, joining the National Health Service Corps (NHSC) was an easy choice. Most medical school graduates believe they're Rambo and can do almost anything with their medical training. I was no different. However, once reality set in, a little bit of panic set in. I had just completed one of the last "iron man" internships with comprehensive training in many disciplines; I cared for many high-risk patients. But I always had a backup.

I asked myself, "Do I know enough? How will I do in the real world?"

I concluded that responsibility was *highly overrated.*

Dr. Bill Berryman came from a training program in internal medicine only. He did not like babies, surgery, bones, or pregnant women. He too was anxious.

Here we were, two young GMO's (general medicine officers) in a small town with minimal backup except ourselves. How would we do? "Just fine thank-you," we thought.

Bill and I complimented each other well. I should say he complimented my deficiencies very well. I had a real life, flesh and blood, walking and talking encyclopedia of medicine at my fingertips. What a luxury! I would learn more from Bill in the next few months and years than I could ever pay for in classes. He was a tremendous teacher for everybody and me. I owe him a perpetual debt of gratitude.

Bill and I discussed our plan of action soon after we arrived in Lusk. Unlike the previous physicians, we planned to care for as many people in Lusk as we could. Remembering the suggestions of Dr. Gudgel in Spokane regarding my training for the Board exams, I made arrangements with a surgeon in Scotts Bluff, Nebraska, to perform surgery in our hospital once a month. In return, I helped him in Scotts Bluff one day a month. I made similar liaisons with the orthopedic group in Scotts Bluff. Kay Breckinridge, an attractive blonde obstetrician in Torrington, Wyoming agreed to provide my obstetric backup. Since we did not have routine anesthesia services in our community, Torrington was the closest for obstetrical emergencies and operations. A pathologist came up from Cheyenne once every two months. An urologist and a cardiologist from Casper routinely visited our hospital as consultants.

Soon, Bill and I became acutely aware of substantial deficiencies with the training of our hospital personnel. I guessed that this might have been the reason the previous docs used to transfer most of their ill patients. Anyway, as Dr. Bill would say, "We're going to bring these people screaming and hollering into the twentieth century!" So we were going to try.

We started courses in reading electrocardiograms, Intensive Care Unit (ICU) care, and trauma care. We trained the staff in cardiopulmonary resuscitation (CPR). With surgery being done, I had an ongoing course in postoperative management, intravenous (IV) fluids, pain management, and so on. We taught everybody and anybody who would listen. Dr. Bill and/or I made hospital rounds morning, noon, and night to keep a close watch on our patients and our students. We made ourselves available 24/7 (24 hours a day and seven days a week).

This effort required more work than my training programs, but it was a lot more fun and challenging.

Our educational efforts in Lusk, Wyoming proved beneficial to our co-workers and our patients in a short period of time. These efforts were the beginning of lifelong commitments for both of us to teach others.

Another Heart Spell

This weekend, Kay, our daughter, Jennifer, and I had just settled in at a local motel when I received a call from the switchboard operator; she said was transferring a call from the hospital. The person on the phone identified herself as the emergency room nurse. She said that I was the only doctor in town and that she had received a call for help from a local resident. The ambulance driver was not available for a few hours; she wondered if I could visit the lady at her home. The nurse told me that the lady had a long history of heart disease and was having some breathing trouble.

I advised the nurse that I did not yet have my Wyoming license.

She responded, "But you're the only one in town!"

I consented to go; I asked the lady's address.

The nurse told me the lady's address, but then followed up with, "Our homes in town don't have numbers. You just have to know where to go."

I then said, "O.K. Just tell me how to get there."

The nurse instructed me to go to the light green house on Oak Street. She said I couldn't miss it because it was next to a pink house.

I advised the nurse that I had a color deficiency, and I did not see green and red colors well. I asked how else I could find the home.

The nurse informed me that the house had a big tree in the front yard.

I had not been in Lusk long, but it seemed that *every house* had a big tree in the yard. I asked, "What else could I look for?"

The nurse asked me to hold on the phone while she found someone who could give me better instructions. Soon, a male voice came on the phone and said, "You can't miss the house. It has an old International Harvester tandem axle truck parked across the street in front of a bright yellow house." He then gave me detailed instructions on how I could get to the yellow house, which I wrote down.

I hopped into our Mustang and set out with my doctor bag in hand. I arrived at the yellow house in short order, made the appropriate deductions regarding which house to pick, and walked up to the chosen home. When I knocked at the door, I heard a weak voice ask me to come in.

Inside the home I found a woman I guessed to be about 60-years-old who was having a lot of trouble breathing. Gasping for air, she told me that she was having another heart attack. She complained of bad pains in her chest (she clenched her fist between her breasts), and trouble breathing.

I took the lady's blood pressure and pulse, which were normal. Her respiratory rate was about 40. (It should be 12-15.) She was sweaty, and her clothes were wet. Using my stethoscope, I heard no air movement in her lungs on my brief examination. I decided that this woman needed to be in the hospital ASAP. Not knowing the status of the ambulance in this little town, I told the lady that I would get her to the hospital.

The two of us made our way to the new ambulance in town, my Ford Mustang.

Upon arriving at the emergency room, the nurse who had called me greeted us. Our introductions were brusque at best because I thought the lady needed my attention now! I started some oxygen and performed an EKG (electrocardiogram or heart tracing). The EKG looked normal to me. "This woman supposedly had a history of multiple heart attacks?" I thought to myself.

I had the nurse get some albuterol (a respiratory drug) for a nebulizer treatment and administer it to the patient while I inserted an IV (intravenous catheter) and obtained some blood for analysis. (The lab tech lived out of town, but the nurse assured me that he was coming.) I wanted to do an arterial blood gas to see how the patient's lungs were working, but I had to wait until the lab tech arrived.

After a few minutes with the nebulizer treatment, my lady's breathing improved markedly. Air movement had returned to her lungs. She was now able to talk in more than just a few syllables without gasping for air. However, her "*chest pain*" persisted.

The woman said she liked to be called Mattie (short for Matilda).

After a more thorough examination, I determined the pain to be in the upper abdomen and not in the chest. I obtained a sample of stool that tested positive for blood.

By now Mattie appeared markedly better and told us that she had not been able to breathe this good for as long as she could remember.

I thought to myself, "Hell's Bells! This lady has asthma and an ulcer, not heart disease".

I had the nurse prepare and give Mattie a "GI cocktail," a combination of an antacid, a local anesthetic, and an antispasmodic. Mattie's abdominal pain resolved within moments of drinking my potion. The nurse, Mattie, and I were all impressed with the results of these simple treatments.

When things had quieted down and my patient was dramatically improved, I spent some time taking a history. It seemed that Mattie had been seeing the "old family doc" in another town. He apparently made the heart disease diagnosis without any testing, such as an electrocardiogram. The older physician had never tested her for asthma despite her lifelong problems with "allergies" and "trouble coughing at night" (common findings in asthmatics). Mattie told me that she had been home bound for several years because of her "heart failure."

I kept Mattie in the hospital for almost a week for lung and stomach treatments, observation, and education. All her tests for an acute heart attack were negative. I could not determine whether or not my patient had suffered a small heart attack in the past. However, now I was convinced that her breathing troubles were caused by untreated asthma, not "heart failure".

I released the Mattie from the hospital with a regimen of antacids, a few days of oral cortisone, and some inhaled asthma medications. Her heart medicines were stopped.

I asked Mattie to visit me in the clinic in a week or so. If she had issues, I told her that I knew where she lived.

Mattie came to the clinic a week later as I had requested. She walked all eight blocks!

The Ballgame

I had always thought that I wanted to practice general medicine in a small community "a la" Marcus Welby, M.D. Lusk was indeed a small town with all the idiosyncrasies. I soon found out that people thought they knew everything—*before it happened.* Confidentiality was a foreign concept. Privacy was an obscure notion. The man down the street in the grocery store thought he knew what was discussed in my clinic just minutes before.

Chuck and Dave were the two NHSC physicians who preceded us in Lusk. They had been well trained and came from quality training programs. However, it became apparent to me my first day in Lusk that these two physicians had used their time in Wyoming as a prolonged vacation instead of furthering their careers. I learned that they cared for few people in the hospital. To the dismay of the hospital board and the administrator who were trying desperately to keep their small facility afloat, 85 percent of the emergency room patients seen by these physicians at the Lusk hospital that required hospitalization were transferred out to other hospitals. In addition, I did ascertain that this duo was pretty good at socializing by arranging ski trips, community events, outdoor activities, and ball games.

The town now had two new young physicians and their families from the West who were living together in Lusk, Wyoming. The townspeople wondered, "How could these two be better than our beloved pair that had just left? Were these new guys any good?"

Dr. Bill and I and our families were the talk of the town.

The first few weeks in Lusk were uncomfortable for me. The people were standoffish. Almost daily someone reminded me "how good" the two previous physicians had been. The clinic had few scheduled patients. Dr. Bill and I spent a lot of time reading. Along with our housing concerns, we were having a little lot of trouble settling in smoothly.

Then one day, our families, Bill, and I were invited to play in a community pickup softball game on the coming weekend. We thought this should be a good icebreaker for us with the community. We accepted the invitation.

On Saturday the participants gathered at the ball field. Bill and I were on the *other team.* Kermit Adkins headed up the #1 team. I am not sure our team had a leader! Kermit Adkins was a tall thin man who looked quite fit. He was quiet and did not say much. I was told that Kermit was the town's universal guy, the super fixer, the jack of all trades, an ambulance driver, and, by reputation, the best pitcher in the county.

As I recall, one of the ladies on our team was our pitcher.

Bill got to play shortstop because of his prior experience as a youth. I was assigned to play first base because I was tall. Bill was selected to bat #5; I was put in the #6 slot on the roster.

The first inning produced no runs for the Adkins team. Bill ended the first inning making quite a good play at shortstop to prevent a hit.

On our team's first at-bat in the bottom half of the inning, we were three up and three down, two by strike out.

In the second inning, the Adkins team leadoff player hit a single. The next batter, however, hit the ball to Bill who threw to second base for an out and then on to first base for a double play. Batter three hit a fly ball that was caught by our right fielder.

In the bottom of the second inning, our first batter struck out. The crowd was really getting into the game by now and encouraging Kermit to strike out another batter. Bill came to the plate and promptly swung and missed for strike one. The crowd was becoming loud and yelled with approval.

Bill crushed the next pitch. After two bounces, the ball landed at the base of the centerfield fence. Bill had a double.

I came to the plate with Bill on second with one out. I fouled off the first pitch. Kermit's second pitch was high and inside; I hit the ball squarely with a loud crack. It sailed over the fence at the 300-foot marker for a home run! (Later I was told that Kermit had not allowed a home run in years.)

Neither Bill nor I received another good pitch from Kermit the rest of the game. We each managed to get singles, but nothing more. The *other team,* our team, won the game.

Once again, Bill and I and our families became the talk of the town.

Our clinic was booked full the next week. The town's folks now wanted to visit with the new docs who could play softball. (Maybe they wanted to see if we were O.K. doctors too.)

Kermit Adkins turned out to be a wonderful guy and a marvelous handyman. We would need his services more than once during our stay in Lusk

Double Excitement

Dr. Bill Berryman was an internal medicine specialist. He really did not like to do anything that would be bloody. He refused to do surgical procedures in the operating room. Reluctantly, he sutured a small laceration or applied a splint to an injured extremity. Dr. Bill *really* did not like obstetrics. He did not like newborn care. Since we were both general medical officers in this small community, patients naturally expected both of us to perform the full spectrum of general practice. This placed Dr. Bill in some interesting and difficult situations.

One day I was asked to come to the hospital emergency room to see a pregnant lady in labor. The patient was at term with her first baby. I had not seen this young lady, and she had had no prenatal care. When I examined the patient, I found the baby to be in a frank breech presentation. Good obstetrical care at the time mandated that a first time pregnancy with a breech presentation have a Cesarean section (C-section).

I gave the young lady my explanation of what I thought was appropriate. Since we did not have anesthesia services on staff at the hospital, I advised the patient that it would be prudent to transfer her fifty miles away to the Torrington hospital where the local obstetrician and I could perform a C- section.

The patient refused!

She told us that all of her family had delivered in the Lusk hospital, that having a baby was a natural process, and that she was going nowhere!

I was in a quandary. I wondered to myself, "Now, what should I do?"

Since the patient was not about to go anywhere, it became apparent to me that the breech delivery was going to occur in the Lusk hospital; whatever the consequences would be, I had to deal with them. I knew we would need some type of anesthesia, but a spinal anesthetic was out of the question because the mother would be unable to push. I called the anesthetist in Torrington who was not available to drive to Lusk that evening.

A nurse overheard my thinking out loud and told me that the local hospital administrator had been an anesthetist at Cook County Hospital in Chicago. Promptly, I called the hospital administrator, and after confirming her experience, asked her to come to the hospital as soon as possible.

I then called Dr. Berryman for his assistance; there was silence on the other end of the phone. Dr. Bill said, "Are you putting me on? I was just about to have a Chevas on the rocks." When I reassured him that I was not making a joke, he said he'd be right up.

Dr. Berryman arrived before the hospital administrator. By now, the pregnant woman was in the throes of strong labor, and her cervix was dilated to a diameter of about 7 centimeters. (About 10 centimeters is fully dilated.) I discussed with Dr. Berryman the maneuvers for delivering a breech baby and how he could assist me.

We also discussed the possibility that the baby may need to be resuscitated. I told Dr. Bill that I had been unable to find any pediatric resuscitation equipment; apparently, it had been thrown away!

About this time the hospital administrator arrived. She advised us that she was not an anesthetist, but she had administered some anesthesia during a two-week training session at Cook County Hospital. I figured this was as good as it was going to get, so I asked the administrator to get ready.

She then went into an adjacent room to check out the anesthesia equipment. Soon thereafter we heard a loud thud coming from the anesthesia room. Our "anesthetist" had opened the valve of an anesthesia gas canister and had taken a few deep breaths to see if any gas was present. She was out for the count.

All the while, I had been keeping my patient informed of the activities around her. I advised her that it looked like she would have to settle for only a local anesthetic. By now, she just wanted to have the baby out of her!

When the time for the delivery came, the nurses took the lady to the delivery room. She moved onto the delivery room table, and I administered a local anesthetic. While we were waiting for analgesia to occur, I could hear Dr. Berryman behind me pacing and whistling. (I learned that whenever Dr. Bill was nervous, he paced and whistled as he concentrated deeply.)

Dr. Bill and I helped this lady deliver a 9-pound breech infant! The baby came out somewhat stunned and required some respiratory resuscitation. Since I had to take care of the mother and repair the vaginal lacerations that had been made, Dr. Berryman had to resuscitate the baby. Since there was no infant ambu bag, Dr. Bill had to administer mouth-to-mouth resuscitation to a slimy, slippery, vernix coated newborn.

He did a great job! The baby cried vigorously after only a few puffs from Dr. Berryman. Dr. Bill, however, was a sight to behold. His handlebar mustache and his large sideburns were coated and saturated with baby goo.

Bill remarked, "I think I'll need a double tonight."

As Bill was finishing with cleaning up the baby and I was suturing the mother's episiotomy, a nurse came into the room and told us that a pregnant lady had just arrived in the emergency room. The nurse said, "The lady *might be in labor.*"

Since Dr. Bill was free from his duties with the baby, I asked him to evaluate the new patient.

His comment was, "I don't do pregnant women!"

I gave him he the choice of suturing the lady's bottom or doing a pelvic exam. For Dr. Bill, neither choice was not good a good one. He elected to perform the pelvic examination.

He left the room and returned about 60 seconds later. He had sweat on his forehead, and his eyes were as big as saucers. I asked him, "What did you find?"

His reply was, "Its right there!" With this statement he showed me his two fingers and pointed to where the presenting part of the baby was. He said, "It is REALLY hard, and it is RIGHT THERE!"

I asked if the lady was having any pain.

The reply was, "Not a damn one."

I asked how many babies the woman had delivered. The nurse replied, "She's a primip." (Primip stands for a woman with her first pregnancy.) I figured I had a little bit of time to take care of the lady who had just delivered before I examined our new patient.

After I completed the episiotomy repair and arranged for our first time mother to be monitored in a postpartum room, I went to evaluate our second patient. Indeed, the baby's head was *right there.* By now, the baby's head could be easily seen, and the mom-to-be was ready to give birth—without any pain!

The mother was positioned on the delivery table; I asked to push when she felt a contraction or pain. We observed her abdomen going up and down with contractions, but the she never pushed. She did not feel a thing!

Bill said, "What the heck is this?" He then started to pace and to whistle.

The Hospital had an old-time unicorn type fetoscope, which had been discovered after our first baby had been delivered. One of the nurses listened to the baby's heart rate after a contraction and noted that the baby's heart rate was dropping into the 80s range. (The normal fetal heart rate is 100-140.) To say the least, this finding was not terribly reassuring to me. Therefore, I had Bill feel the mother's abdomen and tell us when the uterus got hard with a contraction.

When a contraction started and at Dr. Bill's prompting, the lady pushed as hard as she could. She was in excellent physical condition and proved to be a powerful pusher. After each push she would rise up and look in between her legs to see the progress she was making. At no time did she tell us that she felt any contractions or had any discomfort!

After pushing just a short time, the mom delivered an 8-pound, 4-ounce baby with excellent evaluation scores. This first-time mom did not sustain a single superficial skin tear.

After both mothers and their babies were settled in for the night, Dr. Berryman exclaimed, "What a night! It's time for a Chevas on the rocks. In fact, tonight deserves a double, maybe a triple!"

Indeed, the night had a double thrilling adventure for all of us at the hospital.

The hospital administrator, by the way, finally woke up and just went home to bed.

The Hunter

One fall day as I was working in the clinic, one of our front office personnel came back to my office in the rear of the clinic and asked me if I could smell a terrible odor. She thought something must have died in the clinic overnight.

I admitted that I did not and, after concentrating some, could not smell anything unusual.

Indeed, my receptionist agreed that my office had no odor. We concluded the smell had to be coming from the front end of the building.

About this time, a young man entered our clinic complaining of a severe headache that he had had for two days. He told me that he was not predisposed to having headaches so he thought that he should seek some medical attention before starting back to his home on the East coast.

This fellow went on to tell me that he was from New York and that he had been out in our area hunting. (Eastern Wyoming is renowned for its antelope hunting in the fall.) He told me that he had bagged a really nice deer a couple of days before. He planned to have the animal stuffed when he got it back to New York. However, for now, he badly needed something for his headache so he could drive home.

After I examined this man and determined that he probably had a significant muscle contraction headache, I prescribed some aspirin and acetaminophen. I told him that anything stronger might interfere with his driving.

Feeling relieved - or bored - with me, the fellow got up to depart the exam room. He then asked if I would like to see the deer he shot.

I certainly obliged since this fellow was quite proud of his hunting achievement in the wilds of Wyoming.

As we went outside the clinic, the young man's parked his car was parked right in front of our building. On this warm fall day, the smell was almost unbearable. Strapped to the front of this man's car, right in front of the radiator, was his "deer". This "hunter" had not gutted and dressed out the animal in the field after he shot it several days before. Therefore, with the heat of the car engine and the hot fall sun working on it, the carcass was rotting within itself.

The young man proudly discussed with me the quality of the animal he had shot, and then he was off.

I didn't have the heart to tell this young hunter that his prized deer was really a *coyote*. However, I was sure someone would give him the bad news before he got back to New York

Coal man

Along with the fall equinox comes the annual hunting season in eastern Wyoming. Since Lusk was smack dab in the middle of the western high plains and antelope were everywhere, our area became a prime destination for hunters from all over the country. For about six to eight weeks in the fall, the large influx of hunters increased the population of the Niobrara County by three- to four-fold. This was quite a good thing for the struggling economy of our small town. Additionally, this hunting activity generated a burst of activity for our hospital emergency room. The associated revenues assisted our financially challenged hospital.

On a Saturday during the early stages of the "fall experience," I was summoned to the emergency room (ER) about 8 p.m. to evaluate an eye injury. The patient was a 55-year-old man named Jefferson Coleman.

Mr. Coleman said he was an engineer executive for a large coal-mining corporation in Pennsylvania who had never been out of Pennsylvania. To commemorate his thirty years with the firm *and* his birthday, his family and his employer arranged a hunting vacation to Wyoming as a gift. The trip consisted of two weeks of hunting in Wyoming and Montana with guides to insure his success. The company had supplied a refrigerated semi-truck to keep the wild game carcasses cool to minimize spoilage so that they could be transported back to Pennsylvania for a taxidermist to process. Whatever he killed would be mounted on a trophy wall in his office. Additionally, Mr. Coleman had received as a gift a brand new customized Remington rifle. The rifle had his name imprinted on the cartridge chamber housing; the polished wooden butt of the gun was engraved with pictures of wildlife. This magnificent rifle was topped with a high power scope.

Unfortunately, Mr. Coleman had never fired a high-powered rifle. Additionally, he had never fired a gun while looking through a scope. In preparation for the next day's hunt, Mr. Coleman and his friends decided to "sight in" their guns with a bit of target practice before the sun set. By his own admission, Jefferson said, "I pressed my eye against the scope and fired."

His friends reported that the recoil of the rifle against his face flipped Jefferson over backwards. When Jefferson stood up, he was hemorrhaging profusely about the right eye. A pressure bandage to the face and a trip to the ER curtailed his first "sighting in" experience.

Fortunately, Mr. Coleman sustained merely a superficial laceration. The cut was a near perfect half circle around the top of his right eye. After I sutured the wound, Mr. Coleman's face reminded me of the dog with The Little Rascals, the one with the black ring around his eye. I asked my patient to see me again in the morning so I could make sure his eye was uninjured.

Mr. Coleman returned to the ER about noon the next day. Except for the entire right side of his face being bruised and a dark ring around his right eye, he was in good shape for hunting. Jefferson Coleman's big adventure would begin at first light in the morning.

About 10 a.m. the next morning, my nurse, Marilyn, gave me a message to report to the ER for "a hunting mishap."

I wondered out loud, "What the heck is a "hunting mishap? Is it a bloody nose, a sprained ankle, a gunshot wound? What?"

Marilyn didn't have a clue.

Since I was not told to go immediately, I finished caring for a patient before I drove to the ER.

To my dismay, Jefferson Coleman was sitting in a chair in the emergency room with a sling on his arm. I queried, "What happened this time?"

He retorted, "You're not going to believe this, Doc."

I replied, "Try me anyway, O.K.?"

Mr. Coleman told me how the hunting party of six men had arisen at 3:30 a.m. that morning to drive to the prime hunting location some 40 miles out in the country under the cloak of darkness. Two hunters were in the pickup cab. Four others were in the box. Just before sunrise, the guide located a herd of antelope with his spotting scope and started to maneuver his pickup downwind of the herd so the animals would not smell them.

Jefferson figured that the pickup was traveling about 30 miles per hour cross country when all of a sudden a "whole bunch of critters was right there!" In his exuberance, Mr. Coleman stood up near the tailgate, the pickup hit a bump, and the next thing he knew his compatriots were asking him what day it was. Now he was in the ER again!

Mr. Coleman sustained a fracture of his left radius (forearm) that I realigned and encased in a plaster cast. I advised him he would have to wait a few days before he went hunting again.

The patient responded, "Longer than you might think, Doc."

I asked, "What do you mean?"

Jefferson's response was, "My gun." which he said with a most depressed look.

The worst part of the episode was that during the fall Mr. Coleman landed on his custom made Remington rifle and snapped it in half.

I saw Mr. Coleman a few days later getting ready to mount his refrigerated semi truck with his casted left arm in a sling. I asked, "Goin' home today?"

"Nope," he asserted, "before I go home I'm headed due north to the Rocky Mountains in eastern Montana to shoot an elk, a bear, a goat, and a sheep." And off he went in his semi-truck to the mountains of eastern Montana.

I didn't have the heart to tell him the Rocky Mountains were in western Montana, 400 miles farther west.

Panic

One afternoon before Thanksgiving in 1975 a pair of newlyweds presented themselves to our clinic in Lusk. The fellow came from a town of several hundred people in Nevada; the wife grew up in Detroit along with several million people. The husband enjoyed the wide-open spaces; the wife enjoyed the excitement of the big city. The two met in Las Vegas, fell in love, and were married Las Vegas style: a preacher, two witnesses, and a five-minute service.

After their wedding, the pair traveled to the groom's hometown to inform his parents of his big step and to have them meet their new daughter-in-law. All went well in Nevada; so after a few days the twosome decided it was time to show off the groom to the bride's relatives in Michigan.

Instead of traveling the interstate highways from Nevada to Texas and then to Michigan, the husband decided to journey along state roads through the desolate parts of southern Nevada, Utah, Wyoming, and South Dakota so his bride could learn to appreciate his love of the wide-open spaces (so he thought).

The pair had started out the day in the southern Utah desert in the morning and ventured up to Green River, Wyoming by way of the back roads. At Green River, they encountered a blizzard, poor visibility, and a sparsely occupied freeway. The blizzard intensified as they journeyed eastward. Somewhere around Laramie, the wife became hysterical as they drove through a totally isolated area in the blizzard.

By the time the pair arrived in Cheyenne, the storm had subsided, but the wife was no better. As they turned north along the Wyoming-Nebraska state lines, she became convinced that nobody lived in this God forsaken country and that she was going to die of exposure on a lonely desolate road in the middle of nowhere. She needed to be around some people!

When the duo pulled into Lusk, the wife was a "looney-toon out of tune." She was paranoid, agitated, and delirious. The husband wanted to know how far it was to the next "big city".

When I inquired as to what he meant by big, he exclaimed, "At least a million people!" (Twice the population of Wyoming).

Our receptionist said, "Hey, Bucko, you're talking about Minneapolis."

He asked her, "How far is it?"

She replied, "A day and a half straight through."

In dismay, he said, "God, I'll never make it. She is going nuts on me!"

After looking at his young wife, Dr. Berryman and I reassured the fellow that his wife was having nothing more than a panic attack. She was getting anxious about having nobody around just like he got anxious in crowds and big cities.

We concluded that the wife would benefit from a large dose of people and a small dose of a sedative. We "neutralized" the wife in the office with some medication; we gave the husband a prescription for Valium and directions on how to get to Minnesota.

We all wished him well.

We told the husband that after he got to Detroit and mingled with its millions, he may need to take some of his wife's Valium.

Uneventful Procedure

Delores was a 56-year-old secretary at one of the local businesses. Previously, I had seen her several times in the clinic for hip pain. She had been born with a congenital hip dislocation that was not detected until later in her childhood. Consequently, she had a deformed arthritic hip associated with a substantial loss of motion at the hip. She walked with a limp and occasionally needed a cane when her hip pain was severe.

My wife and I visited with her one weekend in the local grocery store. Delores wanted to ask me about a "new problem" she had developed. Since I did not want to discuss her private issues in public, I encouraged her to call for an appointment on the next Monday. I advised her that I would leave a message for the clinic receptionist to get her in as soon as possible. Afterward, I walked to the clinic, which was only a few blocks away, and left a note for my receptionist.

A few days later Delores came in to see me. She related that her "new problem" was bleeding, the feminine kind. She had not had a menstrual period for at least three or four years. She had experienced symptoms of menopause for about five years. Delores told me that she had been spotting daily for almost two months. She was annoyed, anxious, and fearful of what this meant. When Delores was a child her, mother had died of "uterine cancer".

On this day my examination of Delores was not remarkable from a gynecologic standpoint. Obtaining a specimen from her uterus for a PAP test was a challenge because of her immobile hips. On the PAP request form I wrote, "postmenopausal bleeding."

I advised Delores that we would proceed further after I got the report back.

About a week passed before the report returned. The pathologist reported some "adenomatous changes" and "atrophic changes consistent with estrogen deficiency." It further said, "Clinical correlation needed," and "biopsy was not discouraged."

The pathologist and I both knew that vaginal bleeding in a menopausal female was "cancer until proven otherwise." Therefore, a sample of tissue from the uterus should be obtained.

When I met with Delores again, we discussed the PAP report. I encouraged her to consider having a D&C so we could get a definitive answer for her bleeding.

Delores had spent almost two months worrying, and she needed no more time to think. She wanted the surgery as soon as possible.

Surgery in our small hospital was a major scheduling event. An anesthetist had to be scheduled to come in. An extra nurse was needed to assist in the operating room. (We only had a couple of nurses.) I made all the arrangements; I figured fewer minds made fewer mistakes. I was able to schedule the procedure for the next week.

The morning of surgery was unremarkable; in fact, it was markedly uneventful considering all the folks involved. Dave Alderson, an experienced anesthetist, arrived early and in plenty of time to prepare for surgery and to insert an intravenous line into Delores. I checked over the surgical supplies and the instruments. I then double-checked them with Meredith, the hospital's head nurse, who was going to be my surgical assistant. Meredith informed me that she had been a part of "many surgeries" when two previous physicians practiced in Lusk a few years back.

By 8 a.m. we were ready to go.

I assisted Delores onto the operating table. While Dave gave our patient some oxygen, I donned my surgical gown and gloves.

Delores complained of hip pain as Meredith and I attempted to put her contracted legs into the gynecology stirrups.

Dave asked us to wait a minute while he gave her "something" for pain.

Within moments Delores was sleepy and in no distress.

After our patient was in the correct position on the surgical table and was covered with sterile drapes, I asked Meredith to hand me a speculum. Nothing happened. As I looked to my left, I saw my glassy-eyed nurse drop to the floor like a stone.

I was a bit unnerved to say the least. Anxiously, I thought to myself, "Now I have *two* patients! Which one takes priority? Should I abort the procedure?"

However, within moments, Dave was on the floor tending to Meredith. Soon from beneath the table I heard Dave's voice say, "I'm fine. The patient is fine. Our new patient is fine and resting comfortably. Doctor, if you are fine, please proceed with the operation."

The procedure required a short time to complete. Afterward, Dave revived Delores without incident, and the two of us transferred her to a gurney for the journey back to a hospital room.

Meredith remained somnolent on the floor until Dave patted her on the cheek and asked her to wake up. Then we placed her on a gurney and sent her to a room.

Afterward, as Dave and I were cleaning up the operating room, he said to me, "Doc, nice case. I think your assistant is drunk."

I was incredulous. "How could I miss that?" I thought.

Before I could speak, Dave said, "Its hard to smell booze through a mask."

Delores did well. Her tissue pathology report revealed only non-cancerous findings. She and a lot of her family and friends were relieved.

I reported Meredith to the hospital administrator who knew of her "problem," but said in her defense, "She had been doing so well."

Meredith was suspended pending "the cure."

The anesthetist documented in the chart an "uneventful procedure".

Turn up the heat

Dr. Bill Berryman had admitted a man in his 70's for an acute myocardial infarction (heart attack). Soon after admission, the gentleman developed a heart arrhythmia, which was not an uncommon complication. Additionally, the man's heart failed to pump adequately. These new problems required resuscitation with copious fluids and medications. Dr. Berryman managed these problems expertly, as usual. The man's condition stabilized over the course of a few hours; his patient then required vigilant observation.

Within a few hours Dr. Bill's patient had another "episode" associated with a cardiac arrest. Fortunately, Bill and I were in the hospital to direct and coordinate the resuscitation efforts. Again, the fellow survived our chemical and fluid assault upon his body.

After the man's blood pressure and other vital signs stabilized, our examinations revealed substantial fluid in his lungs. While reviewing the chart regarding the resuscitation, Dr. Bill noted that the patient had been given a large quantity of IV fluid; consequently, the primary reason for the fluid buildup in the man's lungs became obvious to us.

We thought a small dose of a diuretic should take care of this problem easily. We gave the man some Lasix. (Dr. Bill always said you could give enough Lasix "to make a rock pee.") He did not pee. He received more Lasix. Still, he did not pee. Finally, he received 400 mg of Lasix, 10-20 times the usual dose. The catheter bag contained only 10 cc (two teaspoons) of urine. Dr. Bill remarked, "Nothing but bladder sweat!"

By now, some lab reports returned for our review. On admission, our gentleman had normal kidney function tests. Now, after two episodes of low blood pressure and resuscitation efforts, his kidneys showed signs of failure. (Acute kidney failure is not uncommon with hypotension insults.) We knew that injured kidneys frequently undergo a "low output" phase, then a "high output," and finally normalize as the injury heals.

Our problem was that our patient needed water, a lot of water, out of his lungs. The kidneys are the body's water spigots, and they were shut off.

Conservative care of kidney failure includes minimizing fluid intake, maintaining blood pressure with medicine, and *patience*. We tried this for a day, but our efforts were fruitless. Besides, the man's heart failure worsened, and his breathing became more labored.

We thought our patient needed kidney dialysis. Bill discussed the case with our regional nephrologist who agreed with our assessment. Bill and I agreed that we should transfer our patient to a hospital with dialysis capabilities ASAP (as soon as possible).

Together Bill and I visited our patient to explain his and our dilemma. (I thought our discussion was most convincing.)

The patient emphatically said, "No!"

He pointed out that if it was his time to go, then so be it. He was not going to spend every penny he ever earned to become a pincushion for some doctors. He would not leave our hospital.

Bill and I were taken aback. I had not experienced a patient refusing to be transferred. Bill, however, WAS NOT going to let this stubborn old guy die on his watch.

We sat down and brainstormed ideas to make this guy better. We discussed drugs, physiology, blood letting, and anything else we could remember, or think of, that might have an effect on fluid balance and a failing heart.

We concluded (hoped) that if we could remove enough fluid, a lot of fluid, then over time the kidneys would heal and correct the problems naturally. Our dilemma became, "How do we do it?"

While we were in the ICU room, it occurred to us to "just turn up the heat." So we did. Unfortunately, it was summer, and the air conditioning was on. We could not get the room temperature above 74 degrees; we knew more heat was needed. Besides, our patient had developed increased difficulty breathing, AND maintaining his blood pressure had become a challenge.

I said to Bill, "Let's ask Kermit. Maybe he can help us."

Kermit Adkins was the hospital's maintenance man, Mr. Fix-it, and all around wizard. Bill thought it couldn't hurt to ask him.

After discussing our heating dilemma with Kermit, he asked us to give him a few minutes to see what he could do. He said he would have to convert the ICU room to winter function while keeping the rest of the facility on air conditioning.

Not much later, Kermit came into the ICU and said, "Let's give it a try." He then turned the thermostat on the wall to full heat. Within moments, hot air was coming from the air vents. Within a short time, the ICU was a dry sauna.

The nurses weighed our patient so we could keep track of any weight loss caused by sweating, and we asked the nurses to weigh our patient twice daily. Dr. Bill ordered lab tests to be done every 12 hours to keep track of our patient's electrolyte and kidney status.

Overnight our man lost four pounds from sweating (about two quarts). His blood pressure became more easily controlled. His breathing was not much better, *but not worse*! The lab values were no worse. The kidneys still were not making urine.

The weight on the second day revealed an additional six-pound loss. Our patient's breathing was improving. His heart required less medication support overnight. The lab values remained stable. The kidneys still made minimal urine.

The third day brought complaints from the ICU nurses about "the heat." However, our patient had lost another eight pounds. He had started to produce urine.

The amount of heart medicines was decreased. Our patient was less short of breath, *and* he asked us to turn down the heat. He wanted to go for a walk!

From this point forward, Dr. Bill's patient continued to improve. He got his wish to stay put. Dr. Bill did not have to see his patient die on his watch. We all learned good lessons in physiology, perseverance, and teamwork.

The nurses got their air conditioning back after a few more days. Kermit received our thanks and a pat on the back.

We had sweated our patient out of heart failure!

Shocker

When Dr. Berryman and I started at the Lusk hospital in the summer of 1975, it soon became apparent that the nurses were behind in updating their skills. The hospital had cardiac monitors, but no nurse knew what to do with them or how to read an electrocardiogram (EKG). The ICU room had a defibrillator unit that had never been used. The nurses had not been allowed to insert IV's (intravenous catheters) without supervision. We knew things had to improve if we were going to take care of patients in the hospital.

As an intern at the Sacred Heart Hospital in Spokane I set up an EKG reading file for all the interns. I had kept copies of the pertinent EKGs for future reference; these would come in handy for our teaching program. Dr. Bill or I met with the nurses three times a week in a crash course of simple EKG interpretation and monitor strip evaluation. Whenever we had a patient in the ICU being monitored, we asked the nurses to keep copies of the monitor recordings for discussion and to call us if any rhythm on the monitor was worrisome to them.

During the first few months one or both of us were at the hospital at all times of the day or night checking monitor strips or rhythm patterns for the nurses. I lost count of the number of times I was called in the middle of the night to evaluate a pattern on the monitor caused by a loose lead, a dry conduit pad, or in-house electrical interference. In one-way or another, all of our ICU patients became de facto cardiac care instructors for the nurses.

This time was before the era of clot busters and routine angioplasty for cardiac events. A new cardiac patient was observed in the ICU room, given oxygen, and given intravenous heparin (an anticoagulant drug). The patient's activity was limited. If his heart rhythm deteriorated, anti-arrhythmic medications were given according to an Advanced Cardiac Life Support (ACLS) protocol.

I admitted a middle-aged rancher who had suffered a small myocardial infarction. He was a robust gentleman with excellent musculature and global body hair. I learned that he was known around the area as a big practical joker. One morning as I was making rounds, the patient said, "Doc, watch this." Pointing to the monitor, the man wiggled his monitor lead over his hairy chest to produce some artifact. Then he watched the nurses scramble outside around the monitor desk attempting to identify the abnormality they saw on the cardiac monitor screen. Just as the nurses got settled into position, he would stop moving the wire. The monitor pattern normalized. The nurses looked frustrated; my patient had a big smile.

This game continued for several days, and my patient was having a grand time. I never let on to the nurses that I knew what was happening. When the nurses asked about the monitor tracing abnormalities, I just reassured them that they were looking at static patterns again.

All the while our EKG classes continued and the nurses were becoming more proficient at interpreting suspicious EKG patterns.

One day while I was at the nurses' station observing the monitor, my patient's rhythm turned ugly and promptly became ventricular fibrillation. A CODE was called, and all available personnel scrambled to help.

When we entered the ICU room, which was just a few feet away, our patient was pulseless, breathless, unconscious, and having ventricular fibrillation (V-Fib). This was no drill! Dr. Bill and I had trained the nurses for this emergency; now was going to be a moment of truth. We wondered if we had taught these people anything or not?

The ICU nurse promptly pulled the defibrillation unit to the bedside, unhooked the paddles, and yelled out, "V-FIB! Set to 300 joules!"

Another nurse pulled out two saline soaked pads from a stainless steel container on top of the defibrillator and applied them to the patient's chest wall in the correct locations on the right upper chest and left lower chest. Just like reading the ACLS manual for a test, the ICU nurse then yelled out, "Everybody clear of the bed!" She then placed the paddles over the saline soaked pads, looked at the monitor again, and said, "Shock!" She pressed the buttons on the paddles, which sent 300 joules of energy into the patient's body.

The electrical charge also set the patient's hairy chest ablaze!

Apparently, one of the cleaning personnel thought the small containers of *saline pads* were for *alcohol swabs*, and filled the stainless steel containers with *alcohol*. The electrical shock went through chest hair soaked with alcohol, not saline, and set the poor man on fire.

Fortunately, the man's rhythm normalized after a single shock. One of the nurses shouted out, "It really works!"

We were able to put out the man's chest wall blaze by smothering him with a blanket. However, his chest looked like it had been part of a forest fire with first and second-degree burns.

Fortunately, all the patient remembered was that he was playing with his monitor leads once again when the "lights went out."

My patient did not play with his monitor leads again. He left the hospital after a few more days without further incident. He resumed his ranch work after a few months.

The hospital nurses replaced the saline pads with a gel that was made specifically for defibrillation.

Dr. Bill and I became encouraged that we had made a difference in Lusk, Wyoming.

Failure to Progress

On a late summer evening an unmarried 19-year-old girl presented herself to our hospital in active labor with her first child. She lived with her parents on a ranch outside of town and had received no prenatal care. She figured it must her due time since she was having pains; she came to town after she completed her daily chores.

After an evaluation, I admitted the lady to our obstetrical area in labor. Her cervix was dilated to 2 centimeters. (During labor the uterine cervix dilates in diameter from 0 to 10 centimeters according to a usually predictable pattern. One does not know how long it will take to go from 0 to 5 centimeters, but the time to progress from 5 to 10 centimeters is usually about 2 to 4 hours. If it takes longer, one has to determine a reason for the delay.)

This lady's labor was uneventful until her cervix dilated to about 5 centimeters at about 4 a.m. I estimated that she would deliver her baby in the morning before lunch.

Over the next few hours, my patient's labor was intense, but her cervix did not dilate past 5 centimeters. After repeat examinations, I attributed the delay to the patient having a larger than average baby and her never having had a vaginal birth. I told the patient that she was progressing slowly, but I was hopeful she could deliver her baby "the right way."

I watched and waited.

By 8 a.m. my patient's labor continued to be intense, but there was no progress with the baby coming down the birth canal. She had been at 5 centimeters for about four hours.

It became time for us to consider an operation to deliver the baby. I talked to the lady about our situation and suggested that we proceed with a C-section. (Cesarean section is an abdominal operation used to remove the baby when it cannot be delivered through the birth canal.)

She declined! She informed me that having a baby was natural; nobody in her family had ever needed an operation; and she was NOT going to be the first.

We agreed to wait a bit longer as long as we knew the baby did not show signs of distress.

While I was waiting, I started to make arrangements to perform a C-section in our hospital. Unfortunately, the closest anesthetist, who lived about 50 miles away in Torrington, Wyoming, was the only one on duty at his hospital that day and would not be able to assist us. Any operation would have to be done in Torrington.

I then called Dr. Kay Breckinridge, the obstetrician in Torrington, to advise her of my situation. As always, she was ready to help at any time.

By noon, my lady was having excellent labor. However, she was becoming weary, and her cervix had not dilated past 5 centimeters. She had made no progress in eight hours. We had another discussion about an operation.

Again, the lady was reluctant. However, she agreed to an operation if she was no different in two more hours.

So, we waited some more.

I knew from experience that my patient probably would not progress further, so, while we waited, I made arrangements for our ambulance service to prepare for an orderly transfer of my patient to the Torrington hospital.

The U.S. Highway 85 between Lusk and Torrington was not a good road and was always under repair. A normal travel time for the 50 miles between the two towns was about 70 minutes or so depending upon the amount of construction and the time of day. I took these facts into consideration when I made arrangements.

By 1:30 p.m. my lady was pooped; she finally relented to having an operation. She was not happy that we could not do the surgery in the local hospital, but by now she was ready to "just get the kid out." After she called her family to let them know the situation, she was ready to go.

By 2 p.m. my patient was in the ambulance ready to go. I called Dr. Breckinridge and the anesthetist to let them know that we were departing.

They said they would make the necessary arrangements for surgery as soon as we arrived.

I planned to follow the ambulance in my car so the crew could return to Lusk in the ambulance after they had delivered their patient at the Torrington hospital.

The ambulance and I started out of town together. At the city limits the ambulance crew started up the vehicle's lights and sirens, and took off. I do mean they *took off*!

I tried to keep up going 70 miles an hour (the speed limit was 60 miles per hour), but I could not. The road was beating up my car, so I decided to slow down and BE ALIVE when I arrived at the Torrington hospital. I arrived after 50 minutes.

I ran into the Emergency Room looking for my patient. A nurse directed me into the obstetric area, not the surgical suite. I found my patient up on a delivery table with Dr. Breckinridge sitting at the end of the table. A newborn baby boy was in the bassinet next to her.

Dr. Breckinridge said, "This lady didn't need a C-section. She just needed a little help, like a 35-minute ride in the back of an ambulance through a construction zone at 100 miles per hour! Ha!" Dr. Breckinridge told me that when she examined my lady in the ER, the cervix was fully dilated, and the baby's head was showing. "It took just a little pull with the forceps, and the kid was out." "He's a whopper! Just look at him! No wonder mom had a time!"

I examined the baby. Except for forceps marks over his ears, he looked great. He weighed about 10 pounds.

I bent over and told my young mom that she had done a marvelous job and that I was proud of her. I offered to call her family, but the nurse had already done that duty.

My patient told me, "I knew I could do it."

Dr. Breckinridge said she had "a little repair work" to do on our new mom, but she should be ready to go home in no time at all.

As I walked out to the emergency room, I found the ambulance crew still hanging around. They wanted to hear "the results."

I told them all was good with mom and babe.

They informed me they made the 50-mile trip in 35 minutes. That's an *average* of about 86 miles per hour over horrible roads. The driver said, "The faster I drove, the more the lady screamed; so I just drove faster."

I figured that the ride essentially *bounced the baby out!*

I had the opportunity to see the new mom and baby in the clinic after a few weeks. Mom's bottom had healed up nicely. Breastfeeding was going well. The baby still weighed almost 10 pounds. The new mom reminded me that, "Having babies is a "natural" thing."

Mom showed me something else, her *new ring!*

Apparently, the baby's father decided to assume some new responsibility after he saw his baby boy. The couple were to be wed in three weeks, the same day their baby was to be christened.

Target Practice

Del and his wife operated quite a large cattle ranch southeast of town. During the fall months they opened up a bed, breakfast, and hunting business on the ranch. For a significant fee, hunters from out of state were allowed to stay on his ranch just like a bed and breakfast. However, the hunters also were *guaranteed* a live kill of an antelope, or they got their money back. Over time, the word spread of this "deal" in Wyoming. If you didn't shoot anything, you didn't pay.

Over the years, hunters with various levels of expertise as riflemen came to hunt on Del's ranch. Some were so bad that Del finally painted a Bull's Eye 10 feet in diameter on the side of his barn for the hunters to have target practice. Del also wanted to know how "good" his customers were at shooting high-powered rifles.

One day just before noon, Del came into the clinic. His complained that his stomach ached, and he had a terrible headache. Del told me that he had no history of stomach issues or headaches. While taking a history, I happened to ask, "How are things on the ranch?"

Del told me that the ranch was in good shape. Moisture had been good during the fall, so he expected good pastures in the spring. His animals were healthier than usual. Next year's prospects were looking good if prices for cattle held up. Then he blurted out, "They almost shot me in my kitchen!"

I asked, "What?"

Del explained that he was in his kitchen the previous morning when a bullet went right past him and landed in the refrigerator. His newest bunch of hunters was out sighting in their guns by the barn early that morning. Del then said, "One of them not only missed the Bull's Eye, he missed the whole damn barn!" "Hell, my wife or I could have been killed! I've been shaking since." Del went on to tell me that the house was not even close to the barn.

Del explained to me his "guarantee." He was fretting over the fact that he would have to refund the clients' money (his first time ever) because he was afraid to take these guys out hunting. Del stated, "Who knows what the hell they'll shoot! Or who?"

I could see why Del had his physical ailments. He didn't need any medicine. He needed less stress.

After we talked a bit more, I asked Del if he was a drinking man.

He said he had been known to drink a beer or two in his day.

I asked him to go home, take some antacids, have a beer or two, and, if his stomach was still hurting after two days, to come back and see me for some testing.

He agreed.

Del returned to the clinic four days later to tell me that now he was fine. After drinking the beers (actually four of them), Del told me he came upon a solution, *a very good solution.*

Del said, "Since I was afraid to take these guys to the antelope, I decided to bring the antelope to them."

He went on to tell me in vivid detail how, in the early morning hours the next day, he lined up the four hunters with one knee on the ground facing his cornfield (just like a firing squad). He then had his wranglers stampede a herd of antelope into the cornfield running right at the hunters. On his command, Del ordered the men to "fire" into the herd of antelope.

"All four men shot their antelope. It was just that simple!" exclaimed Del.

His workers were safe, his property was again out of harms way, and he kept his money.

The four men spent the next two days drinking, telling tall tales about their "hunt," and left town with their trophies.

I figured Del's headaches and stomach pains should be gone for another year.

SIDNEY, MONTANA:

THE EARLY DAYS

*"There are those who look at things the way they are,
and ask why...
I dream of things that never were, and ask why not?"*

Robert Kennedy

*"Whenever a doctor cannot do good, he must be kept
from doing harm."*

Hippocrates

The First Visit

The National Health Service Corps (NHSC) sent the Berryman family and our family on the 500-mile journey from Lusk, Wyoming north to Sidney, Montana, a town of about 5,000 people, in March 1976 for a "visit." Prior to going to Sidney, we had had discussions with Ron Jackson, the hospital administrator, who encouraged us with his positive comments about the community, the town's physicians, the hospital, and the community's need for physicians. We drove through the day and arrived in the early evening. Rooms were reserved for us at the Park Plaza Motel.

Upon entering our rooms, we found a bouquet of flowers, a nice welcoming note, and an itinerary with the events planned for us over the next several days. I was impressed.

The following morning an individual escorted us to a breakfast gathering with a few of the hospital board members. These folks also put a positive spin on the community and its needs. Afterward, one of the board members gave us a short tour of the hospital facility. One of the local realtors followed with a quick tour of the town.

At noon, we had another gathering with "*important*" local residents. After a short time by ourselves to reflect and to sightsee on our own, we met a fellow named Earl Neff, a researcher at the local agriculture research station. Earl took us to the local airport where we were introduced to a pilot named Paul Phillips who had an aerial tour of the area planned for us.

I thought this was a great idea. Kay, my wife, however, was pregnant at the time and declined the invitation. Bill, his wife Kathy, and I climbed into the back of a small airplane while Paul and Earl occupied the control seats.

The flight took us north and west over the vast farms of the area. Paul then veered south and then east to show us the area south of town including the power plant, the towns of Savage and Crane, and the dam at Intake which supplied the diversion of water for irrigation from the Yellowstone River. Our trip continued east across the Yellowstone River over the North Dakota badlands and then headed north. At this point Paul advised us that, "It gets a little bumpy this time of day, so make sure your seat belts are tight."

A roller coaster ride was more like it! Up front, Paul and Earl were having a grand time pointing out items of interest. We passengers in the back, however, were just trying to keep our lunches down. When Paul suggested that we fly "under a bridge," we promptly nixed the idea. I think our pilots looked at us, figured we had had enough "sightseeing" for one day, and headed home.

After we landed, Dr. Bill struggled out of the plane and kissed the ground. After we talked about our adventure in the air, Kay said she was *really glad* she did not come with us.

As we gathered our wits and our stomachs, Earl told us that the next part of our agenda was a meeting between Bill and me and the hospital administrator. This would to be followed in the evening by a reception with more of the "*important locals.*" Earl took the wives to the motel; Bill and I continued on to our meeting at the hospital.

As we walked into Mr. Jackson's office, I noticed that he was sweaty and visibly nervous. After we sat down, he quickly said, "Our town really needs you two young doctors, but *our doctors don't want you here.*" He continued to tell us about the medical staff: two of the physicians were from Ireland and wanted nothing to do with what they perceived as *socialized government medicine* (i.e. us!); one of the physicians was getting up in years, had been in town about 40 years, and needed to retire; a physician from Cuba who practiced in a nearby town "didn't do very much"; a pathologist on staff serviced the hospital lab and all the hospitals in northeastern Montana; and a general practitioner who was "working his butt off."

Bill and I were not impressed by his comments. We wondered why the town had asked us to visit if their doctors had made it known we weren't wanted? We decided right then that it made no sense to go to a reception that the physicians would not attend. We told Mr. Jackson the banquet would have to go forth without us. We wanted to talk to the doctors—that night!

Mr. Jackson said that he appreciated our position. After a few minutes on the phone, he arranged a meeting with the doctors at 7 p.m. at one of their homes.

Bill and I were a bit upset after this conversation. However, we concluded that we needed to hear what the local medical staff members had to say before we did anything else.

The physicians were all present when we arrived at Dr. Shea's home; each one was cordial. I noted that the older physician had been drinking considerably. Essentially, these physicians informed us that we were needed, but NOT as government employees. They would welcome us with open arms only if we came as their employees or as private physicians.

Essentially, if we joined with them, Bill and I would be treated as equals. If not, we would not exist in their eyes.

The physicians openly expressed their views. Bill and I had to decide what we would do pronto.

Bill and I talked for about two hours that evening with our wives. It had been a very long day, in more ways than one. Multiple options open to us were hashed over and over again. Whatever we did, both of us planned to stay just one year to complete our two-year commitment to the National Health Service Corps.

We decided to tell the NHSC folks in Denver the next morning that we would come to Sidney, Montana. With what we had endured so far in our short careers in medicine, Bill and I rationalized that we could tolerate another year of aggravation.

The next morning we contacted our supervisor at the Denver office of the NHSC. We informed him of our decision to stay in Sidney.

He asked somewhat astonished, "What are you doing up there?"

I replied, "You guys sent us up here. You made the arrangements. You sent us the travel vouchers!"

His response was, "That's not possible. Sidney IS NOT a corps site!"

Bill and I were dismayed and befuddled by the government *once again*. I told Bill that I had had enough with the government, thank you! I told him that I would resign from the NHSC when we returned to Wyoming, and I would consult with the Sidney docs to see if they would salary me for a year.

After some thought, Bill related, "That might not be such a bad idea. At least, it won't hurt to ask."

We arranged a meeting with Drs. Smyth and Shea about our "situation." Dr. Shea was currently employing Dr. Larimore and was reluctant to take on any more responsibility. Dr. Smyth then agreed to employ each of us for one year at $3000 a month, if we were willing. He agreed to pay all of our expenses related to a medical practice. The hospital agreed to have housing available for us when we came.

This amount of money was about one-third more than I was getting from the NHSC. It looked like a no brainer for me. Bill had a similar impression. We tentatively agreed to come to Sidney for one year pending our review of the contracts.

The discussion on our way back to Wyoming was energized with excitement about a new adventure.

The First Weekend

I had been in Sidney, Montana just a short period of time when it was time for my first weekend rotation for emergency duty at the hospital. Dr. Smyth, who was my employer at the time, had been on call for weeks before I arrived. He related that he wanted to visit his family in western Montana for the weekend and asked if I would please visit his patients in the hospital during his absence. Of course, I agreed.

Kay was staying with her family in Bozeman, Montana; I was a bachelor for a few months while our newly purchased home was being vacated for us. In the interim, I was sleeping in the basement of Dr. Berryman's home in a sleeping bag.

Call started at 7 a.m. on Saturday. I was there at 6:30 a.m. I got some curious looks from the nursing staff because the other doctors apparently did not come in early on the weekends. I met with Beatrice "Betty" Katy, R.N., the charge nurse. She escorted me to the B-wing side of the hospital to get started with patients.

The Sidney hospital was built like a cross and had 55 acute beds. A letter represented each arm of the cross: A-wing was for medicine; B-wing was for surgery and obstetrics; C-wing was for administration; and D-wing was for dietary, engineering, and pharmacy. At the crossroads was the four-bed intensive care unit.

As I sat down at the nurses' counter, I noticed a string of messages taped to the counter. The first message read, "Dr. Smyth says Dr. Ashcraft will be covering for him this weekend."

Message #2 stated, "Dr. Shea is gone for the week. Dr. Smyth will cover for him."

Message #3 read, "Dr. Larimore went to Regina for the weekend. Dr. Shea is covering."

Message #4 said, "Dr. Hastings is gone. Whoever is in town will cover for him."

Message #5 tersely stately, "Dr. Montoya is gone."

Turning to Mrs. Katy I asked, "What is this?"

Her reply was, "Doctor, You get to see everybody."

I inquired, "How many?"

"46." was the answer.

Well, I had nothing better to do, so I dove into the 20+ patient records on B-wing, the surgical and obstetrical floor with the newborn nursery. I soon made a curious finding; *these charts had no documentation.* The charts for the obstetric patients and the surgical patients had no histories and physicals, no operative notes, and no progress notes. Some of the patients had been in the hospital for a week and the charts had not one word from the physicians. I thought to myself, "What the heck was going on here?"

I questioned nurse Katy, and all she offered in explanation was a smile and to say, "That's the way it is here."

Well, the two of us managed to figure out what was wrong, or what had been wrong, with the patients on B-wing. I wrote notes on all the patients. I discharged 14 patients because I could not figure out why they were still in the hospital. (These were the days when the hospital got paid by the number of days a patient stayed, not by what was done or by the diagnosis.)

On our way to A-wing, where the medical patients resided, we passed through the ICU (Intensive Care Unit). The single patient, who had suffered a heart attack several days before, seemed stable. My encounter with this patient was uneventful.

Mrs. Katy and I continued on to the A-wing.

22 patients resided on A-wing this Saturday. Only one patient had a history and physical on the chart – my patient who I had admitted the day before! Again, the nurses and I pieced together the patients' reasons for being in the hospital. To my amazement, six elderly patients were *boarding* in the hospital for the weekend while their relatives were out of town. I did not have the heart to send these folks home until I found out the real scoop. Of the remaining 16 patients, I discharged 12 of them.

It was now a little after noon. I had not received one call from the emergency room, thank goodness. I was about ready to put on my coat and leave for home when Betty hooked my arm with hers and said something like, "Not so fast Doctor. It is now time for Saturday Clinic."

I had not been told about Saturday clinic. "What gives?" I thought to myself.

Nurse Katy informed me that if patients were unable to see the doctors during the week, then they could come up to the ER on Saturday and see the doctor on call for only $4.

I thought, "My gosh, an office call was $6! Who thought up this hair brained idea anyway?"

Well, it didn't matter what I thought. There was a pot load of folks waiting to be seen by me in the ER. No wonder I had not had an ER call all morning. If the patients just waited until the afternoon, it would cost them only four bucks.

I finally finished seeing all the people about 7 p.m. on my first Saturday on call. On my way home to my basement abode, I stopped by the local A&W to get a chilidog and a root beer. I had no emergencies the rest of the night.

I knew Sunday had to be a better day. I would not have another "clinic." I had discharged 26 patients the day before. All was looking good for a smooth day on call.

First, I saw the patients on B-wing and all was good with the moms and their babies.

The man in the ICU looked great.

No catastrophes had occurred on A-wing during the night. All the boarders were well fed and had slept well. The hospital staff was pretty laid back as well.

As I was taking a shortcut through the ICU to get back to the doctors' library to get my coat, I happened to glance at my patient who had been just fine 15 minutes before. He was ashen in color and having trouble breathing. The cardiac monitor displayed a major heart rhythm irregularity. "Where was the nurse?" I thought. "There was NO NURSE in the ICU!"

The man then stopped breathing. I climbed up onto the bed and started one-man CPR. As I was pumping on the man's chest and in between breaths I tried to summon someone to call a "code."

Nobody came!

I thought to myself, "This was supposed to be an ICU, an intensive care unit! Where was everybody? Where was ANYBODY?"

Finally, I got the attention of a teenage girl who was passing by the open ICU door. She was in a striped uniform; I presumed a volunteer. I yelled at her to call a CODE!

She looked at me curiously, turned around, and, as she walked away, quietly said, "Code."

After what seemed hours, but was actually minutes, some nurses arrived to lend a hand. After one of them took over the chore of chest compressions, I inserted an endotracheal tube in the man's windpipe and had another nurse ventilate the patient with an ambu bag.

The man was now in ventricular fibrillation. I called for the defibrillator, but nobody knew exactly where it was. An all out search began around the ICU. It wasn't there! The unit was found in the *emergency room* nearly a half block away. (The hospital did not think it needed more than one was necessary, I guessed.)

The man received electrical countershock three times without resolution of the rhythm irregularity. Damn!

I asked, "Where is the Crash Cart?" I received a lot of blank looks from the nurses present. I yelled out, "Where is the cart with the heart drugs?"

I heard a high pitched voice from the back of the throng of people say, "Oh, doctor, I know where it is." A young lady then left the ICU.

The young lady returned a minute or so later with a shoebox labeled "*Doctors Heart Drugs.*" Inside the box was some I.V. tubing, a vial of morphine, a vial of Coramine (a stimulant medication that had not been in use for 15 years), a bottle of lidocaine for local anesthesia, and a bottle of nitroglycerin pills. I found nothing at all in the box that would slow down or stop a cardiac arrhythmia. My efforts were doomed, and so was the patient!

In retrospect, I concluded that the man probably had another heart attack. That did not make me feel any better. The man died on my watch.

I kept asking myself, "Where were the nurses? Where was the equipment? Where are the drugs? This is an ICU. That stuff is all supposed to be right here. Where was everything?" I was frustrated beyond comprehension.

After everything had settled down, the patient's family had been notified, and the funeral home had been called, I sat down with the nurses to figure out what could be done to prevent future disasters. A crash cart was required for sure. A second defibrillator was required in the ICU. ACLS (Advanced Cardiac Life Support) protocols needed to be posted and followed. Cardiac drugs had to be *in the ICU.* ICU patients had to be attended at all times by a nurse trained in cardiac care.

The bigger items would require my visiting with the administrator on Monday. However, I figured the drugs could be placed in the ICU that day if they were in the pharmacy. One of the nurses said she had seen the pharmacist in the hospital and that he should be able to help me.

It was now about noon, so I decided to go out for a breath of fresh air and some lunch at the local Dairy Queen. Upon my return to the hospital, I went straight to the pharmacy to talk with the pharmacist before he went home for the day. I found him, drunk as a skunk and asleep with his head on his desk! Holy Cow!

I thought to myself, "What kind of a place was this? What had I gotten myself and my family into? This place was a nightmare!"

I wandered through the pharmacy picking up the items I wanted and took them back to the ICU. The pharmacist never noticed me.

I went home about 6 p.m. I did not see one real ER patient all weekend. But goodness, WHAT A WEEKEND! I was pooped.

On Monday morning I asked the Chief of Staff for a special meeting to get "some on-call items squared away," and this meeting was scheduled.

I went to the hospital administrator to tell him my story. When I asked for a crash cart, he retorted, "The hospital could not afford one."

When I spoke of the drunken pharmacist, his reply was, "Again?"

I then went down to the local Sears catalog store and purchased a Craftsman tool chest for the new crash cart. (It was still in use 25 years later when I closed my office.)

I had experienced a very stressful four days. That cool basement floor at Berryman's sure felt good that Monday night.

The pharmacist left town and never returned.

The administrator "retired" two months later because of a *quivering heart*, a diagnosis made by the older physician in town.

Dr. Berryman and I started classes for ICU nurses that week, just like we had done in Lusk, Wyoming.

Heart Attack

On a fall morning in 1977, I was in the clinic across the parking lot from the hospital attending to patients. Georgia, my nurse, interrupted me in an exam room and told me I was needed in the emergency room right away. Someone had collapsed at the sales yard, and the ambulance was bringing him in.

I promptly apologized to my patient and excused myself from the room. I then ran across the parking lot to the emergency room.

As I was coming around a corner in the hospital toward the emergency room, I could see the ambulance crew pushing in their stretcher with a patient on it. One of the ambulance crewmembers was performing external chest massage on a patient. I overheard the ambulance crew tell the waiting nurse that the man was watching the cattle sale and just slumped over. He was about 45-years-old with no known medical history. His name was Benson Morgan; he operated a local sand, gravel, and asphalt business.

By the time I arrived in the emergency room, the man's shirt had been removed, and he was on the cardiac monitor. Oxygen was being administered through a mask. The man was sweaty, unconscious, had a barely detectable pulse, and had labored respirations. The cardiac monitor pattern was that of a significant myocardial infarction. The man was in obvious cardiogenic shock.

The patient's rhythm promptly converted into ventricular fibrillation, a lethal rhythm if not stopped promptly. The defibrillator was charged and ready to go. Promptly, I administered an electrical countershock three times in succession without any change in the rhythm.

By now, the anesthetist had arrived from surgery. Skillfully, she inserted an endotracheal tube into the man's windpipe and started to ventilate the patient with an ambu bag.

The patient had no blood pressure, and it was impossible to start an intravenous line. I asked a nurse standing by the medication cart to hand me the cardiac needle along with the vial of cardiac adrenalin. I withdrew about two milliliters of the adrenalin into the syringe. I selected a spot just below the rib cage and a little bit left of the middle to insert the long cardiac needle. I inserted the needle until blood could be withdrawn into the syringe; I ejected the adrenalin directly into the heart. (This was done in the days before the use of endotracheal administered medications was acceptable.)

Within moments, the cardiac monitor showed a normal sinus rhythm. The patient developed a blood pressure and an intravenous line could be started. Benson started to breathe spontaneously, and the anesthetist was able to remove the endotracheal tube. *We had a save!*

I then heard a man's voice from somewhere behind me pronounce, "Well I'll be damned! I have never seen that work before."

When I turned around, I saw Dr. Lasater standing against a wall with his arms crossed. Dr. Lasater was the local pathologist whose office was in the hospital. He frequently came to codes. Since he did not practice clinical medicine, he was an observant bystander and another good pair of hands when needed.

The team observed the man in the emergency room for a short while. When I thought he was stable, he was transferred to the intensive care unit.

As I was cleaning up and getting ready to go back to the office, Dr. Lasater came by me and said, "Well done young man. Well done. I just didn't know that cardiac adrenalin ever worked. Well done."

As I was walking back to the office, I had recollections of my disastrous first weekend on call in Sidney, Montana. I kept thinking, "How things had changed in the past a year-and-a-half."

After one year, Dr. Berryman returned to Oregon for more training. However, had he been here for this resuscitation, I thought he would be proud. At least for Mr. Morgan, we, the team, had made a difference today,

Mr. Morgan survived and left the hospital. However, the damage done to his heart by the heart attack was extensive. He would be a cardiac cripple, but he continued to participate in his usual routine as best he could.

Several months later I received a similar call while I was working in my office. A man had collapsed at the sales yard; the ambulance was transporting him to the hospital. This time, we could not help Benson. He was dead on arrival at the hospital.

Later, a family member told me that we gave him some precious time to take care of some business dealings and to get some important family issues addressed.

Politics

Enlightening and educational are appropriate words to describe my first months in Sidney in 1976. I learned an awful lot about how medicine was practiced in the 1950s and 60s; because a lot of what was done in the Sidney hospital was the standard of medical care a generation before me. I became acquainted with the local medical politics. I was intrigued with the lengths people, not just physicians, would go to obtain or maintain status, wealth, political power, or all three. I was naive for sure.

When Dr. Bill and I went for our interviews with the Board of Medical Examiners, the board members spent little time asking about me; the Board had my credentials, and the President of the Board already had interviewed me. Instead, the Board members asked me about the activities of Dr. Larimore. I responded to them candidly about what I had seen or what I had been told. I related to them that Dr. Larimore was presented to me as an obstetrician who had worked in Australia before coming to Montana. Dr. Shay had recruited her. She performed surgeries, delivered babies, and took general ER call. She covered for Dr. Shay's surgical patients when he was out of town, which was just about every Thursday through Sunday.

The Board members thanked me for my candor. They then advised me that Dr. Larimore was NOT an obstetrician, but a general practitioner. She *did not* have a medical license and had failed to pass her qualification examination *twice*! She supposedly was acting only as a physician assistant for Dr. Shay who was to observe all her procedures personally.

I told them that the situation they described to me was not reality.

I received my medical license and left the meeting.

On the way home, Bill and I discussed our "interviews." His experience was essentially the same as mine. Our stories were similar. We felt by the doctors and the hospital in Sidney had betrayed us.

On the next Monday afternoon, Dr. Shay asked Bill and me into his office for consultation. His only comment was, "What did YOU tell the Board?"

I said, "I told them what I had been told, what I had seen, and what I understood about Dr. Larimore."

Dr. Bill agreed with me.

Dr. Shay responded, "I see. That will be all." He then dismissed us like we were his children.

The next day, Dr. Larimore went on "sabbatical" indefinitely. (Later we found out that her PA certificate had been revoked, and she had gone away to study for another examination to obtain a medical license.) Dr. Shay took a "vacation" for several months. (Apparently, the Board had reprimanded him.)

With two physicians now gone, Bill and I had plenty to do, and to learn, and to teach.

The hospital had an ICU, but only one nurse worked in it. She had been the only nurse to take ICU-nursing training classes, and she *would not* teach the others. Bill and I had a battle on our hands with the hospital administration and this particular nurse when we demanded that the ICU be staffed 24 hours a day by "qualified nurses." The alternate solution was that we would not take care of seriously ill patients in the hospital. The hospital relented; we won our complaint, and Bill and I started to teach nurses how to care for critically ill patients. We made sure that other nurses were sent away for training at the hospital's expense. As Bill often said to me, "We're going to bring this bunch into the twentieth century if they like it or not." Bill even arranged for a world famous expert in electrocardiography, Dr. Henry Marriot, to give presentations in Sidney for the doctors *and* the nurses.

It soon became obvious to me that the elderly physician on our medical staff had a significant problem with alcohol. Not infrequently, he came to the hospital in the morning smelling of alcohol. It became apparent that other physicians had issues with the elder physician as well. He occasionally arrived at staff meetings inebriated.

At one meeting, Dr. Shay had some unresolved issues with the elder physician from an encounter the previous night. Dr. Shay pointed out firmly in his stately Irish accent, "And it is not appropriate to urinate on a colleague's door when you leave his home!"

The meeting then continued as if nothing happened.

One day I saw the elder physician stagger out of the operating room quite intoxicated. He was barely able to stand. I got him to lie down and take a nap before he hurt himself. I related this experience and others to the hospital administrator who responded, "What's your point? He keeps the hospital full!"

The local pathologist, the senior member of the medical staff, told me that this issue had surfaced before. The old guy "has friends" he told me, and " He always wins. Many others had tried to change things, failed, and left town in disgust."

Another concern I had was the "doctor" on the medical staff from Cuba. I did not see much of him, but I knew he could not have gone to medical school the day he asked me for help with the removal of the gallbladder from a 9-year-old boy with diarrhea. (The surgery was never done!)

The pathologist again became my historian. This fellow came across to Florida during the Cuban exodus in the late 1960s. Many Cuban "doctors" obtained Florida medical licenses when their documents and credentials were not scrutinized. This fellow got a Montana license via a reciprocity agreement Montana had with Florida (so the State of Montana to save a few dollars). His credentials were never checked in Montana. How he ended up in Sidney was anyone's guess.

I took my concerns to the Hospital Board about these three physicians.

The Board members already knew that Dr. Larimore *did not* pass her tests and *did not* have a medical license. They knew that the elderly physician had "issues". They knew the Cuban physician was "weird", but considered him harmless. The hospital Board's position was: "The hospital is doing fine financially, and the issues I brought up did not concern them! They were medical staff issues. You deal with them!"

Through the first year, I remained very busy in the many disciplines of my general practice. My efforts generated much more revenue than my salary plus all expenses by double. Dr. Smyth felt obligated to compensate me more, but I wanted to abide by my contract. In April, at the end of my first year, Dr. Smyth asked me to consider being a part of a combined organization that would include his corporation, Dr. Shay's corporation, and the clinic building, which was a partnership between the two physicians.

I told him I would be interested.

In May, Dr. Berryman left for a two year sabbatical in internal medicine; I became even busier when I assumed a lot of his ICU work.

During the summer months negotiations continued between the various parties needed to perform the legal and accounting activities of the proposed consolidation. On a Friday in August, we remaining physicians had a late afternoon meeting to discuss preparations for the consolidation.

In my office the next Thursday, a drug representative told me, "I am sorry to hear that Dr. Shay was leaving."

I told him he must have heard a rumor. I informed him that the community had known for some time that we physicians were working on a plan to consolidate all the folks in the clinic under a single legal umbrella.

The very next afternoon, Friday, Dr. Shay invited Dr. Smyth and me into his office. He said, "I have been looking at moving to the Black Hills for years. My wife and I are going to move, *soon*."

I thought to myself, "He had been planning a move for *years*. The discussions to form a group practice had been a sham!"

Dr. Shay would not give us a timeline for his move to make our transition smoother.

About 7 o'clock the next Monday morning, before I went to the hospital to make my patient rounds, I walked into the clinic. *The whole place was empty*! I mean empty! Every desk, chair, exam table, stethoscope, and tongue depressor was gone! In my office, only my black bag and a foot basin remained on the floor. The entire business area was stripped as well.

I called Dr. Smyth to tell him to get to the clinic ASAP; everything was gone!

Dr. Smyth was incredulous. He was incensed. He wanted to know who, what, when, and why?

He called Dr. Shay at his home, but nobody answered. He too was gone! He had skipped out in the middle of the night with all the clinic's equipment.

The police investigated the incident, but concluded that they had no jurisdiction. Since the partners owned the equipment and the building, each one got something.

Dr. Smyth and the office staff spent the rest of the next two days trying to obtain equipment from any supplier possible. Since the clinic never had an inventory, the ordering process had to be done one catalogue page at a time.

While Dr. Smyth ordered the clinic needs, I assumed the hospital and clinic duties for both of us. The patients that could not be rescheduled in the clinic were examined in the emergency room. Surgeries were postponed until our situation stabilized. By Wednesday, enough equipment, furniture, and supplies had been obtained for us to see patients in the clinic again. The clinic was running at full capacity in two weeks.

Dr. Larimore, who had been Dr. Shay's employee, was no longer welcomed in the clinic by Dr. Smyth. She took refuge with the elder doctor in his office.

Our five-physician clinic now had new equipment, just two physicians, and a lot of work to do.

Catastrophe

Kristen Easton came to my office during my first autumn in Sidney. She was a 28-year-old attractive mother of three girls who had missed her menstrual cycle for two months. She had the usual complaints of pregnancy, i.e. nausea, breast tenderness, moodiness, etc. She told me that she really did not want to be pregnant again. When a pregnancy test was positive, she cried. We discussed her options with an unwanted pregnancy, including termination. She would have nothing to do with such talk.

Through the fall of 1976 and early winter of 1977, Kristen never missed a prenatal visit. Each visit, however, seemed to convince her more and more that she did not want another child. My nurse Georgia, who had recently delivered her first baby, spoke positively about having a baby. However, she could not deter Kristen's feelings. We tried multiple times to get Kristen to "open up" about her feelings, but neither Georgia nor I were successful.

Kristen's pregnancy progressed without a hitch, except for her mental state. Her home life, as far as we could tell, was unremarkable. She was managing with her other children just fine as far as we knew.

About noon on February 28, 1977 Kristen came to the hospital in labor. After the nurses finished admitting her, I sat down with Kristen to review obstetric procedures, pain medications, IVs, etc. During this visit, Kristen apologized to me for having been such an awful patient. She had decided that she really did want to have her baby.

I was very pleased with her attitude change.

Kristen went on to tell me that her husband was abusive and drank heavily. They had been having marital problems to the point that she was seeking a divorce when she got pregnant. She related that her husband came home one night drunk, beat her, and essentially raped her. That was how she got pregnant. That was why she did not want this baby.

I just listened and told her that no one in the hospital would know her secret.

I asked about her husband. She had no idea where he was; she had left her children with a neighbor friend before coming to the hospital.

I left Kristen and returned to my office. The nurses would monitor her labor.

In the early days, the Sidney hospital had a curious routine for a woman in labor. The woman was allowed to labor in a regular room until the cervix was dilated to about 4 to 5 centimeters. At that time, the patient was transferred to a "labor room", a small alcove room just outside the delivery room and across the hall from the operating room.

The hospital had two of these rooms facing each other and separated by accordion doors and a small entryway. When the time of birth was near, the pregnant woman was transferred once again to a delivery room.

About 5 p.m. Kristen was transferred to a labor room. Another obstetric patient of mine named Chris, who was pregnant with her first child, was transferred to the other labor room about the same time.

I checked on the ladies about 5:30 p.m. when I got out of the office. All was going smoothly. I took time to call home to let Kay know I would not be home for a while; I would eat at the hospital.

About 6 p.m. I looked in on the moms-to-be once again. Kristen was doing well and in good spirits. Chris was having some difficulty with back labor pains, but was holding up quite well for a first timer. All appeared to be in order.

As I came out of Chris's labor room, I glanced at Kristen through the half open door. Our eyes met. She was smiling. Then, all of a sudden, Kristen's mouth drooped, her eyes became glassy, and she turned gray! Promptly, I went in to examine her. My God, she had no pulse! She wasn't breathing! What in the world was going on? I called a CODE as I started to perform one-man CPR.

The area was filled with people quickly since it was change of shift time and a lot of help was available. Dr. Larimore and Dr. Smyth arrived within a few minutes. Because of the small space in the labor room, Kristen and the resuscitation effort was transferred to the operating room across the hall. 5 minutes elapsed, then 10, then 20, then 30. Nothing we did was helping: not the drugs, not the shocks, not even intracardiac adrenalin. The baby had been without heart tones since the mom went into shock. I had lost a mother and her baby!

The entire team was dumfounded. I just wondered, "What went wrong? She was healthy. The labor was proceeding without a hitch. She was happy at last."

I wanted to find a hole and hide, but I had to notify the family. When I went to the obstetrics wing of the hospital, I was told that the husband was not around. As I was about to call him, a nurse tapped me on the shoulder and said, "Doctor, I'm so sorry, but Chris is ready to deliver."

I had forgotten all about Chris! Thank goodness for nurses.

When I reached the delivery room, I tried to apologize to Chris for all the commotion outside. However, I know I didn't do a good job. I was still stunned.

Chris just looked at me and said, "Doc, it's going to be all right, trust me."

A short time later, Chris gave birth to a screaming little boy. I could not believe the feeling of relief that came over me. I must have been smiling ear to ear under my mask! I had tears in my eyes. After Chris was cleaned up and with her new baby resting on her chest, I leaned over, gave her a hug, and said, "Thank you."

Kristen's husband finally arrived. He was drunk. I conveyed to him as best I could my condolences and my desire to determine the cause of his wife's death. I advised him that the coroner would request an autopsy to help find the cause of death.

It was now about 11 p.m. I went into the doctor's lounge, sat down, put my head in my hands, and tears came to my eyes. I had experienced the nightmare of all obstetricians, the death of a mother and an unborn child.

I sat for another 30 minutes or so before I decided to go home.

When I got home, Kay and the kids were in bed. After I had slipped into bed, Kay asked quietly, "How did things go?"

I said, "Both the mom and baby died."

I don't recall Kay speaking. She just hugged me as I fell asleep.

The following morning I looked in on Chris and her newborn. Once again I tried to explain the events of the night before without going into detail. Chris broke into my fumbling speech and said, "I know the other lady died with her baby. You must feel awful. Don't worry about us. We'll be fine." This young lady had made my day.

The entire hospital staff was mum that morning. Questions were many; answers were few. What had happened to Kristen? Why would a healthy female not respond to any therapy?

I met with Dr. Joseph Lasater, the hospital pathologist and assistant county coroner, about 9 a.m. Joe wanted to know "the story" like always, and I did my best to recreate the tragic events of the day before. He had planned an autopsy for noon and invited me to participate.

I agreed.

The autopsy theater was located at the local funeral home. I joined Joe at the appointed time and place in hopes of finding "the cause" so I wouldn't feel so guilty.

The gross findings were a normal pregnant female with an unborn male fetus. The only anomaly was lung congestion, which Joe attributed to the resuscitation effort. I would have to wait several more days to get a report on the microscopic tissue analysis.

The days went by oh so slowly. I had trouble keeping focused. I read anything obstetrical I could find to give me some reassurance that I had not really missed anything. But everything rested upon the final autopsy report.

Several days after the autopsy, Dr. Lasater asked me to stop by his office; he had something that may interest me about the autopsy. When I arrived, Joe was pretty excited (for a pathologist). He said, "I've never seen anything like this! She has goddamn *squames* everywhere! Here, take a look."

With this, Joe moved away from his microscope so I could view the slide and participate in his excitement. The slide revealed a piece of lung tissue that was packed with layers of cells filling the blood vessels, all the blood vessels. These were the "squames." Joe explained to me that the "squames" represented a massive amniotic fluid embolism that had shut down Kristen's cardiopulmonary system in a heartbeat. There was nothing that we, or anyone, could have done to save this woman and her unborn baby. The cause of amniotic embolism was unknown.

I gave the news to Kristen's husband who did not take the information well. By now he was sober and was confronted with being a single parent with three kids.

Dr. Lasater told me a few weeks later that he had received a call from an attorney inquiring about Kristen's death. Joe said he told the guy, "Go to hell. You don't have a case!"

In January 1978, I learned from the State of Montana that Kristen was one of two maternal deaths in Montana for 1977. This disclosure did not make me feel any better. This revelation aroused a lot of bad memories. "Why are government statisticians so compulsive anyway?" I thought.

In the fall of 2000, my office nurse asked if she could bring two women back to my office to talk. When I inquired about the topic, she said, "They want to talk about their mother, Kristen Easton."

I got a lump in my throat. Memory flashes from 23 years before became as clear as day. I thought I was done with this episode in my life! I hesitated, but then I agreed to see them.

Two young ladies soon appeared in my office. They promptly apologized for bothering me and for possibly resurrecting painful memories. However, they wanted to know about their mother. They said were so young when she died, and their father never would tell them much. They informed me that their father had died recently, and they were seeking some closure about their mom too.

I told them what I could recall about their mother, her pregnancy, and how she died.

They asked if their father had ever hurt her.

I said, "Yes."

Their reply was, "We thought so. That's how our dad was."

The ladies then thanked me for what I had tried to do for their mother. Then they left.

I thought about Kristen daily for months afterward.

Something or Nothing

The winter weather this particular day was ridiculous. The wind chills were around 60 degrees below zero. A blizzard had been going on all day, and I could barely see across the street from my office. No travel had been advised since early morning. Our clinic closed just after lunch to allow the employees and me a chance to get home safely.

A nurse summoned me to the emergency room in the early evening to see a lady with a sore abdomen. I reminded the nurse on duty that I lived 5 miles outside of town, the weather was horrendous, and I was not on call that night. I asked if any of the other doctors who lived in town could see the patient.

She related that the other doctors were either out of town, would not come, or could not get out of their driveways because of snowdrifts. The nurse then told me that the lady seemed to be having a lot of pain, and she essentially begged me to come in.

As always, I said yes. However, I advised the nurse it might take me a while because of the blizzard. I then stepped into our Dodge Ramcharger and headed toward the hospital.

I found that the visibility to be really pretty good for a blizzard. The wind was blowing so hard that there was not a lot of snow drifting onto the highway. When I reached the edge of town, however, I noticed snowdrifts of four to five feet deep around homes. I had to plow through a few drifts on the city streets on the way to the hospital, but they were no match for my big Dodge 4x4.

Upon arriving at the emergency room, I heard a wailing noise coming from behind a curtain from someone in obvious distress. The nurse thanked me for coming in to see the patient. After I briefly discussed the weather conditions with the nurse, she presented to me the patient's history and vital signs.

As I opened the curtain I saw a massive woman in front of me. She was wider than the bed! I guessed her weight to be well over 300 pounds. Her face was sweaty, and her gown was soaked with sweat. She would talk to me only in truncated sentences because of her paroxysms of abdominal pain.

Knowing that her vital signs were good and that she was coherent, I briefly examined her heart and lungs, which were not remarkable. Her back was not tender. Her legs were not abnormal except for their excessive size and weight.

As I exposed the lady's abdomen, I immediately saw the problem. This lady had a hernia about the size of a volleyball sticking above her mid-abdomen. The skin overlying the mass was thinned and blue. I could hear bowel noise in the mass. I concluded that this lady had an incarcerated and perhaps a strangulated bowel in this hernia. (Incarcerated means stuck through a small hole and strangulated implies being stuck with a loss of blood supply to the tissue.)

Gently, I attempted to reduce the mass, but the patient's persistent grunting made my efforts fruitless. I gave the lady some pain medication in the hope of relieving her pain and getting her to relax—No such luck.

I informed the patient and the nurse that to relieve the obstruction an operation would be necessary. I advised the patient that I was not a general surgeon, but I did have surgical experience. Because of the weather, no travel was advised. Therefore, I could not send her anywhere. She was stuck with us.

The lady wanted to wait a while longer to see if the hernia would reduce itself after I gave her more medication. Since she was stable, her request was not unreasonable. Besides, the added time gave me an opportunity to get my own consultation, to obtain some lab work, and to prepare the patient for surgery.

I called Dr. Smyth who was at his home. After I advised him of my patient's situation, he came to the hospital promptly. After he examined the patient, he concurred with my assessment. He agreed that surgery was required.

Dr. Smyth had a lot of experience with orthopedic surgery, but he had much less experience with bowel surgery. I had done some bowel surgery, but it had been a while. We came to an agreement that we would tackle the surgery together, but I would do any bowel resection if one were needed.

About this time, the nurse noted that the lady's pain had increased and her vital signs showed an increased pulse with a significant lowering of her blood pressure.

I knew that she was getting worse. (I was getting cold feet!)

I knew something had to be done soon. This lady was massive, and her chance of having a bad result because of her size was exponential. My stomach felt like a massive knot ready to explode.

I called the Billings Clinic for a surgical consultation.

Dr. Peter Edwards was the surgeon on call that evening. I had never met Dr. Edwards, but after I introduced myself and briefly presented my patient's, and my, dilemma, he asked, "Do you feel like your going to crap your pants?"

I replied, "Can you tell?"

After a chuckle, he said, "I've been there. It shows me that you care. That's what counts." Then Dr. Edwards went on to tell me, "In surgery you have only two choices: you do something or you do nothing. Now, if you do nothing, this lady may survive, but most likely she may die. If you do something, she may still die, but at least you give her a better chance to survive. So what do you want to do?

I responded, "I think she needs an operation pretty soon."

Dr. Edwards then said, "Good. Now, when you operate on this hernia, you will find dead bowel or you won't. If its dead, you cut it out. If not, you leave it alone. If you find black fat, cut it out. If not, leave it alone." He then said, "Call me back with what you find. Good luck."

Dr. Edwards made the decision making seem so easy. I already knew the decision making process, but he, in that short conversation, eliminated most of my trepidation.

By now, the lab technician, who lived within walking distance of the hospital, had arrived and had completed the requested lab tests. The hospital anesthetist and the surgical tech had braved the elements and plowed through snowdrifts to the hospital. When all the preparatory chores were completed, the operating room team took the lady to the operating room.

The anesthetist advised Dr. Smyth and me that because of the lady's size, it might take a few extra moments to get her asleep and cautioned, "So be patient."

We were in a hurry to get started; yet we weren't.

When our patient was fully asleep, I made an incision in the thin skin covering the mass. Delicately, the skin was loosened from the underlying mass and retracted aside. The mass was a black ball of fat. Carefully, we released the scar tissue holding down the mass so we could examine the tissues beneath it. To our relief, the intestines connected to the fat underneath were intact and totally *pink!*

The opening in the abdomen was only the size of a silver dollar. The quart-sized piece of black fat, about two pounds, had extruded through this small opening, became stuck, lost its blood supply, and died.

We removed the dead fat, re-evaluated the bowel to make sure nothing bad had been missed, and closed the hole with reinforced sutures so this problem could not happen again.

When the surgery was over and our patient was stable, I called Dr. Edwards to tell him the results of our efforts. His only response was, "Congratulations. Have a good night's sleep. Call us when we can be of help again."

Afterward, the patient did just fine.

I sent her home with a weight reducing diet that I knew would never be used - but I had to try.

Looking Right

The Richland County Fair takes place the first full week of each August in our farming community. Its timing is such that usually it occurs after the grain harvest and before the sugar beet harvest. Its a time when area residents have an opportunity to display their efforts in cooking, sewing, woodwork, the arts, and husbandry for their neighbors to appreciate their talents and in hopes of the receiving one of the sought after ribbon prizes. I personally enjoyed the critters in the 4-H barn and the big boy "toys" in the farm equipment displays.

While visiting the animal barns about midday during the fair in the late 1970s, an elderly lady named Eva approached me. Eva and her husband Emil were in their 70s and still farmed and ranched with their children about 50 miles west of town. I had met Eva and her husband the previous year during the county fair only in the hospital emergency room; Emil had "gotten sidewise with a heifer" and required a few stitches to his head to repair the damage. On this occasion, Eva told me that she knew something was wrong with her husband, but she could not put her finger on it. She asked if I would not mind seeing him.

I asked Eva a few more questions about her concerns, but I received only vague replies. Eva told me I could find Emil looking at the big John Deere tractors.

I made my way to the center of the fairgrounds to the farm implement display area. I found Emil inside the cab of a monstrous, new, 12-tire, four-wheel-drive International tractor. I greeted Emil and told him that I had spoken with his wife who wanted me to talk with him; she was concerned about him.

Emil countered with, "I feel fine. I have no pains. I eat good. I sleep good. I go to the bathroom just fine. I have not been sick. I just don't know what's got into that woman!"

About this time, Eva arrived and entered the conversation. The two had a feisty exchange in front of me before I suggested that I examine Emil in my office the next day. I thought that if I found nothing wrong with him, then Eva would be happy, and I found something wrong, then perhaps we could remedy the problem.

After another round of a brisk, one-sided conversation, Emil relented to be evaluated. However, it had to be early the next day because he had work to do on the farm.

My receptionist made a "special spot" for Emil at 9:30 the next morning. The pair arrived at the office and was ready to be seen at 9 a.m. Fortunately, I had my hospital work done early, and I was able to see the pair at 9 a.m. After I got the two septuagenarians into an exam room, I asked Emil a battery of the usual questions to get some idea of any potential issues. Just like at the fairgrounds, Emil produced only non-helpful answers. I directed similar questions about Emil to Eva for her point of view. She gave me essentially the same answers.

I then asked Eva, "What is he doing that's bugging you so much?"

Eva's reply was, "*He always makes right turns!*"

I queried, "Everyone makes right turns. What do you mean?"

Eva said, "Just like yesterday. We were in the truck just across the street from the grocery. All he had to do was turn left, and we would have been there. But NO! He makes a right turn and drives all over creation to get to the store.

Emil interrupted with, "I like to check things out. I enjoy looking at things."

After some further inquiry, I determined that Emil had taken a "scenic route" through town to the grocery store during which he made five right turns and no left turns. The pair started to get feisty again, so I asked Emil to get up onto my exam table. First I took his pulse and blood pressure lying down, and these values were normal. I did the same while he was sitting with the same result.

Now staring at Eva, Emil said, "See woman, I told you so. I'm fine."

As I started to evaluate Emil's head and neck area, I noticed that he looked at me a bit off center. Emil's head was facing me, but his eyes appeared to point left toward my right ear. I noticed that my nurse had recorded his vision as "20/20 each eye and together" so I knew his visual acuity was good. I thought that perhaps it was just the way he postured his head. With a penlight I determined his pupils reacted appropriately to light stimulation. As I moved my light horizontally to Emil's right side, his eyes moved appropriately to follow it, and he said he could see the light just fine. However, when I moved the light to Emil's left side, his eyes stopped in the middle, and his head moved to the left.

I thought to myself, "Something is amiss."

I proceeded with multiple other standard maneuvers to determine Emil's total field of vision. With my gross estimations, I determined that Emil had some type of left sided visual field loss. My examination of the back of his eye with my ophthalmoscope (a fancy name for a lighted magnifier for the eye) was normal.

The remainder of my total body examination was essentially normal for a man in his mid 70s.

I advised the pair that I found some abnormality with how Emil was seeing things. I wanted him to have a more formal evaluation of his eyes before I made a final diagnosis.

Eva wanted to get it done at once. Emil was a bit more reticent and was not interested. After another brief "discussion" between the two, Emil agreed to another evaluation.

I was able to get Emil an appointment with a local optometrist that morning for a visual field mapping examination. The pair agreed to return right after lunch to discuss the findings.

Just before noon, the optometrist called. He said, "This guy is fascinating! He has a classic left homonymous hemianopsia. I have never seen one! I will have Emil bring the pictures to you." (Left homonymous hemianopsia means there is a defect in the nerve tracts, the optic tracts, in the brain on the right side that manage visual signals for the left side. This is one defect that I recall a neurology professor telling my class that we probably would never see.)

Apparently, Emil had developed, probably from a silent stroke, a symmetrical visual loss encompassing the entire left visual field of each eye. Therefore, he could not see anything to the left of the midline of his eyes. Subsequently, he had adapted unconsciously to his disability by aiming his head a bit to the left and *by making only right turns when driving.*

When Eva and Emil returned, I gave them the news. The good news was that Emil was not going to die. The bad news was that Emil did not meet the legal visual requirements for driving a vehicle.

Eva was stunned. She did not drive. She asked me, "If Emil cannot drive, how will we get to town?"

I called the local law enforcement center to get some advice on how to proceed with my patient's predicament. I was referred to a lady in the Driver's License Bureau who told me that Emil could obtain a license if he received a waiver by a certified driving performance evaluator.

Fortunately, our hospital physical therapist had just started such a program.

I referred Emil and Eva to the physical therapist for an evaluation. After just a few sessions, Emil proved he could indeed make left turns and operate his truck safely with some adaptive mirrors mounted on his vehicle. About a month later, and after some practice, Emil retook his driving test with the Highway Patrol and passed. He could drive Eva into town once again!

Emil died a few years later at 82. I a family member told me that Eva made sure the funeral procession made a lot of right turns out in the country on the way to the cemetery so her husband could "check things out" one last time.

Revolution

When Dr. Berryman and I agreed to come to Sidney, we just wanted to be doctors. All we wanted was to take care of people the best way we knew how. Unfortunately, we took care of patients much differently than the people on the medical team that were present at the time. I found that most wanted us to come. But after a short time, a good number in the hospital wanted us to leave. We did things differently. We promoted excellence instead of mediocrity. We promoted team effort instead of a "king of the hill" hierarchy. We wanted everyone on the team to know what we knew. We found that there were a good number on the health care team who would not, could not, or did not want to change. In a very short period of time, Bill and I found ourselves in the middle of a major transition. We became the leading edge of a revolution to, as Bill would say, "bring these people screaming and kicking into the twentieth century."

Bill and I appeared on the scene just as an oil boom was starting in the area. Along with "economic prosperity," the boom brought drugs, crime, trauma, and a very busy hospital. This increased activity in the hospital with many more severely ill and traumatized patients added more stress to this sea of change.

The hospital nurses became the most obvious first avenue for change in the new environment. Most were quite good at giving back rubs, taking vital signs, and sitting at the bedside to comfort patients. However, our *new healthcare* first asked, and then demanded, that they become more responsible for the care they delivered. This meant that they had to learn a lot more about drugs. This meant the nurses had to become more adept at observations, physical evaluations, and correctly documenting their findings. To keep up, the nurses had to change significantly. Some made the transition readily. Most, however, struggled immensely. As with any significant change, some could not or would not keep up. A significant number of the nurses decided to retire.

Our hospital undertook an unprecedented effort to recruit and retain new nurses. Over the next few years our team was blessed with a new generation of nurses. Tabatha, Pamela, Naomi, Mary Beth, Kay, Judith, Melanie, Georgia, and many others who came, stayed, and upgraded our level of care. Our hospital changed nurse administrators several times as these folks also withered under the storm of stress and change. At times the atmosphere at the hospital was tumultuous. In the end, however, all the new nurses wanted to do was to show people what they knew, and what they could do. (Sound familiar?)

Another area undergoing major upheaval was the lab and radiology department. Previously, a single person, Thomas, manned these separate areas. Along with the massive increase in patient volume came increases in the number of x-ray and laboratory procedures ordered and completed. This development required splitting the department into two distinct units, the laboratory and radiology. Thomas became the chief, and only, radiology technician.

Thomas was an amazing worker. He came daily at 5 - 6 a.m. and did not leave until late. He was always available, day or night. Later, Adelle trained onsite as an assistant. After a period of time, the hospital recruited our own radiologist along with a steady stream of new technicians who could operate the new tools of the trade: the ultrasound, the CT scanner, and the nuclear scanner. These workers also wanted to show the world what they knew and what they could do.

To keep the lab afloat, the hospital was fortunate to hire two new lab technicians, Donna and Cheryl, who worked like dogs and seldom complained. Not only did they have to perform an increasing number of basic lab tests, but also they had to obtain and test new equipment that would perform the ever more complex tests that the physicians were requesting. Since I had been a lab technician in medical school, I found myself trying to help out during "crunch times" by doing some of the simpler tests. These ladies were new, young, motivated, dedicated, and very good!

Eventually, Donna and Cheryl moved on with their families, and different lab techs arrived. The latest and future techs continued to build upon the foundation these ladies had lain.

The hospital pharmacy was in a shambles. It was covered only part time by one of the local private pharmacists who had little experience with intravenous therapies and acute care drugs. Somehow, the hospital found a young pharmacist from North Dakota named Grant to head up the pharmacy. Soon after his arrival, Grant asked me to be part of a formulary committee to clean up and update the pharmacy. No other physician volunteered, so Grant and I were the committee. At our first committee meeting we had to decide which one of the *37 brands of vitamins* in stock should be kept.

Grant developed a system of drug evaluation and review so the pharmacy would not become loaded again with the latest "drugs of the week" promoted by drug company salesmen. Additionally, he presented training sessions to nurses and physicians about IV additives, feeding through IVs, and drug pharmacology. He just wanted to do a good job and show people what he knew. He became an integral addition to the new team.

Other departments had their changes along the way. The food service added a consulting dietitian for our ill patients and the nursing home. Engineering added Pete and others to lead the charge to fix up and maintain the aging physical plant of the hospital. Medical records enlarged to four new people from a department of one. This department added expertise in coding and record keeping efficiency. A new financial officer came on board to make sense of an antiquated accounting system and to get the financial data onto computers. Respiratory therapy services were added for our onslaught of intensive-care patients and the large number of local patients with asthma and emphysema. Physical therapy was added for our trauma and orthopedic patients.

Our emergency room, all 20 feet by 20 feet of it, became one of the busiest in the state of Montana. Our hospital provided an ever-increasing flow of patients requiring critical care to the regional referral hospitals. One year our EMS system averaged one flight a day just for trauma. This activity came from a 50-bed hospital in a community of only 5,000.

Saying that our small emergency area was overused and overcrowded was an understatement. In 1981, after substantial effort and input by our physicians, a new trauma based emergency area with significantly more space was completed. This much larger space would be a blessing on more than one occasion.

Under the direction of Earl Neff, the Richland County EMS system was transformed into a model admired for excellence by many statewide.

The Hospital Board changed too. Those who had been on the Board for a social "feather in their cap" left and were replaced with others who became more engaged with the issues, concerns, and dilemmas of health care delivery in the "new era" of Medicare and prospective payments.

Finally, there was a dramatic turnover in our medical staff during this time. Issues continued to surface with the older physician and our Cuban born physician. After some very public episodes, both these men lost their medical licenses. Dr. Larimore moved, and eventually made it back to Ireland. Dr. Smyth left in 1980 for a surgical residency. Dr. Bill left for a residency in internal medicine and returned. He added just another dimension to his previous efforts for quality care and improvement in the "system". Over the years, many more new physicians came and went. Each one added something to the team while they were with us. (Over the next 25 years close to 50 doctors would come and go from our small community.)

Following the end of the oil boom of the 1970s and early 1980s, our sleepy little hospital transformed into a regional center of excellence for health care. Certainly a revolution had occurred to produce this transformation.

Little did Dr. Bill and I know what we were walking into in the spring of 1976.

THOSE DARN KIDS

"There are only two things a child will share willingly — communicable diseases and his mother's age."

Benjamin Spock, M.D.

"A child is a curly dimpled lunatic."

Ralph Waldo Emerson

"When you have children yourself, you begin to understand what you owe your parents."

Japanese Proverb

Puppy Girl

Late one afternoon my office staff and I heard a lot of screaming and crying in the hallway outside my office. A child was obviously in distress. Into the office ran a mother with her four-year-old daughter in her arms who was screaming vigorously and not moving her left leg.

The mom quickly informed us that she was called away from work by the preschool attendant who said that her daughter had been playing with some of the other children and all of a sudden started to scream. The worker noted that the girl did not want to use her left leg; she assumed that an injury had occurred. According to the daycare attendant, none of the other children were hurt, the kids had been getting along just fine, and no traumatic event had been witnessed.

The mother and the screaming young girl were promptly escorted out of the reception area to the nurses' area of the clinic. As soon as the child saw my nurse, she stopped crying. The pain apparently vanished!

As the mother held the child, I quickly checked the left leg. I found no tenderness. There was no redness, bruising, or swelling. The leg did not recoil from pain. The leg seemed to be just fine to me. We were all befuddled.

The mother set the child down only to watch her briskly jump onto the scale *without pain.*

The child then ran back to exam room #6. She got up on the exam table and waited for the adults to follow.

The mom and I looked at each other in bewilderment to say the least.

When the mom and I entered the room, I asked the youngster, "Where do you hurt?"

She pointed to her left ear.

Now I wondered, "How can an ear ache make your leg have pain?" I decided to bypass the leg and look at the left ear first because that seemed to be the culprit for this whole adventure.

As I began to put my otoscope (a fancy name for a flashlight) into the child's ear canal to examine the ear canal and the eardrum, she whispered something to me that I could not understand. I pulled back and asked her, "Tell me again only a little louder because I am getting old."

The little girl said nicely, "The puppy peed in my ear."

I said, "What?"

She then got a disgusted look on her face and said with her hands on her hips, "THE PUPPY PEED IN MY EAR!"

I was bewildered.

The mother started to giggle and then to laugh. The mother informed me that someone had brought a new puppy to the preschool, and the puppy had been licking her daughter about the face. Apparently, the puppy unloaded in the child's ear, and the little girl thought I should know about it.

I guessed that no one ever would have taken her to the doctor for "pee in the ear," but certainly a painful, limp leg did the trick.

We all had a good laugh.

I thanked the little girl for letting me know about her fun day.

I thought this little girl and her mom deserved some commendation for brightening my day. So, I gave them coupons for the local Dairy Queen.

Pretty Darn Rare

After an unremarkable labor, Michael was born in late summer to a young couple who farmed a few miles outside of town. His birth weight of 7 1/2 pounds was a substantial relief to his mother who had feared delivering yet another large infant. (She had delivered two 9-pound baby boys previously.) Except for some facial bruising, Michael appeared by all the physical parameters to be a "normal" newborn.

Since medical school, where I spent a substantial amount of time in the newborn intensive care unit, it had been my custom to obtain a blood sample from all my newborns to test for blood sugar, since a low sugar could cause severe issues with newborns. Since the lab technician was already obtaining blood, I had her obtain a little extra blood to determine a hemoglobin and a hematocrit, which determine the amount of red cells in the blood and subsequently the oxygen carrying capacity of the blood. This testing was most often done within the first four to six hours of birth if the baby appeared healthy.

Michael's initial hematocrit was 37 percent. (Normally, it would be 50 percent to 60 percent at birth.) The morning after Michael's birth, a repeat hematocrit was only 31 percent. I was perplexed since I noticed no obvious reason for him to be anemic. The mother was healthy. The pregnancy was not complicated. There was minimal blood loss with the birth process. I called the regional neonatologist for a consultation.

The specialist was not terribly concerned as long as the baby appeared healthy and vigorous, which he did. The neonatologist said, "Sometimes things just happen, and we just don't know why." He suggested that I give the baby some blood to bring him up to a "normal" hematocrit level. Then he suggested that I watch the baby closely and repeat the blood test in a few weeks. If I had concerns, the neonatologist said I could call him at any time.

After I discussed with Michael's parents their baby's blood tests and my conversations with the neonatologist, I gave Michael a transfusion of about 60 milliliters of packed red cells (about four tablespoons). Afterward, his blood count was 60 percent.

He was no longer pale from his anemia. His examination remained normal. I allowed Michael to go home with his parents, and I planned to see him again in three weeks.

At his three-week examination, Michael looked great. At his six-week exam, not only was Michael growing and developing according to plan, but also his hematocrit was still 50 percent. (The hematocrit decreases with age, and the numbers normalize to a range between 38 percent and 48 percent.) I figured his low blood count at birth was some sort of fluke, and that the single transfusion had corrected the mystery problem.

.When he was 10 weeks old, Michael caught a cold and became quite fussy. The mother brought him to the office where I noticed that the infant was growing normally but had developed a severe ear infection with his respiratory infection. I prescribed an oral antibiotic for the child, I gave the mother my usual precautions about illness in young babies, and I asked her to bring the child back to the office in a week to have his ears reevaluated.

The mom brought Michael back after just two days because his fussiness had worsened. This time, the baby was much more agitated. He was also markedly pale. I had a complete blood count performed which showed normal white cells (cells that fight infection), normal platelets (cells to help blood clot), and a hematocrit of only 7-8 percent!

I admitted Michael to the hospital for a blood transfusion and an evaluation of his anemia.

Soon after his admission, I inserted an intravenous catheter into Michael's leg, and I gave him enough blood to bring his hematocrit back to about 50 percent.

Afterward, Michael was a new boy. His fussiness resolved. Despite his cold and ear infection issues he was considerably happier.

I then performed a bone marrow aspiration from the baby's pelvic bone. Dr. Lasater, our hospital pathologist, evaluated the samples and told me the bone marrow had essentially no erythroblasts, the primitive cells that make red blood cells. He said this could mean the child had a temporary problem, called Transient Erythroblastopenia of Childhood or TEC (a temporary condition during which normal cells in the bone marrow that make red blood cells stop working for an unknown reason), or a more serious problem called Congenital Red Blood Cell Aplasia or Diamond-Blackfan Syndrome (a condition at birth of unknown cause where the bone marrow cells that make red blood cells do not exist or are critically diminished in number). Dr. Lasater said each of these problems were "pretty damn rare" and that I had better talk with one of the "Big Boys" at a medical school.

Subsequently, I spoke with a professor in the pediatric hematology department at the University of Washington Medical School on two separate occasions. This physician reiterated Dr. Lasater's comments. He told me that the first condition, TEC, was reported about 1000 times per year in the U.S. Its treatment consisted of a blood transfusion and observation for several months. Typically, TEC resolved spontaneously for no known reason when the body resumed making normal red blood cells after 2-3 months.

The Diamond-Blackfan Syndrome, however, occurred only about 20 times per year in the U.S. There were only about 500 known cases worldwide at the time. The disease was so rare that not enough was known about what should or would happen in the long term. The doctor did say that it appeared that giving cortisone early might improve survival. With no treatment, the life expectancy was less than 20 years and about 20 percent of patients died by the age of three years. At the time, no patient had been known to live past 26 years. The physician suggested starting Michael on cortisone as soon as possible.

I discussed all the information I had with the parents. With considerable reluctance, and understandably so because of the potential side effects of cortisone, the parents agreed to start their son on cortisone therapy. Following a protocol given to me by the hematologist in Washington, Michael was started on a specific dose of cortisone determined by his body weight; his blood would be evaluated every two weeks after starting the medication.

The parents brought Michael into the clinic after two weeks. His growth remained good. However, his hematocrit had dropped to 32 percent. More importantly, his reticulocyte count, which is a measure of how many new red cells are being made, was only 0.2 percent. (Normally it should be 1-2 percent.) I was hoping for 3-4 percent to demonstrate a good response from the bone marrow. The tests showed that Michael was not making new red blood cells. However, as directed, I continued with the protocol after more discussions with the parents.

Two weeks later, Michael's hematocrit had increased to 36 percent. His reticulocyte count had increased to 0.9 percent. I thought things were looking up, but we still did not have a final diagnosis. Michael was not "out of the woods" yet.

After two more weeks, the lab results were no better, but not worse. By the protocol, we still had to wait at least another month to distinguish between TEC and Blackfan-Diamond Syndrome.

The next month was a nightmare for the parents. Michael was now about four months old and seemed to catch every infectious bug that came into the family home. He had the croup. He had vomiting and diarrhea. He had ear infections. I had no idea how much of his cortisone medicine, if any, he had been able to keep down for a month. At the end of the month, Michael's blood tests had not changed. We still did not have a diagnosis.

In late February, I saw Michael again when he was about five and one-half months old. The mom related that her son had an awful time with the cortisone medicine and did not get *every dose.* I was not sure how much medicine, if any, he had received or had kept down. This situation proved to be most beneficial to me, however, because Michael's tests plummeted. His hematocrit had dropped to 28 percent, and his reticulocyte count had dropped to 0.6 percent. I concluded that his bone marrow was failing. He appeared to have Diamond-Blackfan Syndrome.

I had a long talk with the parents about my thoughts, and the fact that they should develop a relationship with a hematologist. I also suggested they make sure Michael received his cortisone as prescribed.

Over the next few weeks, the parents and I communicated a lot. They had to deal with a mountain of information, a lot of uncertainty, and a lot of fear. Importantly, over this time frame and with a full dose of cortisone daily, Michael's hematocrit rebounded to 36 percent and his reticulocyte count jumped to 4 percent! His bone marrow had started to work.

Finally, the parents elected to see a hematologist in Billings instead of going to a university.

I made inquiries with a pediatric hematologist in Billings. He told me that he *might* have seen a Diamond-Blackfan kid when he was in training some 20 years before. He said, "Those kids are pretty darn rare! He would have to hit the books before they came." He was anxious to see Michael as soon as possible.

The rest, as they say, is history. Except for periodic medication changes, Michael blossomed. His blood counts remained stable through illness and health. As he grew, Michael proved to be smart and athletic. He participated in *everything* according to his mom. Yet, as he grew, he never had to increase the dose of medication.

The hematologist told me that not he, nor anyone else, had any idea of the correct course of treatment for Diamond-Blackfan Syndrome. But as long as Michael was doing well, and he was, the doctor was more than willing to allow Michael to "grow out of his medicine."

The hematologist stopped the cortisone when Michael was about 18-years-old because he was taking "almost nothing."

Michael graduated from high school as an honor student and headed off to college to become an engineer.

As of 2006, only about 600 cases of were known in the U.S., Canada, and Europe. The incidence remains at about 5 cases per 1,000,000 births. Considering the number of babies born in our town every year, I figured some lucky physician in our community *might* see the next case of Diamond-Blackfan Syndrome in about *150 years.*

Its cause remains a mystery.

Vegetables

The grandmother noticed that her grandson Jeremiah had really bad breath one morning. First she thought he must have a cold because his nose was runny. However, as the day progressed, the odor from the boy's face became just plain awful! Just before suppertime, the grandmother had smelled enough and brought Jeremiah to the emergency room at the hospital.

Jeremiah was about a two-year-old boy with bright red hair and a face full of freckles. He was one busy boy in the ER as he ran around trying to get into everything and anything not locked down or closed. On my first view of Jeremiah, I knew "this was not a sick child."

I too smelled the odor coming from his head and neck area. With further observation, I noticed that mucous was coming only from the left side of his nose. This was the source of the odor.

Using an otoscope (a fancy flashlight) with a nose adapter I detected a foreign body deep in the nasal cavity on the left side. By using an instrument similar to a very small pair of pliers, I was able to retrieve a macerated pea.

The grandmother told me that the father had been getting ready to plant some peas, and Jeremiah must have decided to experiment with some planting of his own.

We all had a good chuckle. Grandma went home with a much better smelling Jeremiah.

The very next day, the mother returned to the ER around suppertime with Jeremiah. She said they were eating when she told Jeremiah to eat his peas. He promptly put a pea in the right side of his nose. The mom told us that she had tried to retrieve the pea, but she succeeded only in pushing it in farther.

After I had retrieved another pea from his nose, Jeremiah seemed none the worse for wear. However, the mother admonished her young boy, "Never put a pea in your nose again!"

The next day was Saturday. I was about ready to leave the hospital just before lunchtime when the ER nurse paged me and said, "Guess who's back. Its Jeremiah again."

As I walked into the ER, I saw a most exasperated woman with a most content Jeremiah sitting on the exam table.

I asked if Jeremiah had put another pea in his nose. The mother replied, "No. This time it's a *piece of corn*. I can see it, but I just couldn't get it out."

Again, I removed the foreign object from the boy's nose. As they were leaving the ER I heard the mom exclaim, "Don't you EVER put ANYTHING in your NOSE again!"

I thought to myself with a chuckle, "Yeh, right."

To my amazement, or perhaps not, the mom, the dad, and Jeremiah returned the very next day to the hospital. This time their little boy had put stuff in his *ears*! I could see that dad was not a happy camper.

On this visit, from Jeremiah's ear canals I plucked a pea, a corn kernel, and several small seeds, which mom said looked like tomato seeds.

I commented in jest, "It appears that your little boy likes his vegetables."

The parents were not amused by my wit.

The family left without incident. However, before they got into the family pickup truck in the parking lot, Jeremiah experienced dad's board of education to his seat of learning!

Jeremiah had learned his lesson, or had he? At least, I never plucked another foreign object out of him.

Kati

In the spring of 1979 a father brought his daughter to the clinic because she had a nosebleed that he could not stop. The parents told me that the youngster's nose had been bleeding off and on for about three days. The dad said he and the mother figured that Kati just had a cold with a sore nose. The other kids had been ill too.

Kati was about seven-years-old. She was thin and profoundly pale. My examination of this youngster revealed evidence of previous bleeding in the nose, which had now abated. Her mouth had many small hemorrhages under the mucous membranes. Finally, she had multiple bruises on her arms and legs.

My first impression was that this girl had been abused. The parents were shown the skin lesions. They thought she had just fallen while playing with the other kids.

Because she was so pale, I had the lab perform a CBC (complete blood count). While the lab was processing the test, Kati fell asleep on the exam table because she was so tired. The lab results showed a few platelets (cells for clotting), a normal white cell count (cells for infection fighting), and a hemoglobin (a measure of red blood cells) of only 3! (Anemia is defined as having a hemoglobin less than 11.)

I thought, "This girl almost bled to death. She needs a transfusion."

I explained the situation to the parents and advised them that Kati should go to the hospital for the transfusion. The father became most upset. He accused me of just trying to rip him off. The parents asked for a few minutes to discuss my suggestion in private. Outside the door the entire clinic staff and I could hear a heated conversation between the parents. Afterward, I was asked to come back in.

The parents said they had no insurance. The family income was subsistence at best; another large bill would be a hardship.

I told them I was more concerned about their daughter than my pocketbook. I thought that is where their priorities should be too.

They agreed to take their daughter to the hospital.

Before Kati received any blood, more of her blood was obtained for testing. After a two-pint transfusion of blood, the child showed considerably more energy. Unfortunately, one test called a reticulocyte count, which estimates the body's production of new red blood cells, was zero. I had the test repeated. It was still zero. (Had Kati been normal, this test should have been elevated, not absent.)

I asked our pathologist, Dr. Joseph Lasater, to review the blood slides. He confirmed the previous reports. He said he saw a few "atypicals" as well. Additionally, he related her iron studies proved she should be able to make red cells. After a short discussion, we concluded that our patient should have an evaluation of her bone marrow. After obtaining consent from her parents, Joe and I performed the bone marrow aspiration from her posterior pelvis bone.

After a short time, Joe had reviewed the blood slides and told me, "This girl has no red cell precursors in the marrow. She has aplastic anemia."

Nothing else seemed to be wrong in the sample we had obtained. For some reason, Kati's bone marrow cells that produce red blood cells did not exist. I knew that this situation could have been caused by a number of things including infection, chemicals, or early leukemia. Whatever the reason, I knew that this girl needed to see a specialist.

The parents were not happy with our findings. I never knew if they were mad at me, mad at Kati, upset about their sick daughter, or just basically unhappy people. The parents consented to take their child to Billings to see a pediatric hematologist. Dr. Lasater sent along his pathology slides with them.

Over the next few weeks, Kati's condition worsened. A repeat bone marrow test confirmed my worst fears, "acute lymphocytic leukemia presenting as an aplastic crisis." The life expectancy of this disease untreated was only three months.

The pediatric oncologist administered medications to acutely stop the cancerous process with only some success. Kati would require much more care and many more medications at a specialty center if she were to be helped for the long term.

I saw Kati in our hospital a few months later for another blood transfusion. Supposedly, this transfusion was to improve her status before yet another course of chemotherapy could be started.

At some point over the next few months, Kati's parents became unconcerned with finances. No treatment was too good or too expensive for their daughter now. My thought was that since the family was so far in debt, the parents would never get out of their financial hole without a bankruptcy. The parents fired the Billings physicians and headed to the Mayo Clinic.

I last saw Kati about a year later when she came to our hospital in another crisis. This time she was in need of red cells and platelets, both of which had to be irradiated before they were given. The doctors at Mayo wanted her to get to the clinic in Rochester, Minnesota as soon as possible.

I thought the best thing to do was to fly Kati and her family to the Mayo Clinic. However, I found out that no ambulance service would fly Kati or her parents until they were paid *in advance*. The parents had literally run out of their financial rope. The family would have to drive to the Mayo Clinic about 800 miles away.

With the assistance of Donna, our chief lab tech, we found a place to get the blood products Kati required. It was the middle of the night when I called and woke up the radiation oncologist near our blood bank outlet. I asked have him irradiate the needed blood products for Kati.

He was delighted to help us. He told me, "This is my first emergency call in 15 years!" He agreed to prepare the blood and send it by airplane as soon as it was ready.

The blood we gave to Kati in Sidney would not last the time it would take to drive to the Mayo Clinic. Therefore, I arranged for her to receive transfusions in Bismarck and Fargo, North Dakota, and in Minneapolis before she arrived in Rochester, Minnesota.

The irradiated blood arrived from the blood bank about three hours later. Kati received one transfusion in Sidney. The remainder of the blood was kept in a cooler for transport. Her IV line remained in and was secured so that "she would have to break her arm for it to come out." I handed a sheet of instructions to Kati's parents and wished them a good trip.

The family made it to the Mayo Clinic about 14 hours later where Kati received the last of the blood we had prepared for her. Unfortunately, her condition deteriorated thereafter. She died within a short time.

Some time later, I received a call from the billing department at Mayo because they were trying to locate Kati's parents regarding her bill.

I informed them I had no idea where they were, or where they lived. I told them that my clinic and our hospital had written off their debt a long time before.

I did not see the parents again. Not once did I hear them say any words of appreciation for what we, the medical team, had tried to do to help their daughter. I guess they figured it was their *right* to have medical care, and it was our *privilege* to serve them at *our* expense.

Anyway, I felt good about what our team had tried to do for an unfortunate child.

Speechless

Tom and Mary Thompson were the proud parents of three wonderful children. They had decided that their family was complete, and they successfully relied upon natural birth control methods after their third child was born. They were successful, that is, for six years. Then along came Matthew, a gorgeous child who was loved dearly by parents and siblings alike.

The other children seemed to develop normally and by all accounts were performing well in school. In his mother's eyes, however, Matthew seemed to be a laggard in his development. He seemed to eat, sleep, and play all right. He would giggle and grunt and cry, but not a word came out of Matthew. But he just did not talk.

When Matthew was about 15 months old, Mary brought him in to see me to figure out why he was not talking. I figured that language skills would come eventually. When my physical examination of Matthew was benign, I encouraged the mother to be patient for another three or four months. If Matthew was not talking by then, I asked her to bring him back.

The time went by, and Matthew still was not talking.

The child was now 18 months old and no "Mama" or "Dada" was forthcoming. I relented and made arrangements for the child to be seen by Dr. Paul Crellin at the Child Study Center in Billings. Dr. Crellin was one of the pediatric gurus of Montana. Surely, if something could be found, I thought the folks at his clinic would find it. They tested and tested and tested Matthew. The report came back "No substantial developmental abnormalities noted except mild speech delay. Recommend observation for six months, and reevaluate." This note came from *the experts.*

Mom was not pleased, but she agreed to another observation period.

When Matthew was 24 months old, Mary called me to say there was no change. She spent a lot of money in Billings for nothing and did not want to go back. I arranged for this boy to be seen by Dr. Olden at the Development Assessment Program (DEAP) in Miles City with two more days of testing. The final report said," Normal child with a mild speech delay. Recommend period of observation of four to six months."

Mom was getting more aggravated each day her child said nothing. This mother wanted an answer, but again she agreed to more observation.

About four months went by when I received a speech evaluation report from the CARES (Clinical Assessment and Rehabilitative Services) program in Williston, North Dakota. Apparently, Mrs. Thompson wanted a third opinion. This report said, "Normal child with speech delay of unknown origin. Repeat evaluation in three to six months. Family may want to consider speech therapy."

When I called Mary with the answer, she cried. She was convinced there was something wrong with her baby; she was going to find someone, somewhere who could help Matthew.

Another several months went by before Mary called the office again about Matthew, who was now almost three-years-old. Mary was quite excited and said she had to see me right away.

I told her to come right up to the office. I let my receptionist know that Mary was coming in now!

Mary arrived within minutes. She was smiling, crying, laughing and talking simultaneously. When I got her to slow down a bit, she exulted, "He talked! Matthew talked!" She was so happy it was contagious. My entire office staff was smiling.

I asked, "What did he say?"

"Hamburger, fries, and coke!"

I replied, "He said what?"

She repeated, "Hamburger, fries, and coke!"

Apparently, she and Matthew were in the drive-up line at the local McDonald's. When the attendant asked for their order, there were no siblings around to speak up for Matthew. So from the back seat came, "Hamburger, fries, and coke!"

Matthew continued to talk and talk and talk.

Failure to Thrive

New parents-to-be have nothing but high hopes and expectations for their new baby. Susan's parents were no different. The mother was healthy, and her pregnancy was not complicated. No one in the family had any known "weird" diseases. Mom's labor and delivery were uncomplicated. The newborn baby girl seemed normal when she left the hospital.

The mom was so excited about her new little girl. In addition to breastfeeding her new baby, the new mom tried to do everything that was good and natural. At her three-week examination, Susan seemed to be fine. The parents reported that Susan was playful and alert. Her growth was acceptable. Unfortunately, the breastfeeding had not gone as well as mom had expected. The mother had changed her diet, but Susan still did not feed well. I suggested that Mom might try regular infant formula.

The mom changed her baby's diet to a cow's milk based formula and tried this for a few weeks. Still, Susan remained fussy, and she was not gaining weight. Mom then tried a soybean-based formula; the baby continued to be fussy and developed loose stools. Despite being sickly a lot, Susan did gain some weight. By two-months of age, this child seemed to be rebounding. I decided to take her measurements every two weeks.

Susan seemed to have a perpetual cough and a stuffy nose. Except for a few nonspecific symptoms, I did not appreciate any major physical findings. She continued to gain weight, but *very slowly*.

When she was about four months old, Susan became ill with what appeared to be just a simple upper respiratory illness. Within a short time, however, she was having trouble breathing most of the day, and her mother brought Susan into the clinic to see me.

When I examined her, Susan appeared quite ill. She was wheezing like she was having an asthma attack. She was a pale blue color, which indicated to me that the lungs were not keeping her body oxygenated. At this time, her oxygen saturation was only 80 percent (normal is 95 percent).

Additionally, Susan was not gaining weight again. Her height was at the 40th percentile while her weight had dropped to the second percentile for her age. With all these persistent problems, Susan met the criteria for failing to thrive. I sent Susan from the clinic to the hospital with the diagnoses of acute viral illness, respiratory distress, and failure to thrive.

After a few respiratory treatments, Susan's breathing improved, and her color turned pink. Because of her apparent food intolerances, I gave her a special formula used for kids with feeding problems that she appeared to tolerate formula well.

During my evaluation of Susan in the hospital, I noticed that her stool looked like gray paste, not normal stool. This raised a diagnostic flag for me. I thought to myself, "I've seen this before."

During my internship, I had the opportunity to care for "T Bear" (Theodore Barrett Hollingsworth) for eight weeks. T Bear, a 9-year-old boy with cystic fibrosis who had his nickname coined by the pediatric nursing staff, died after his 10th birthday after spending almost two consecutive years in the hospital. I recalled that T Bear had stools that looked like Susan's.

Over the years since my internship, the treatment for cystic fibrosis had changed dramatically. Cystic fibrosis patients, when supported with good pulmonary care and enhanced digestive and nutrition management, had an increase in their average life expectancy of 5 to 10 years. The average life expectancy was now 15 years.

The evaluation of her breathing issues and failure to grow prompted me to order a series of tests to include a sweat chloride test. (The sweat chloride test determines the amount of salt in a person's sweat. When the test result is elevated, it is diagnostic for cystic fibrosis.) The result was quite high. The lab repeated this test daily for three days, and the results remained high. I diagnosed Susan with cystic fibrosis!

Cystic fibrosis is an inherited inflammatory disorder of all the body's secretory glands. The glands that secrete digestive chemicals are abnormal and function poorly; therefore, the child has feeding and digestive problems that lead to poor development and growth. Stools look can like gray paste. The glands in the lungs secrete thick, tenacious mucous instead of a watery mucous. This produces various types of pulmonary problems including making the person susceptible to frequent bouts of infection.

I knew that my Susan needed to be seen by a pulmonary specialist.

After consultation with the Denver Children's Hospital, Susan was referred to Billings to be seen by the local pediatricians and by a pediatric pulmonology consultant from Denver. In Billings, she received the immediate care she needed for her acute respiratory illness.

After her initial acute illness had resolved, Susan spent time in Denver with their cystic fibrosis team. The Denver team told me that Susan was the youngest child diagnosed with cystic fibrosis on record at their clinic, a mere four and one/half months.

The pediatric pulmonologist congratulated me on my "nice pick up."

I told him that actually I had remembered the stools that T Bear had, and I just "did the test."

Afterward, for whatever reason, Susan's parents decided not to follow up with me. I heard verbal reports about her status over the years from various sources. The parents had taken her to see multiple pediatricians in search of "the one." But I did not have the opportunity to participate in Susan's care directly.

Over the years, this youngster had many problems relating to her disease. She had a feeding tube in her stomach for years to supply her with 24-hour nutrition. She needed to eat certain foods along with handfuls of digestive enzymes and vitamins. She required respiratory treatments and chest physiotherapy every four hours daily for years. When Susan was not in the hospital, her parents provided most of her care under the phone supervision of the Denver CF team.

Susan grew oh so slowly, but she did grow. I had the opportunity to observe her development from afar as the years passed.

The last time I saw Susan was at her high school graduation before she left for college. She was 18-years-old.

Miracle Child

Annette was the first-born child to a young couple who had a farm west of town. The mother's pregnancy was unremarkable. The mom always seemed to be delighted that she was going to have a baby. In midsummer Annette was born without much trouble considering this was her mom's first delivery. Weighing almost eight pounds, she was almost perfect except for some bruising on her face and head.

Except for a few incidental issues, Annette's first 18 months passed uneventfully. She had grown in height and weight appropriately. She was meeting or exceeding normal developmental milestones. She started to talk and to walk and to be a normal little playful person.

When Annette was about 21 months old, her mom noticed that her infant had bruises for no apparent reason. Annette would be playing with other kids when she would become bruised and the others would not. She did not appear ill in any way. She remained playful. She was just developing bruises.

The bruising continued for only a short time when the parents decided to have Annette examined. The mom knew something *just was not right.*

I examined Annette on a Friday morning in May. She was a robust, playful youngster who seemed quite pale to me. Additionally, she had bruises in some most unusual places where one would not expect trauma, such as inside her mouth, under her arms, and on her lips. In addition, I appreciated many bruises of various sizes on her arms, legs, and head. Annette's mom was questioned again about unusual trauma or vigorous play, and again she repeated that Annette was just as active as the other kids.

I ordered a complete blood count and some clotting studies to be done that day. Initially, the first lab report was normal except for *low platelets* and a *low red blood cell count.*

I thought this child might have a relatively benign disorder called ITP (idiopathic thrombocytopenic purpura). (Now you know why doctor's use alphabet soup when they talk.)

As I was about to chat with the parents about the lab tests, I received a call from Dr. Joe Lasater, the pathologist in the hospital, who informed me that the lab report was only partly correct. After personally reviewing the blood smear slide, he concluded that something ominous was afoot. He reported that the blood picture was one of an acute myelogenous process, probably leukemia of some sort. He said he could not be more specific because the blood required further testing, and the patient needed a bone marrow aspiration to view the activity in the bone marrow itself.

I advised the parents of my discussion with Dr. Lasater and that I would have to consult with a specialist in blood diseases of children. I then contacted a pediatric hematologist in Billings regarding my Annette's situation. He kindly informed me that he did not administer the initial treatment for new cases of leukemia but rather referred patients to regional centers for initial care. Only then would he assume aftercare, if it were requested. The physician gave me the names of the physicians in Denver that he found to be the most productive for his patients and their families in our area. Subsequently, I called the physicians at the oncology department at the Denver Children's Hospital who said they were ready and willing to accept Annette in referral as soon as possible.

I returned to talk with the parents. I informed them of my multiple discussions with the various physicians. I advised the parents that Annette appeared to have a serious blood disorder that required prompt evaluation by specialists. After this conversation, the parents, made arrangements to be flown to Denver as soon as possible.

About 10 days later I received a call from Dr. Gary Brian, the pediatric hematologist in Denver caring for Annette. He stated that she had a most rare leukemia called acute megakaryocytic leukemia, a leukemia of the cells that make the platelets needed for clotting. She had incurred a bone marrow aspiration and many more blood tests to identify the disease; he started Annette on her initial course of chemotherapy. Dr. Brian told me that if all went well, Annette would need to be on chemotherapy for two more years. She would need to be seen in Denver again in about two weeks to evaluate the effects of the first course of therapy.

In the meantime, I researched megakaryocytic leukemia. I talked with Dr. Lasater and the Billings hematologist. I looked up the latest type of chemotherapy and its consequences. I contacted the National Cancer Institute and the National Institute of Health. My research was not comforting. Annette's disease occurred in children under 20 years of age at a rate of only about *3 cases per 10 million per year!* That meant there were only about 20 cases per year in the country! The more common types of leukemia occurred at a rate 100 times this. Furthermore, the cure rate, defined as surviving five years after diagnosis, was about 20 percent only if the patient had a remission in the disease after the first course of chemotherapy. If the first trial of chemotherapy failed and a second course of primary chemotherapy were required, then the survival rate dropped to about 5 percent. In other words, if the disease did not kill the patient primarily, and the patient survived the chemotherapy poisons, then only about *four* of the 20 patients would survive with a successful first trial of chemotherapy. However, if a second course of therapy were needed, then only about *one* of the 20 patients would survive.

Dr. Brian called about two weeks later to tell me that another bone marrow test showed 30 percent abnormal cells, the first trial of chemotherapy had not been successful, and Annette was going to receive a second round of chemotherapy.

Afterward, Dr. Brian told me that Annette would be coming home, and he asked me to be his eyes and ears for her. He also gave me instructions for follow-up lab tests for our patient. Again, she would be on chemotherapy for two years.

I queried Dr. Brian about my research, which he essentially confirmed. However, Dr. Brian's phone demeanor was contagious and positive. I asked him how he kept up such a positive attitude.

He just said, "I have to or all would be lost. We can only do our best."

Annette returned home with essentially no immune system; it had been suppressed by the chemotherapy. Consequently, she was susceptible to major infections from the smallest of concerns like a scrape on her skin or an ear infection or just a mild viral illness. Over few weeks and months that followed, I hospitalized Annette multiple times for high fevers and infections. Fortunately, these all resolved without major problems with the blood recurring. Each time I treated Annette, I informed Dr. Brian, or one of his partners, and Annette's parents of all my conversations.

Annette with her family made multiple trips to Denver over the remainder of the first year. Through it all, her parents remained positive, at least outwardly. However, I just knew that they were worried sick on the inside.

As time went on Annette seemed to be tolerating the chemotherapy as well as could be expected. Caring for her became *routine*. That is, she saw doctors a lot, she had a lot of tests and treatments, and she, with her family, made trips to Denver Children's Hospital.

During the entire first two years, Annette continued to grow and develop normally. Her growth remained at about the 75th percentile for her age and sex. In fact, Annette's total development did not seem to be hampered one bit by two years of chemotherapy, and this did not change.

After two years of therapy, Dr. Brian officially declared Annette to be in remission. The next goal, for statistical purposes, would be the 5-year mark or when she was about 7-years-old.

About Christmastime after her seventh birthday, Annette presented to my office acutely ill. She was fatigued, had a sore throat, and had a sore neck. She had enlarged lymph nodes everywhere! I feared the worst. (Of course, that is what doctors do.) A blood test revealed atypical lymphocytes, but *normal platelets.* A second test confirmed that my young patient had *infectious mononucleosis*, and her body seemed to be fighting it well. I think I knew right then that Annette was going to be just fine.

Over the coming years, Dr. Brian's letters confirmed that Annette was prospering and *cured.* She continued to grow, develop, and mature into a marvelous young lady. Before her high school graduation I talked with Dr. Brian about her. I had calculated that her chance of getting such a rare disease and surviving two initial courses of chemotherapy was about *2 in 10 million*!

He agreed with me that she was indeed a "miracle child."

Annette graduated from high school near the top of her class and went off to college to become a veterinarian.

Sucker

Late one afternoon I heard a tremendous commotion outside in the hallway of the clinic. A child was screaming and carrying on so that anyone within the complex could probably have heard him. Soon thereafter a young mother opened our clinic door holding a male child who was definitely distressed about something. He acted as if he were having severe pain someplace.

When my nurse and I saw the screaming, flailing child in the reception area, we assumed the worst (as medical people do). I promptly had my receptionist ask the mother to take her child back into the exam area. My nurse greeted the mother at the door.

The mother said she had no idea what the problem was. She had been called away from work by the babysitter who related that the child must have hurt himself. The baby sitter did not see any accident, but all of a sudden the little boy started screaming and rolling on the floor. The panicked mother raced from work to get her child. She was unable to soothe whatever was bothering her three-year-old youngster. The mother just knew something must be terribly wrong.

The mom related that this was really bad timing. She said that she was behind at work and had to get some things done before the end of the day! The day had been going poorly, and this was the frosting on the cake. She looked frustrated, tired, and mad!

As my nurse extended her arms to assist with holding the young boy, he stopped crying. I mean he stopped like a switch had been turned off. The little boy smiled. His flailing and thrashing ceased. His total incapacitation was over. He hopped onto the scale to be weighed and measured.

"What the heck?" I thought.

The mother said something like, "What in the world is going on?"

My nurse escorted the now quite mobile, content child to an exam room as I stood as a bemused bystander in a hallway. The nurse left the door ajar just in case. Upon entering the room, I asked the young boy to climb up onto the exam table, which he did without any problem. I asked him if he hurt anywhere; he pointed to his ears.

The mother said her son had not been ill, but maybe he got an ear infection. My examination of his ears was normal. Ditto for the throat, neck, chest, abdomen, and extremities.

As I was about to console the mother and tell her that I did not have the faintest idea of why her child caused such a ruckus, the child loudly exclaimed, "I'll have my sucker now!"

I thought to myself, "All he wanted was a sucker! What a little con man."

As you can imagine, the mother who had already had one miserable day, was beside herself. Her hair was messed up, her make-up was smeared, she had lost time at work, and she was worried to death for no reason. Now her face was getting *really red* like Mount St. Helens was gonna blow.

I knew I had to think quickly, so I started to laugh.

I assessed the situation and decided that this child was going to wish he were dead by bedtime if the mother's mood did not change. Therefore, I did what doctors do best. *I wrote a prescription!*

This prescription was for a pizza at the local Pizza House. I gave it to the mother and told her this was her family's "bonding coupon" for the day. She did not have to worry about dinner (another stress). Her family could have a dinner out on me.

Mom's furrowed brow smoothed out; the down-turned corners of her mouth started upward; she reached out her arms, grabbed her little one, and said, "You little stinker. Wait till your dad hears about our day!"

The mom gave me a hug, thanked all my office staff, and was on her way.

Just as she was opening the clinic office door, I called out for her to wait. I said that I had forgotten something.

I grabbed a handful of suckers and gave them to the little boy. I hoped that these might prevent another "attack."

The Blessed One

I was taking call for our local obstetrician on a morning in March when Rebecca, one of his obstetrics patients, presented to the hospital. She had two children from previous uncomplicated pregnancies. I was summoned to the obstetrics wing to examine Rebecca because she was agitated and crying, appeared to be in labor, and was only 26 weeks pregnant by her records.

Upon arriving, I reviewed the fetal monitor strip that indeed showed regular contractions and a reassuring fetal heart rate pattern. Since Rebecca did not appear to be in imminent danger of delivering, I reviewed her prenatal papers that had been obtained from the obstetrician's office; I obtained more history from the patient and her husband.

It appeared that Rebecca had conceived with an IUD (intrauterine contraceptive device) in place. The IUD had been removed soon after the pregnancy was verified. Otherwise, the pregnancy had been unremarkable until today except for a "little discharge."

The nurse and I then proceeded to set up a sterile pelvic examination with a speculum *just in case.* After Rebecca had been set upon the examination table and draped, my preliminary external examination revealed more than a *little discharge* on her genitalia. There was a lot of discharge that was foul smelling pus!

By inserting the speculum into the vagina, I exposed a pool of pus draining out of the cervix. The cervix was soft and about three centimeters dilated. The baby's head was the presenting part. Rebecca's uterus and ovaries were tender to my palpation. I knew that she was infected and most likely was going to deliver an infected baby.

I talked to the parents about my findings. My first inclination was to airlift the mom and baby to a perinatal center. However, a winter storm was in progress and potential flying conditions were atrocious. Therefore, I decided to discuss the case with Dr. Bryan Salvino, a perinatologist in Bismarck, North Dakota, to whom I had referred newborns many times. After I presented my case, and knowing the technology at the time regarding 26 week septic babies, Dr. Salvino said the chances of having a good result was only one percent or less. However, as usual, he offered to manage the child if I, and the parents, were so inclined to transfer the baby.

Subsequently, I talked to the parents. I offered discussions of the weather, flying concerns, outcome probabilities, potential risks for mom and baby, and anything else I could think of. As it turned out, however, I was venting to deaf ears. Rebecca and her husband had discussed their options as I was consulting Dr. Salvino. If the probability of having a good baby was not high, then they were willing to let Mother Nature take its course. They would deal with the consequences. They would have the baby in Sidney. They wanted *no extraordinary care* for the child.

After verifying what they told me, I agreed with their wishes.

Since the baby was so early and small, Rebecca's cervix would not have to dilate completely to give birth. It was just a short interval before Rebecca was dilated to six centimeters and felt like pushing. Fortunately, Rebecca had been kept in the delivery area anticipating such an event. Rebecca maintained her composure until the baby's head was coming out. She then started to cry and shout at the same time, "I don't want to see it! I don't want to see it!"

The shouting proved to be a good pushing maneuver that expelled a pus-coated small male infant followed by a gush of foul smelling goo. The baby made a weak cry with its first gasp of air, but then the sound turned into a whimper. The baby was already showing chest retractions of respiratory distress. After I suctioned the baby's mouth and nose and wiped the purulent material off the entire body, the newborn baby boy was wrapped in a blanket and set beside me per the parents' request.

I obtained blood from the umbilical cord for no other reason than it was my routine. I anticipated no other need for the blood for this premature infant. After the placenta was expelled, I cultured the membranes, the vaginal goo, and the uterine cavity. Then I started Rebecca on intravenous antibiotics while I awaited the results from the cultures.

The nurses escorted Rebecca to her regular hospital room; the baby was kept warmly wrapped up in a bassinet in the nursery and given *no extraordinary care.* His weight was two pounds, six ounces.

After about an hour, the baby was still breathing! His respirations did not seem to be as labored. I asked the parents if they would mind if I applied a little oxygen to the baby's face. After conferring, they reaffirmed that they wanted no extraordinary measures taken.

I reassured them that all newborns received supplemental oxygen at our hospital.

The parents agreed.

The nursing staff then applied an oxygen mask to the baby.

I kept checking on the baby throughout the day. He had some mild chest wall retractions, but his blood oxygen levels remained good with minimal additional oxygen. I kept the parents informed of their baby's stabilizing situation. Rebecca, however, still did not want to see the child. I decided to just keep the baby warm through the night. I asked the nurse in the nursery to keep everyone's fingers crossed.

Amazingly, soon after Rebecca had delivered her baby, another obstetrics patient of the obstetrician came in with the same problems, i.e., purulent discharge, premature labor at 28 weeks, and, by now, worse weather conditions. I knew the data by heart for the child's potential poor outcome and related it to the parents. These parents, however, wanted to go to Bismarck only *after* they determined their insurance would pay the costs!

When I called Dr. Salvino again, I advised him of the status of the first child and the situation with the second patient. He said he would call the flight team for transport possibilities. The air transport team called me soon thereafter relating that their weather was satisfactory in Bismarck, but a storm front was coming from the northwest. There was only small time window of opportunity to transport before a blizzard hit, so the transport team was deployed.

Preparations were made for the mom by giving her some medication to slow her labor, starting antibiotics at the request of the receiving obstetrician after culture swabs had been obtained of the purulent discharge in the vagina, and giving the mom some medication for anxiety. She left the hospital about 90 minutes later just as the blizzard was arriving. Whew!

I had the nursery personnel call me every two hours during the night with updates on our little boy. Each time the report was, "No change."

The following morning, the baby was about 16-hours-old and holding his own. He was sucking because he was hungry, but he was too weak to suck for long. He had a meconium stool during the night and had urinated. All systems seemed to be working.

I talked with the parents after my examination that morning to update them. Since the baby was hungry and stable, I asked permission to give him some fluids through a vein.

Again, the parents wanted nothing extraordinary done.

We then had a discussion about what they meant by "extraordinary" so if I tried to care for their baby, I would know my boundaries for rendering care. We came to an understanding. The intravenous fluid was in.

I inserted an umbilical catheter with a maintenance rate for fluids. Since watching an IV in a wrapped up baby in a crib was not practical, the infant was transported to a radiant warmer unit. Here, the nursing staff could apply an oxygen hood over the baby to provide a more regulated amount of oxygen.

Rebecca finally saw her baby for the first time that morning and sat with him for several hours. What a great picture!

The baby continued to do well. Hyaline membrane respiratory disease of premature infants worsens with time after birth and frequently requires ventilator support within 12 to 48 hours. This baby, however, got better! I surmised that the baby had been stressed for such a long time by the mother's sepsis that his lungs had matured prematurely as well. Whatever happened, I was pleased.

By the third day, the baby was faring quite well. Having had considerable experience in newborn ICUs in training, I knew that this child was going to require a lot of time and care if he was going to survive. I relayed my thoughts to the parents about transporting their baby to a pediatric center.

They did not want to have him transported. If I was willing to care for their baby in Sidney, so were they.

I professed that the nurses and I could only do our best. That was good enough for the parents.

About this time the parents decided upon a name for their baby. It was Bennett, which, in my loose Latin translation, meant, "the strong blessed one." What an appropriate name I thought. I just hoped his blessings continued.

Bennett did famously. So did his parents and our nurses! I was proud of all of them.

Bennett grew and gained weight with Rebecca's breastfeeding. The parents were proud of their little boy, as they should have been. The nurses in our little hospital gained extraordinary experience managing a premature infant.

I was just the overseer of God's work in progress. I marveled often about how amazing the human body is.

When Bennett was about a month old, his mom was breastfeeding him when all of a sudden he turned blue and stopped breathing. A CODE was called for the nursery. Fortunately, all that was required was a few puffs of air in the baby's mouth.

Babies are nose breathers when they are young to enable them to continue breathing while feeding. On this occasion, Mom's breast tissue apparently occluded Bennett's tiny nose so he couldn't breathe. He just needed a quick jumpstart.

All was faring well in the nursery with Bennett until he was about 10 weeks old. All premature infants should have an eye examination before they are discharged to make sure that no damage has occurred as a result of oxygen therapy. Since Bennett was doing so well and getting near a discharge, I asked a visiting ophthalmologist to examine our baby boy. The doctor instilled a drop of medicine into each of our little boy's eyes to dilate his pupils.

Bennett took exception to this, had a reaction to the drops, and stopped breathing!

The ophthalmologist was mortified! A CODE was called for the nursery!

The medication caused Bennett's heart rate to drop below 60 from 160. However, with some ventilation, cardiac stimulation, and a few minutes of time, Bennett was as good as new. Ah, the blessed one!

I could not say the same for the eye doc. He called me every day for a week for updates. He was terribly concerned, which was good. I told him, "Stuff happens! The baby is going to be fine. I'll have you see him again when he is six months old, but don't use the drops!"

Bennett remained in our hospital for 98 days, my longest acute care stay. As far as I could ascertain, his was the longest acute care stay in the history of our hospital. He exited weighing just over six pounds and doing well.

As time marched on, it became apparent that Bennett had some neurological problems involving one side, i.e. cerebral palsy. However, it also became apparent that he was quite intelligent.

Years of physical therapy would help Bennett to maximize his physical capabilities and minimize his disabilities. Continual assistance, perseverance, and encouragement by his parents and his sisters would produce a 4.0 student who was fluent in several languages.

In the fall after his high school graduation, Bennett would enter college at Princeton on an academic scholarship.

When I closed my practice, Bennett insisted on being my very last patient.

A family doc could wish for no finer gift than a final hug from the blessed one.

HOME VISITS

"The practice of medicine is an art, not a trade;
a calling, not a business;
a calling in which your heart will be exercised equally with your head.
Often the best part of your work will have nothing to do with potions and powders, but with the exercise of an influence of the strong upon the weak,
of the righteous upon the wicked, of the wise upon the foolish."

Sir William Osler

The Delivery

I was working my weekend rotation in our hospital's newly opened emergency room. The ER had been exceptionally quiet for a Saturday in oil boom country. In the early afternoon the ER nurse took a call from a frantic man who said his wife was having a baby. He said she needed some help *right away*. The nurse offered to send the ambulance, but the man refused. He was insistent that someone needed to come right away to help his wife.

The nurse handed me the phone. The man sounded frantic. In this conversation I deduced that the home was just a few blocks from the hospital, so I said I would come as soon as I could. I advised the nurse of my intentions. I told her I would call back to the ER after I was able to assess the situation. I then grabbed my medical bag, and I was off. (Now I would grab a prepared obstetrics pack.)

I arrived at a house in the correct location, but the numbers had been removed. The front yard was full of junk and garbage. A young, agitated, foul-smelling man met me at the door and guided me through the house that looked very much like the yard. I could hear a female screaming that she wanted some pain medicine.

The young man did tell me that he would like to help me if he could. He advised me that he had been a medic in Viet Nam. He and his wife had planned this home delivery for their first child. He apparently became faint of heart when his wife started screaming and there was more blood than he expected.

I followed the woman's shrieks re-tracing an open path into the depths of the house. When I got to the bedroom, I found a young, nude woman who was most distraught. She was lying in a filthy bed covered with blood. Her legs were spread apart revealing a substantial *bloody show* (a bloody vaginal discharge common during labor), but I did not notice any active bleeding. Since she was so vocal, I knew her vital signs must be adequate.

I removed a sterile glove from my bag and performed a pelvic exam. The baby's head was near the outlet and about ready to come out. I knew I had to hurry! I remembered that the husband had told me that this home delivery was planned. Consequently, *I assumed* that he must have gathered some necessary supplies for the delivery.

I was wrong!

The bedding was soiled not only with new blood but also with very old dirt and grime. I asked the husband to bring me his clean towels for the baby. I saw a blank stare. He left the room and returned with a towel from the kitchen. I thought it might have been yellow once upon a time, but it was caked with something that smelled awful.

I asked, "Don't you have anything cleaner than this?"

He said, "Unh, unh." as he waved his head from side to side.

I said, "Do you have a newspaper?"

He replied, "Yeh, but I put the dog food on it."

I started thinking, "What have I got myself into this time?"

Just then, the husband said, "Wait, I have an idea!" He then left the room, and I heard a slam as he left the house.

A dog barked outside, and I thought, "This guy's gone out to play with his dog."

The husband returned in about 30 seconds with the neighbor's freshly rolled up newspaper. He said they were out of town and would not miss it.

I took the newspaper from the husband, opened it up in the middle, and spread it under the buttocks of the mom-to-be who, by the way, was pretty much in her own world by now because of the labor pain. I tried to get the lady to focus on something to manage the pain without success. She wanted *morphine*!

I asked the husband what he had planned to use to tie and cut the umbilical cord.

He said, "The what?"

I thought, "This guy was supposedly a medic for God's sake!"

I tried to explain what was hopefully going to happen pretty soon, and what we had to do when the baby came out.

I asked him for something to tie the umbilical cord.

He brought me used dental floss!

I saw some muddy hiking boots by the door. I told him to get one of the shoestrings from the boot, wash it quickly with soapy water, and then give it to me.

He complied.

I requested some scissors.

He countered with, "What for?" (I could only think, "DUH!")

I said, "To cut the shoe strings."

He replied, "Oh, we don't have any of those. How about a knife?" He then went to the sink, took out a dirty butcher knife, and washed it as he had done with the shoestring.

By now, the mom-to-be wanted the kid out of her in the worst way. She was tired of the pain. She said something like, "It's coming out, NOW!" With the NOW, she put forth a tremendous grunt. As I was trying to control the baby's head, she let out another grunt. This time the baby's head popped out. I suctioned the mouth and nose with a bulb syringe that was in my bag. As I was finishing the suctioning, another grunt came forth, and a baby girl squirted out onto the newspaper. The baby cried spontaneously and vigorously.

"Hurrah!" I thought.

I wiped the baby as dry as I could. I cut the shoestring in half, tied it around the umbilical cord in two places, and then severed it between the ties. The infant was placed upon the Mom's chest while we waited for the afterbirth. I covered the pair with a nearby coat. (It seemed clean.)

The placenta came out almost as fast as the baby without incident. I examined the uterus outside the abdomen and noted it to be quite firm. I thought, " I'm out of the woods."

But, as I looked down at the bedding, I noticed a significant amount of bleeding from a large tear through the mother's vagina into her rectum. (This can happen when the baby's head has an uncontrolled explosive exit from the mom's bottom.) I knew that I was not equipped to repair this lesion under these circumstances, and a trip to the hospital was required.

I called the ER nurse to inform her that we had had a good baby, that the mom had a large perineal tear, and to please get the surgical area set up with the obstetrical instruments I needed to make the repairs.

When it was time to go to the hospital, I heard no objections from the new parents. The last thing I had to do was soak up the blood from the vagina for the several block trip to the hospital. I asked the husband to get me several of the wife's sanitary pads.

She replied, "I use tampons."

I thought to myself, "Of course! How silly of me to ask."

I asked where they kept their socks. I located a chest of drawers behind me. I opened a drawer, pulled out a pair of rolled up crew socks, unrolled them, and placed them into a pair of clean panties lying nearby.

The mom put on the panties, and we were ready to go.

The husband insisted that it was his responsibility to take his family to the hospital. After everyone climbed into his sedan, and the car departed toward the hospital, I followed to make sure they arrived.

The surgical repair went without incident.

The mom got her home delivery, her baby, *and her morphine.* The newborn female was doing well - for now. (I could only wonder about her future.)

Dad said he was exhausted, so I sent him home to rest and to spend some time cleaning up his home.

The new mom and her baby went home from the hospital after a few days.

The following Tuesday morning, Dr. Larimore, a female physician in our community, confronted me. She was mad as hell with me! She exclaimed, "You delivered my patient at home! I told her I would not assist a home delivery! Then you go out and stab me in the back! You stole my patient!"

I tried to reassure the good doctor that I had no idea who these people were. I did not know that the mom had been seeing her for prenatal care. Additionally, I tried to explain that I thought the idea of owning patients (people) went out of vogue with our country's civil war over one hundred years before.

She was not impressed with me at all. She stormed off down the hallway. She did not speak to me for a while, but eventually, she got over the incident, I think.

After being discharged from the hospital, I did not see these people again.

Just a Scratch

One of the things that happen when you work as a physician in a small community is that you get called upon to make home visits for your neighbors. Such was the case in the summer of 1976 when I was asked to make a visit to the farm of one of my neighbors on my way home from work. I had not formally met these neighbors. Therefore, I thought it would be a good idea to take some extra time on my way home so I could spend some time getting acquainted.

Only women operated this particular farmstead. The ladies were all related. There was the grandmother, the mother, the daughter, and a niece. The farm had been in operation in the valley for generations. The daughter asked me to stop by to see the grandmother who reportedly had taken a spill and had a scratch on her arm. The daughter and the mother related that the grandmother did not like the physicians in Sidney, and there was just no way that they could bring the grandmother into the office to be seen.

I arrived at the farm at about 6 p.m. Waiting for me at the kitchen table was a small elderly lady who I guessed to be about 80-years-old. She and her family were Hispanic; it appeared that the grandmother spoke very little English. The entire family was extremely cordial and said they were excited to have my family as their new neighbors.

The grandma called me "the little boy doctor."

The grandmother's forearm was covered with a bloody gauze wrap. I noticed that the skin on her good arm was quite thin and atrophic. Even the good arm had a few small scratches and scars on it.

I unwrapped the long piece of gauze covering the injured arm. Underneath, I found a u-shaped skin tear that went all the way from near the elbow to the wrist. This injury produced a very large skin flap that was essentially a split thickness skin graft because of the thinned-condition of the aged skin.

When I saw the size of the injury, I suggested to the grandmother that I take her into the office to put sutures into the wound to close it.

She would have nothing to do with going into town for medical care.

I asked the other family members if they had some steri-strip bandages, but they didn't.

I thought that I could make some steri-strips by cutting up some large Band-Aids. I explained my idea to the daughter and asked if they had some large Band-Aids that I could cut up. The granddaughter knew they had a new box of Band-Aids, and she went to get them.

The granddaughter returned with a box of *miniature* Band-Aids.

I thought, "At least I will not to have to cut them up to make them smaller."

The granddaughter was kind enough to bring in their selection of medicinal products including Merthiolate, Neosporin ointment, iodine cleanser, and gauze wrap.

I proceeded to clean up the wound as best I could with tap water. Afterward, I dried off the skin and approximated the skin edges with the miniature Band-Aids. To close the wound, it took *all 63 of them!*

I then applied some of the antibiotic ointment at the closure line, and I wound the gauze around the arm firmly to keep pressure on the skin flap. I hoped that a firm wrap would minimize the amount of fluid that could accumulate under the skin flap. Finally, I made a sling from a clean dishtowel.

I asked the grandmother to keep her arm immobile in the sling for a few days. I told the family I would check on my patient every day at their home until I was confident that the wound would heal.

The grandmother wanted to know my charge for coming to their home.

I replied that there was no charge. It was just nice to get to know my new neighbors.

The grandmother would have none of this. She pointed out to me, through her daughter's interpretation, that I was just a young man, and I could not feed my family if I didn't get paid. She then pointed her good arm to send the niece in one direction and the granddaughter in another direction as she gave them instructions in Spanish. The two ladies returned with packages in their hands. One carried a box with a dozen eggs. The other carried a package with a lamb roast in it.

I didn't know what to say except, "Thank you."

Each day when I came by to evaluate the grandmother's arm, I received a small package of farm goods as payment.

The grandmother's arm healed quite well. Weeks later, only a very fine scar provided evidence that something had ever occurred.

About a year later, I saw the grandmother in my office. I thought to myself, "At least, I had converted one family into believing that they could be cared for in their own hometown."

Over the subsequent few years, I made multiple visits to the farm to see Grandma and the other women for various issues. Each time I went home with something edible from the farm.

I was quite sad the days when I learned of the grandmother's death and when the ladies had to sell their farm.

Jailbird

I was the only physician on our medical staff that routinely made house calls. I always figured it was often easier for me to get to some patient's homes in our small community than it was for them to get to see me. Taking sick children out into blizzards, having elderly folks try to negotiate slippery sidewalks and streets, or just moving someone who was too chronically ill for a routine visit seemed irrational to me. Because I was close to the hospital and its services, I always felt I could call for help from our ambulance crew.

The local law enforcement office soon found out that I did not mind making a "house call" to the jail if I was truly needed. Therefore, during our oil boom years I would make a trip to the jail about once a month for some acute problem with an inmate.

I was called to the Law Enforcement Center one Thursday morning to see an inmate who was acting "crazy." When I arrived at the jail, I heard a lot of hollering and commotion inside the depths of the jail. The jailer escorted me back into the cellblock where the jail cells surrounded a central area. Numerous law enforcement personnel were present watching, but not saying much, as the inmates jousted obscenities at each other. In fact, some of the police were smiling because the scene was so bizarre and humorous.

One inmate's room was stripped down to the bare walls with just a mattress on the floor. The entire area smelled awful because he had defecated and urinated in the cell. This guy was pacing like a caged animal and talking like a man obsessed. I knew this man was definitely *crazy*. The other inmates took offense to his bowel habits and to the smell he had made.

I was told that one inmate, who thought he was THE MAN in the jail, had threatened to hold the crazed man's face in his own stool. The agitated inmate then proceeded to grab a handful of his own feces and wipe it on this own face while saying "Like this?"

The officer in charge wanted to know what I could do to slow down this crazy, agitated man. The inmate had been seen by the judge that morning and had been declared legally incompetent. He was to be transferred to Warm Springs, the state mental hospital, as soon as possible. However, they wanted a way to calm him down until he could be transferred.

I went to the hospital pharmacy and picked up some Inapsine. (Inapsine is a drug we used to quiet down agitated, psychotic patients. It is extremely safe, quick in onset, and relatively short acting. The dose was two milliliters given by injection every 20 minutes until the patient was controlled.)

Back at the jail the lawmen earned their pay that day as they subdued our patient while I gave him the injection. He was asleep within 5 to 10 minutes. In addition, I gave him an injection of Haldol, which is a similar product that lasts longer. The patient slept until the next day.

The jailer called the following morning to tell me that they were transferring the inmate that morning to the state mental hospital some 500 miles away. He was waking up from the shots I had given him, and the sheriff wanted to know if I would give him some more medicine so he would sleep during the transfer.

I went to the jail, again the lawmen subdued the agitated man, and I administered the shots. Once again, the man soon fell asleep. I gave the officers a booster dose just in case the medicine wore off too soon, and they departed.

Several days later I learned that the medicine did not last nearly as long as it had initially. The inmate awakened and relieved himself all over the back seat of the police car when they were only halfway to their destination.

It was over 90 degrees outside that spring day. The smell in the car must have been overwhelming.

On the way home after dropping off their prisoner, the lawmen utilized Montana's "480 air conditioning system"— *four windows down and 80 miles per hour!*

Just Saving Time

Our home was located on 21 acres of land about five miles north of town. It was aligned directly north and south adjacent to a county road with the front door facing the North Dakota badlands directly to the east. With the long days of summer, the sun rose about 5 a.m. and set close to 9:30 p.m.

Early one Saturday morning during the summer I finished with an emergency call and assisted a woman with childbirth. I got home about 2 a.m. I was dead tired. Since I was still on call for the rest of the weekend, I hoped I would be able to sleep in that morning before I returned to the hospital. I fell asleep as soon as my head hit the pillow, as usual.

About 5 a.m., the doorbell ringing awakened Kay and me. I got partially dressed and went to the front door. The morning sun was just coming up and shining directly into my eyes as I opened the door. Just outside the doorway was an outline of a large man. Because the sun was directly behind him and shining into my eyes, I could not see his face. However, I knew it was my neighbor Jerry when he said in his husky, very characteristic voice, "Good mornin Doc! Did I wake ya?"

Jerry and his family lived on a farm about two miles down the road from us. Jerry was the kind of neighbor anyone would want. He was honest, a hard worker, and would do anything at anytime to help a neighbor.

I said to Jerry, "Its all right. What can I do for you?"

Jerry told me he had been out irrigating his beet fields just down the road from our place in the early morning when something flew into his eye. He figured it must have been a piece of a weed or something. He explained he had tried to rub it out for several hours, but it wouldn't come out. He said, "The darn thing is bothering me somethin' fierce!"

Jerry then said, "Well Doc, I figured it this way. I could go to the emergency room in town, but then they would just call you up. I'd be just sittin' there, waitin' until you finally got out of bed and showed up. 'Bout an hour I figured. It would be another half hour before you were done with me, and another half hour before I got back to irrigating. Then I looked up the road at your house. I figured I would save a whole lot of time just coming to see you here, and you would save time by not having to go to town. So here I am! I'm not bothering ya, am I, Doc?"

What could I say? I asked Jerry to come inside so I could look at him.

In my little black bag I always carried local anesthetic eye drops, eye patches, Q-Tips, and my ophthalmoscope for home visit eye injuries. While Jerry took a seat, I fetched my bag.

With a Q-tip, I inverted Jerry's upper eyelid. This simple maneuver exposed the pain-causing culprit, the outside coating of a weed seed which had become lodged onto the under side of the eyelid. With a quick brush from the Q-tip, the foreign body was removed. I showed Jerry the small dark piece exposed on the white cotton background. I then placed a drop of local anesthetic and a dye called Fluorescein into his eye. (This product exposes abrasions on the front of the eye.)

Sure enough, after several hours of rubbing, Jerry had generated a good-sized abrasion on the front of his eye.

Again I went to my bag to find a small bottle of antibiotic drops that I gave to Jerry.

Usually, I would have placed a patch on the eye, but knowing Jerry, I decided it would be a wasted effort.

Jerry's eye pain resolved, and his eye stopped watering.

Jerry said, "Gosh Doc, I feel great! What do I owe ya?"

I slapped his back and replied, "Go back to work. You saved me two hours, remember."

I was back asleep in no time.

Someone Special

I met Albert in the emergency room. He was a man in his mid 70s who was complaining of being "just tired, weak, and not feeling too good." I soon learned that Albert was a man of few words and definitely not a complainer.

After I put Albert in the hospital, I determined that he had a low blood sodium and concentrated urine simultaneously. Along with some other lab anomalies, these tests suggested that Albert had what is called SIADH (**S**yndrome of **I**nappropriate secretion of **A**nti**D**iuretic **H**ormone) (more medical alphabet soup). This is a problem during which the hormone that regulates water control for the body by the kidneys (ADH) is excreted excessively for some reason with the result being, among other things, a low sodium level in the blood. The cause of SIADH is variable, but often it is caused by a tumor someplace in the body.

In Albert's case, I found a mass in his left lung. Before he knew it, I had Albert and his wife on their way to see a cancer specialist for treatment.

Soon thereafter I received a call from Albert's wife who asked if I would come to see her husband at home. We agreed upon a time to visit the next day, which was a Saturday.

Albert and his wife told me about their visit to the cancer doctor, Albert's problem with an advanced cancer in his lung, and the fact that they decided to let Mother Nature takes its course. Albert wanted his last time on earth to be as good as possible. He said he wanted to die at home *"if that was all right with me?"* Albert and Anna just wanted to make sure that he did not have a lot of pain, and they weren't a bother to anyone.

His request caught me by surprise because it had been my experience that most people wanted to die in the hospital after everything and anything had been done to them. The hospice movement was just gaining a foothold in a few places nationwide, and it had not yet arrived in our community. I told them I would be glad to assist in any way that I could. However, I emphasized that I would not kill him.

Those were the words they wanted to hear. I arranged for Anna to have some pain medication on hand for her husband. I suggested that they make sure that Albert's will was current and any final arrangements be made. I offered to visit every few days and whenever they needed me.

Each time I visited Albert over the next few weeks, Anna had freshly baked goods for me to sample. Albert's only complaint was that he had to sleep sitting up because of his shortness of breath.

I explained to the pair that the breathing would worsen as the left lung filled with tumor and fluid. I pointed out that Albert would probably die peacefully without pain if he were to lie down on his right side with the side of his bad lung pointed up.

I received a call from Anna on a Friday afternoon requesting that I come to see her husband. I thought the worse as I went to their home after office hours. Instead, I found Albert and Anna sitting at a table "discussing things." Anna said, "I think we are ready. The kids will be here tonight to say their goodbyes."

Albert said he was just too tired to go on. He would like to die the next day after he had a last visit with family and friends. He wanted to know *"if that would be all right with me?"*

I asked what time they wanted me the next day - if Albert did not die during the night.

They thought 9 o'clock in the morning would be a good time.

I said I would bring pain medication in case Albert needed it. I cautioned Albert *not* to sleep on his right side.

The next morning I went to visit Albert after I made hospital rounds. Anna was sitting at the kitchen table watching her children saying their goodbyes to Albert. She offered for me to sit down and have a freshly baked breakfast pastry.

I agreed, and it was delightful.

After a few minutes, Albert motioned for me to come by his side. He said he was ready.

I explained once again to Albert and his children that all he would need to do was lie down on his right side. His lungs would do the rest and let him go to sleep. If he had a lot of pain, I would give him some medication. With that said, I helped Albert lie down on his right side and allowed his children to sit beside him.

Albert shook my hand and thanked me for my help.

Anna once again summoned me toward the kitchen table and offered me another pastry.

Soon thereafter, Albert stopped breathing in peace with his family at his side, just like he and Anna had planned.

I thought to myself, "What a nice way to go."

Maribeth

One early morning in March someone knocking on our door awakened me. As I opened the door, I was confronted by a dark figure in the night. He said, "I'm Bob, your neighbor from down the road. I heard you were the new baby doctor in town. Well, Maribeth is having a lot of trouble having her kid. She sure could use your help about now."

I asked why he had not taken her to the hospital.

The man replied, "No time to jaw!" "Are you coming or not?"

I asked the fellow to wait a minute while I got dressed. After dressing, I grabbed my doctor bag and headed off into the night with Bob, my new neighbor.

Bob's farm was a few miles away. Upon arriving, I headed toward the house to see my new patient.

Bob asked, "Where are you going? I need you over here!" He waved me toward him and then proceeded to walk across his yard toward the barn.

In the barn was Maribeth, *a heifer in distress!*

Bob told me she had been in labor most of the day, and the calf inside appeared to be "hung up a bit."

I promptly advised Bob that I was a "people doctor," not a veterinarian.

His response was, "You deliver babies, don't you? " Before I could reply he said, "Well, here's a momma with a baby that needs our help."

I was already there, so I figured I might be of some help. I asked Bob, "Where do you want me?"

Bob pointed to the behind of the cow.

I could see the calf's nose and two feet.

Bob said, "I'll push on the belly while you pull on the feet." He then instructed me on the correct position for calf pulling.

After I placed my feet on the heifer's buttocks aside the calf's head, I grabbed each hoof. Bob then counted "One, two, three." On "three" we simultaneously pushed and pulled; he pushed on the heifer's belly, and I pulled on the calf.

Nothing happened.

Bob yelled, "Put your back into it man!"

After three more push-pull maneuvers, a calf was born.

Bob promptly cleaned the calf's nose, and Maribeth did the rest.

In a short time Bob told me, "The calf is doing just fine."

I, however, was covered with mud and slime and cow poop.

I asked Bob why he didn't call a veterinarian. He said, "You were closer. Besides, I just wanted to see what kind of neighbor you were going to be." He then displayed a mischievous boyish smile.

When I got back home, I left my clothes outside. I showered and went to bed for the second time that night.

I must have passed Bob's "good neighbor test" because we got along quite well afterward. Actually, I learned that Bob got along pretty well with just about everyone if they could put up with his practical jokes.

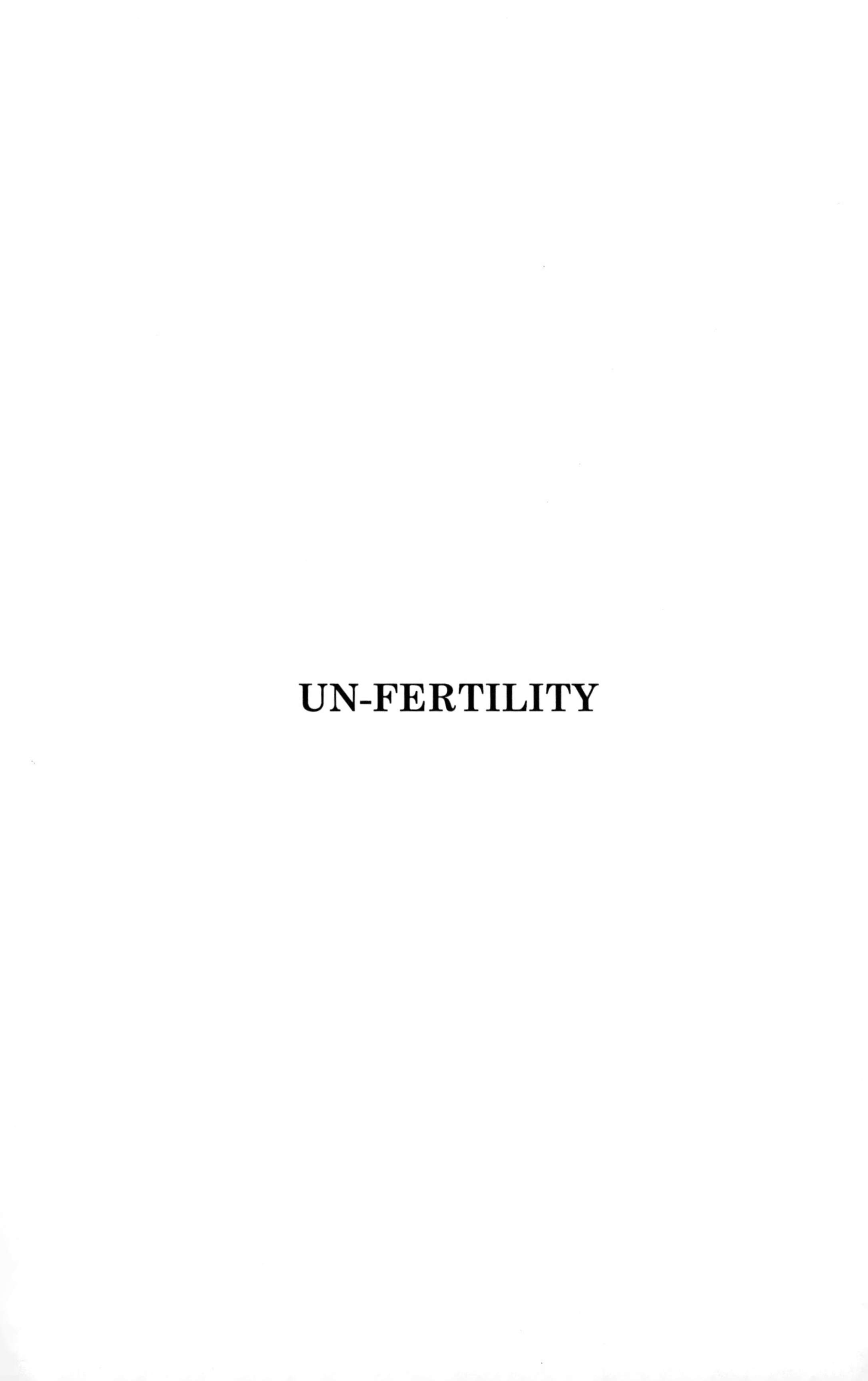

UN-FERTILITY

"You can't fool with Mother Nature!"

unknown

"The thing that a lot of people cannot comprehend is that Mother Nature doesn't have a bullet with your name on it, she has millions of bullets inscribed with "to whom it may concern."

unknown

Rx MAN

I saw Bob in the office one day for my partner. Bob had come in for a sperm count three weeks after a vasectomy. Usually, I checked patients after six weeks (or 12 episodes of sex), but since I was new in town I surmised that my partner had his own post vasectomy procedure.

Bob's sperm count came back as 100 million. I knew that something was amiss because the sperm count should not be that high after a vasectomy. It should be *zero*.

When I talked with Bob he looked depressed. I told him he was going to have to have more sex to drain all the sperm from his storage tanks (seminal vesicles, prostate, etc.).

Bob remarked, "Momma says we can't make love until all my sperms are gone."

Oops, I detected a lack of personal communication here.

I told Bob that he had to have sex more often to get rid of the sperm. When the sperm were all gone, his wife could get off the pill.

He seemed to understand my explanation.

I asked him to go home and practice. I planned to see him again in a few weeks.

Bob returned in three weeks. His sperm count was still 90 million. I knew something had to be wrong. I thought that my partner might have missed the vas (the segment removed during the procedure). Maybe Bob had a sperm granuloma (where the vas regrows itself).

I asked Bob, "What's been happening?"

He replied, "Nothin'."

I told Bob his sperm count and asked how often he and his wife had had sex since our last visit.

Bob said, "None." He then repeated, "Momma says we can't make love until all my sperms are gone."

"Holy Cow!" I thought.

Once again I tried to explain to Bob the facts of life about a vasectomy. I then gave him a pamphlet for his wife to read again (assuming she had read it the first time). Finally, I gave Bob a prescription, which read, "This man needs to have sex four times a week for the next six weeks."

Bob returned about six weeks later; his sperm count was zero.

I was pleased.

When I told Bob the good news he said, "Doc, don't tell momma. Could I get another prescription?"

My nurse and I had a good laugh that day.

The Barber

Before every vasectomy, I talked to the patient to reaffirm their intentions, the risks and benefits of the procedure, and so on. Also, I shave prepped all the patients before the procedure. As my practice became busier, I was always looking for ways to become more efficient. My nurse suggested to me that I allow the patients to prep themselves at home, and maybe I could save several minutes per procedure. It sounded like a good idea, so I felt it was worth a try.

One Friday afternoon I walked into our surgery room to see Wilbur, a slight middle-aged farmer with an appearance much greater than his stated age. As usual, I went through the legal and procedural formalities before performing the vasectomy.

Wilbur informed me that he had shaved himself at home.

I left the room so Wilbur could get undressed and gowned. Upon returning, I asked Wilbur to climb onto the surgery table and lay face up so I could wash his genital area.

When I pulled back the gown to expose his genital area, I could see that a shave prep had been attempted. The genital area was covered with hairs about 1/8 inch long. There were at least a hundred short linear scabs all over the scrotum! Several cuts appeared to have been deeper than the others. I was more than a little taken aback by this sight. I thought, "Should I attempt to operate through all those cuts? What will happen when I try to shave off all those hairs? Was the skin going to bleed from every one of those scabs?"

I quizzed Wilbur, "What the heck happened to you? That's quite a shave job. If you had gone any deeper with some of those cuts, I wouldn't have anything to do."

He replied proudly, "I'm a barber part time!" As I mused over the situation, he inserted, "I used my electric clippers. What do ya think?"

I really did not know what to think.

I decided to go ahead with the vasectomy. However, I explained to Wilbur that I was going to have to shave a few more hairs off before I started.

As I was shaving the scrotum, I asked him, "Didn't you bleed a lot?"

He responded, "I bled like stink! But I got it stopped with good old toilet paper."

I then asked, "Didn't it hurt to get all of these cuts?"

Wilbur retorted, "Hell Yes! But not half as bad as when I put on the Aqua Velva! Now that was pain! I was jumping around like a cat on a hot tin roof!"

We both had a good laugh. I continued to chuckle to myself during the entire procedure.

All went well. No complications occurred, and the scrotum scabs were all gone within a week.

Wilbur went back to being a part time barber on the head only.

A Birthday Present

Late one Tuesday afternoon Jeremy Alderson came into my office. He told me I had to perform a vasectomy that day! He had been thinking about it all day, and he had to get it done NOW. He and his wife had three children, they wanted no more children, and he was the reason his wife had to stay on the pill. They had read all the pamphlets; he had seen the movies; he just had not been able to get up the courage to have a vasectomy done.

I inquired about his wife's thoughts, and he told me that she was all for it. I asked my receptionist if we had time.

She said I could start at 4:30, but I had better be done by 5 o'clock. Three employees had something they *had to do*. (I really did not like to keep my employees late if at all possible.)

I consented to do the vasectomy. (I was always a softy.)

My nurse and I went into high gear to get things ready (we had to make the deadline.) I proceeded expeditiously through the vasectomy, and Jeremy left the office with my usual instructions for follow-up. I was pretty proud of myself that night. I had performed an emergency vasectomy, *and* I had the employees out by a little after 5 o'clock.

About 9 o'clock the next morning, I received a call from Mrs. Alderson. Upon answering the phone I was confronted with the sounds of a hysterical woman. She exclaimed, "Dr. Ashcraft? This is Mrs. Jeremy Alderson. Do you know what you did to my husband last night?"

Suddenly, I wondered, "What have I done now? Maybe she wanted another child. Maybe her husband is cheating. Maybe he had a complication. Of course I knew what I had done. Should I have done it?"

I was still thinking how to respond when she blurted out, "Thank-you, Thank-you, Thank-you from the bottom of my heart! That was the best birthday present I ever had!"

Now, I mumbled to myself, "How can a husband lying down with ice on his scrotum be such a great gift?" So I inquired, "Oh, what happened?"

Mrs. Alderson exclaimed, "He was just sooo cute! After we had dinner and the kids were in bed, I was washing dishes. I thought he had forgotten my birthday since he had been so busy at work. I heard him walk into the kitchen. He said, "Hey, Honey, I've got something for you. When I turned around, there he was standing naked in the kitchen with a red bow on his penis. I screamed, I howled, and when he told me what he had done for me, I gave him a great big kiss. He may have been sore, but it worked pretty good last night!"

She then said, "Thank you again." and hung up.

At last count, they had been married 30 years.

The Mailman

Soon after I started my practice I was asked by my partner to perform outpatient vasectomies. He would perform the procedure only with general anesthesia. (I understood that there were many vasectomy procedures waiting to be done on an outpatient basis because insurance companies would not cover a hospital admission for a vasectomy.)

I had decided to perform vasectomies on Friday afternoons after the patients had completed their workweek. This way they would be able to take it easy over the weekend and usually be able to return to work on Monday. I could check the patients on Monday mornings before they went to work. At least, that was my plan.

Walter, a local postal worker, asked me to perform his vasectomy. On Thursday, we discussed the procedure, answered his questions, and obtained consent to proceed. On Friday morning the vasectomy was carried out with precision, skill, and speed. I was indeed proud of myself about how smoothly the surgery went. Walter was given the usual instructions, and we made arrangements to see him before he went to work on Monday.

Late Friday evening Walter called me to ask if he could go to work at the Post Office in the morning. Apparently, another worker had taken ill, and a replacement was needed.

I was a little anxious about him straining himself a lot. I asked him what he would be doing.

Walter reassured me that his job was to sit on a chair and put sorted mail into the postal boxes. He would be home by noon.

I thought that sitting should not cause any problem, so I gave him my blessing.

About 6 a.m. Monday I got a call from the ER nurse who asked me to see Walt from the post office. The nurse noted that he appeared to be in a lot of distress with fevers and chills.

As I got out of bed, I wondered what went wrong. The procedure was flawless. I tried to guess what the problem could be because I knew it could not be something I did.

When I got to the ER, the patient was indeed having a lot of pain. He told me his sac hurt like hell and Tylenol was not cutting the pain.

I asked Walt to drop his pants and underwear so I could take a look. My eyes almost popped out and my jaw must have dropped wide open. Walter's scrotum was the size of two tennis balls! It was tense, hot, and very tender to touch. I asked, "What happened to you?"

He replied, "Nothing."

I inquired about him falling, sneezing, exercising, lifting, etc. in an attempt to vindicate myself. Surely, I thought, my perfect operation could not have become *this*!

During my interrogation, Walt confessed. He told me he did go to work to sort mail. However, when another employee did not show for work, the postmaster sorted the mail, and he volunteered to deliver the mail. He walked all day Saturday with a 60-pound sack of mail on his back!

So much for my warning against NO LIFTING!

I called Dr. Vince Hughes, a consulting urologist in Great Falls, who made monthly trips to Sidney for family business and for medical consultation. Vince was a seasoned urologist and, when I told him my dilemma, he howled into the phone. He said he knew how I felt because he had been there. Vince suggested a regimen of warm baths, analgesics, antibiotics, and absolutely no lifting or straining. He reminded me that it might take awhile to get a negative sperm test because the patient wouldn't feel too frisky for 3-4 weeks.

Walter followed the new directions to the letter this time. He healed nicely.

His sperm count was negative at three weeks as well; so he did get frisky!

Macho Man

Gary Barber was an intelligent, well-educated young man who worked for a medical care company. He and his wife had two lovely kids, and they decided to have a permanent solution to fertility. Gary was the chosen one to get "fixed".

Gary was an avid exercise enthusiast and was in excellent physical condition. He was a low-key sort of guy and really didn't say much (like most men in our neck of the woods). Overtly, not much seemed to bother him or his wife. So when it came to having a vasectomy, he seemed to take it in stride.

I gave the pair my usual talk about vasectomy, the procedure, and the post-op care. On one Friday afternoon I performed the deed without a hitch. Gary was sent home with a handout of instructions. He offered no queries or concerns.

I anticipated no problems.

About this time, the movie Rocky IV was playing in theaters. You know, the one in which Rocky fights the Russian on Russian turf. Rocky prepares "naturally" for the fight versus the high tech Russian training, and eventually wins the fight. There is a part in the movie when Rocky performs sit-ups over the edge of the loft in a barn.

Did you ever wonder if you could do sit-ups like that?

Gary didn't wonder. He knew he could do it!

I received a call from the ER on Sunday midday. The nurse told me that a man was there who was having severe groin pain. I was not on call, but she insisted that I come, and I did. Upon arriving, I heard moaning and groaning coming from behind one of the curtains in the ER. I pulled back the curtain to find Gary in a V-shape holding his crotch. I asked what had happened.

Stoic Gary said little. A somewhat concerned *and disgusted* wife said that Gary had watched the Rocky IV movie and got a little pumped up. Despite the post op instructions to limit physical activity, her husband decided it was time to work out. He started with sit-ups—over a barn loft. Apparently, after about 20-30 sit-ups, rigor mortis set in, Gary developed severe pain in his genitals, and he had to be extricated from the loft!

I almost started laughing when I heard the story and watched the wife's energetic recounting of the episode. However, I contained myself because poor Gary was in a world of hurt.

Obviously, he had developed acute inflammation in his scrotal contents. I had seen this before. I gave Gary some pain medication in the ER via an injection, some pain pills for a few days, antibiotics, instructions for warm baths twice daily, and a reminder to follow the instructions he had been given initially.

Afterward, Gary behaved himself, for six weeks only.

An Academy Award

Frequently, couples would come in to learn about birth control, and I would talk to both of them about male and female contraception. One such couple was Mike and Brenda Cole. Brenda had delivered their third child about two months before. She really did not want to have a tubal ligation or to take the pill any longer. Her remark was that, "I suffered like hell three times for him. Now he can suffer a little bit for me!"

With this as our premise, I soon realized that the end result was going to be a vasectomy Mike. Additionally, Brenda wanted to watch to make sure that I got it done.

I had no problem with the wife watching the procedure. I had done the procedure with medical students many times without any problems. I figured that having a wife present would not be too much for me to handle.

The day of the surgery arrived. When I went into the exam room only Mike was present. I went through my usual pre-op verbiage and stepped out to allow him time to undress and gown. When I returned, the Mrs. was sitting in a chair next to him.

I offered to let her be at the table next to me to see the procedure, but she politely declined.

I should have known something was up when Mike asked me to be careful shaving. He said, "It was pinching "a bit."

As I injected the scrotum with anesthetic, both of Mike's legs came up, and he let out a loud grunt.

The wife let out a screech. (I had never had anyone scream during a vasectomy!)

As I continued with the procedure, Mike moaned or grunted every time I made even the slightest move. I would ask, "Does this hurt?" as I moved or touched a scrotal part, and he would groan and grimace.

I injected more anesthetic.

I was wondering, "What is this? Do I have a bottle of Japanese Lidocaine or saline? How can he be having so much pain with such a swollen scrotum?"

By now, the wife was crying vigorously. She whimpered, "Had I known you would be having so much pain I would have had her tubes tied. How can I ever make this up to you?"

As Mike was talking, I continued to be quiet and work away. He was no longer complaining? He only complained when I talked about discomfort. I also noted an intermittent little smile on his face.

As I finished the first side, I said something like, "We're half done."

The wife shouted, "Honey, how can you stand the pain? You are only half done!"

He whimpered, "It's all for you, Babe."

I forged ahead knowing that I had some curious personal dynamics going on. When I finished the vasectomy and removed the sterile drapes, I had Mike sit up. He promptly flopped back stating that he was really dizzy.

By now his wife was crying buckets. She came over to the exam table and started to hug and kiss this poor soul.

He rolled his head toward me and gave me a wink and a great big smile.

I thought to myself, "What a showboat."

When I saw Mike back in the office some weeks later, he was still pleased with his performance. He told me that he really did not have any pain.

He complemented me for being a good sport.

And with a big grin he said, "And my love life is 100 percent improved!"

The Failure

Harold and his wife had one child about 12-years-old. They had been trying to conceive another child for 11 years without success. And as Harold would say, "It was not for the lack of trying!" He was now 31 years old, but his wife was 10 years his senior. Therein was the dilemma. They knew that her biologic clock was winding down and pregnancy could cause her some troubles. She was a tad overweight and physically not in good shape. They had come to the realization that one child was going to be their limit. It was time to get fixed to avoid any accidents.

With some trepidation I performed a vasectomy on Harold. The surgery went without incident. He was given the usual postop instructions. In this case the important instruction was *"keep your spouse safe until you are free of sperm."*

Having had no luck in 11 years of practicing natural family planning, I guess Harold decided to ignore this important rule. He did not return for a follow-up sperm count; I forgot about him.

Several months later Harold accompanied his wife into the clinic thinking she had a bad gallbladder. She was acting like the other women in her family at her age. That is, she was having trouble eating, especially in the morning, her stomach hurt, and her attitude "really sucked." She forgot to tell her husband that her breasts were getting bigger, and they too *really* hurt.

A pregnancy test was positive.

I was demoralized to say the least. This was my first known failure of a vasectomy. I looked at the pathology report that said "vas deferens right and left." The specimens were a centimeter long each, more than long enough.

A repeat sperm count revealed 60 million sperm. I thought, "Harold was indeed the fertile father. There was no hanky-panky here."

I was feeling really bad when I broke the news to this couple. I read the reports from the pathologist. I just did not know what to say.

Harold helped me out. He said, "Hell, Doc, if I had known all I needed to do to get my wife pregnant was have a vasectomy, I would have done it 10 years ago! We're tickled pink!"

As she was throwing up, his wife spoke, "Speak for yourself, Buster!"

The pregnancy progressed without incident, and a healthy boy was the result; just what the Dad had ordered.

Harold had a second vasectomy done. The previous vasectomy had regrown itself via a sperm granuloma.

A repeat sperm count showed *no sperm.*

The Sleeper

The first winter of my practice was pretty normal for Montana; it was cold. It was dark when I went to work, and it seemed even darker when I went home. One particularly dreary day, I had hopes of going home early before I had a walk-in patient about 3 o'clock in the afternoon. My nurse shrugged her shoulders as if to apologize for my inconvenience.

When I walked into the exam room, a petite, very attractive lady in a dress and a BIG handsome cowboy met me. This guy had to be about 6 feet 6 inches because he was about the height of the door when he stood up to shake my hand. He was also about the size of the door! After the introductions were over, the three of us settled into chairs. Because his name was on the chart, I turned to talk to this gentleman. But before I could say anything, the wife stated, "We hear you do vasectomies. He wants one!"

I looked at the husband and asked if that was true.

He just nodded in the affirmative.

I excused myself to get the usual information pamphlets, forms, etc. Upon returning to the exam room, I started into my canned speech about vasectomy. The wife cut me short by saying, "We know all that stuff. When can you do it?"

My rhythm had been disrupted. I was out of sync. Looking at the wife, I replied, "I will look at the schedule and see. Would that be all right with you?"

The wife retorted, "We have time to do it today. We just drove in 75 miles in bad weather to get this thing done; let's get it done."

I looked at the husband, and he just nodded his head.

I thought that I could do the vasectomy promptly since he was my last patient. However, when I talked with my nurse about setting up the surgery room, she informed me that more people had come in. I was now booked until 5 p.m.

I thought, "I will just have them schedule it for another day."

Upon entering the exam room, however, I was met with, "Well, what time can we get it done?"

I just could not refuse this pretty lady. I explained my clinic situation to them, but I told them that I would be willing to do the procedure after clinic hours.

The wife said that was a good idea because they had to get some stuff for their critters at the Ranch Supply. They would return to the clinic after they finished shopping.

About 5 p.m., the pair pulled to the back door of the clinic in a large station wagon. (What else for a guy his size?) I had the husband go to the surgery room to undress and gown up. Meanwhile, the wife took me aside. She told me that her husband always passed out at the sight of blood. He would even pass out at the thought of blood, especially his blood. She said, "I am just warning you."

I thought to myself, "Oh, sure."

When I entered the surgery room, the husband was sitting on the exam table. His wife said, "You better lay down Honey."

The big guy complied without comment.

My nurse had set out all the needed materials for the surgery on an instrument stand and had covered them with a sterile drape. A razor for shaving was in a basin with iodine solution near the sink. As I started to shave prep the man's genital area with the razor, he started to quiver. As I looked up at his face, his eyes rolled back, and he started to drool. I turned his head to the side so he would not choke. Sure enough, he had passed out!

His wife said, "See, I told you so."

I suggested that maybe we should abort the procedure for now and try again another day. The response by my now unconscious patient unnerved me.

The wife said, "It won't get any better. Keep on working, Doc. He won't feel a thing."

I had the wife watch his respirations while I worked, but I kept asking, "How's he doing?"

The wife kept saying, "He's just fine. Keep on working."

The vasectomy continued without any more "events." Actually, in afterthought, it was pretty nice having an unconscious patient. However, I did use local anesthesia because I really could not believe the wife when she told me her husband would not feel a thing.

After I finished the vasectomy, I reached over and tapped the big guy on the face, gently. I told him it was time to wake up; he did, right on my command. This massive cowboy was still a little groggy when the little wife and I assisted him to the station wagon. In preparation, the wife had reclined the front seat in the car to a sleeping position.

I retrieved a bag of ice from our freezer that the wife promptly placed on the strategic location. Then they were off into the night.

The wife brought in a sample for a sperm count weeks later.

The result was zero.

The wife conveyed to me their appreciation for my doing her husband's vasectomy on such short notice. She again told me, "My husband just doesn't like that medical stuff."

I thanked her and wished them the best of luck.

Deception

The chart on the outside of the exam room door had an encounter form that indicated a "New Patient." My nurse added a note that said, "New OB ... wants to talk." After briefly reviewing the chart, I noted that no obstetrical data form had been started, which was unusual.

As I entered the exam room, I saw an attractive woman I guessed to be about 30 years old. Just as I extended my hand to introduce myself, she said rather brusquely, "Are you Dr. Ashcraft?"

I stated, "Yes. How may I help you?"

Without further encouragement, this lady verbally laid into me. In a tone of voice that was angry, agitated, and crying, she told me that I had done a vasectomy on her husband, and now she was pregnant *again*! She went on to say that she and her husband already had three children. They did not want, nor could they afford, any more children. She wanted to know what **I** was going to do about it! Vigorously and in no uncertain terms she told me that I was responsible for her pregnancy. She expected me to pay for any medical bills associated with her pregnancy.

Obviously, this lady took me aback. I did not know her or her family. I had no recollection of performing any surgery on her husband. However, I must confess, my memory regarding patient's names was not the best. Since I performed essentially all the vasectomies in town, if there was someone to blame, then, probably, I guess was that person.

I advised the lady that I would get her husband's chart to gather some facts (always a good practice when in a bind, review the record.) I stepped out of the exam room and asked my nurse to locate the husband's chart. Within minutes she returned and said, " We have no record of seeing her husband."

Even though the lady heard the reply, I repeated to her, "*We have no chart*."

She cried out, "That's not possible! You're lying! I brought him here myself!" She then became tearful and visibly more upset.

I told her that occasionally records got misplaced, so we would check again. My nurse would also call the pathologist's office to get the pathology report since *all* my vasectomy specimens were sent for pathology verification. She would call the hospital for medical records as well.

My office staff, who knew everybody I ever saw in the office, related to me that they did not know this lady OR her husband. After about 5-10 minutes, the pathologist called me personally to say he had received no vasectomy specimens for the given name. He was concerned that he had lost it.

I assured him my office was just looking for some medical records and were trying to sort out “an issue”.

The hospital medical records department reported having NO SUCH PERSON in their files.

I returned to the exam room to tell the lady that there were no records of her husband being seen by anyone or anywhere in the clinic and hospital complexes.

Quite befuddled by now, she said, “How can that be?” This lady then gave me a story of how she had dropped her husband off at the clinic one day on her way to work so he could get information on vasectomies. She said her husband came home with brochures, which they both read. That night the pair decided to go ahead with the vasectomy, and her husband “called to make an appointment” the next morning. Several weeks later, she dropped her husband off at our clinic in the morning to have the procedure. (A clue since I seldom, if ever, did a vasectomy in the morning.) The husband asked his wife to wait in the car for him. Since she had some shopping to do, the wife left and returned about an hour later. She then waited for another hour and a half before he “limped out of the clinic to the car.” That evening her husband laid on the recliner with ice on his groin and took some Tylenol for pain.

I interrupted to ask if her husband had any trouble having sex after “the procedure.”

She related that they could not have sex for at least three days, but he was told to have sex at least four to five times a week to empty out the extra sperm. (Apparently, no problems were encountered carrying out these instructions.) According to the wife, after six weeks the husband returned to the clinic to give “a sample” to see if he was “clean”. Again, the wife said she waited for her spouse in the car. He returned about a half hour later and told her “all is good.”

Now she is pregnant, again.

By now the lady and I both started to smell something fishy. I suggested that we had had an interesting meeting. I suggested if she wished to return to me for obstetrics care, it would be best to bring her husband to her next visit.

She agreed to both and made another appointment for several days later.

At the next visit, the lady was still quite emotional. Her husband, however, had a smile from ear to ear. After completing the obstetrical examination portion of the visit, I left the exam room to allow the patient time to get dressed. By my examination and by dates, my patient was about eight weeks pregnant.

Upon returning, my patient was sobbing uncontrollably. Apparently, in my absence, the husband had fessed up to his “misdirections.”

As we talked, it became apparent that the husband still wanted another child; the wife did not. I discussed options with the mom, including pregnancy termination. She would hear none of it. She said she would have the baby, and they would get by somehow. However, she did insist that her husband have a vasectomy before they had another "accident."

He agreed.

The next seven months went along quite uneventfully for the mom-to-be. At each visit I asked about when her husband was going to get his vasectomy.

She always replied, "We are discussing it."

I tried to convince her that having her husband sterile *before* she delivered would give them the best odds of having no more mistakes.

She would always reply, "I know."

On an evening near her due date, my patient presented to the hospital in labor with her husband at her side. The labor and the delivery went smoothly (as one would expect with the fourth birth). The new-again mom did require a few stitches, however, because the new baby boy was about one and a half pounds heavier than her last baby girl. The nurses got the mom and her newborn back to her room about 2 o'clock in the morning.

After performing my customary last examination of the mom and babe before going home, I was about to leave the room when when I heard, "Hey Doc! Aren't you forgetting something?"

Somewhat puzzled, I confessed I could not think of anything.

My new mom pointed to her husband and said, "HIM!" "He gets fixed. Remember?"

The husband stammered, "We will talk about it in the morning."

The wife responded firmly, "It is morning. *We have* talked about it! It is your time— NOW!" She looked at me and said, "Isn't it the right time, Dr. Jimmie?"

Under the circumstances, I could not disagree with the new mother.

Before he could protest, I had the husband in tow toward my office – at 2 a.m. for a vasectomy!

Afterward, I brought the husband *and* his vas deferens specimens for the wife to see. I gave HER his post-operative instructions. I left the room to complete some additional paperwork and to ask the nurse to get a bag of ice for the husband.

About 3:30 a.m. I checked in on my two patients before going home. She was asleep in bed with ice on her bottom. He was asleep in the recliner chair with ice applied "down there" too.

All That Planning

A young woman in her early twenties came to visit me one spring day to discuss family planning. She conveyed to me that she and her husband had been married about 16 months, and she had not been able to conceive a child. She went on to say that they had made plans three times to visit Hawaii as a delayed honeymoon, but not having a baby on time had made her cancel three trips!

I was amused and intrigued. I wondered, "What did *not* having a baby have to do with *not* going on a vacation?"

This lady continued to tell me, "I can tell when I ovulate, and so getting pregnant should be easy." I ascertained that the couple's plans were for her to get pregnant, have a child 9 months later, and then they would go to Hawaii. (She did not mention taking a newborn, however.)

Since she had come in to discuss family planning, I started taking a history. As far as she knew, and could tell by experience, nothing was wrong with her husband. She told me that her husband was a strong, vigorous young farmer who had never been sick. He had a good sex drive and, in her opinion, performed well!

She had been having regular menses since the age of 14. She "always" had cramps when she ovulated. (At least, that was what she had been told by another physician.) Therefore, "planning" a pregnancy should be easy; but it was not working! She had never been in the hospital. She had never used any form of birth control. Her husband had been her only sexual partner. She took no medicines.

Her thought appeared to be "If cows can do it on time, then why can't I?"

Part of a fertility workup is to ask about sexual habits and patterns. When I asked how often the lady and her husband had sex, she promptly replied, "Four."

I asked, "Four what? Four times a month, four times ever, what?"

Nonchalantly, she returned, "Four times a day."

Somewhat incredulous, I asked, *"Four times every day for 16 months?"*

Her response was, "Absolutely! Before we get out of bed in the morning, when he comes in for lunch, right after supper for dessert, and when we go to bed about 10 o'clock."

I must have chuckled because the young lady asked, "What's so funny?"

I countered with, "How does he have enough energy to work? He must get exhausted?"

She responded, "He seems to be doing just fine, thank you."

I discussed some male anatomy and physiology with the lady, and the fact that the male needs time to make more sperm. He does not have a ready made endless supply. I suggested that I could perform a sperm count on her husband first before we continued with her evaluation, which was going to be much more time consuming and costly.

Then I thought that perhaps all this pair would have to do is decrease their sexual encounters. Therefore, I offered the suggestion that perhaps they could curtail their "activities" some so he would have time to regenerate more sperm. I was thinking about four times *a week* instead of *daily*!

The lady pondered my proposal briefly and replied, *"I guess we could stop the one at noon."*

She then left my office to consider our discussions.

She did not return for a fertility workup. However, she did return about six months later for an obstetrics visit.

She delivered her first child six months later.

However, the couple did not make it to Hawaii as planned (Again).

Oops

Mr. Z stormed into my clinic one morning without an appointment. He was in a most unpleasant mood. My office personnel escorted him back into my office so we could talk in private. (They also did not want him to make more of a scene than he had already.)

He reminded me that I had done a vasectomy on him previously. His wife just told him that morning that she was pregnant. He wanted to know what *I* was going to do about it!

I re-advised him that there was always a chance that a vasectomy could fail; that was the why I always asked patients to bring in a semen sample for analysis after the procedure. I reminded him that there was also a possibility that the vas segments could reconnect naturally via a sperm granuloma. I asked Mr. Z if he recalled following the post vasectomy instructions that he had been given.

He replied that he had. Then he repeated, as he pointed his finger at me, "My wife is pregnant! What are *YOU* going to do about it?"

As usual, I suggested that his records retrieved for my review (a good way to stall and to defuse a situation). Mr. Z's chart was pulled, and indeed I had performed a vasectomy some time in the past. There was a note that stated that his post procedure semen sample showed "NO SPERM."

The chart entries did not help this man one bit. He was still incensed at me. He reiterated, "My wife is still pregnant. What are you going to do about it?"

I was never really sure what he was asking of me.

I suggested that he provide us with another sample to check his current sperm count. I said that he might need to have a repeat his vasectomy, which I would do at no cost to him.

He was agreeable.

The following morning I received a lab slip which stated "NO SPERM IDENTIFIED."

Mr. Z was called and asked to come into my clinic later that same day. I did not want to report the findings over the phone. (One never can tell who might be listening.)

As soon as Mr. Z saw me he shouted, "My wife is still pregnant! What are YOU going to do about it?"

Again, I asked him into my office. I told him that the new lab report confirmed that he had no sperm.

His response was, "So what! My wife is pregnant. What are YOU going to do about it?"

I repeated, "You have NO sperm."

He asked, "What are you telling me?"

Again I repeated slowly, "You have NO sperm."

He countered with, "My wife is pregnant! What are you saying?"

I said even slower this time, "YOU—HAVE—NO—SPERM." I almost told him to talk to his wife, but I didn't.

Mr. Z was incensed when he left my clinic. He knew something was not right. His wife was pregnant, and HE HAD NO SPERM!

Later that day Mr. Z and his wife apparently had a "discussion." Apparently, Mrs. Z was not as true to her hubby as he and most folks thought. She had been receiving frequent "packages" from a delivery service driver, one of which impregnated her.

Mr. and Mrs. Z went their separate ways shortly thereafter. Mrs. Z left town with the driver and her children. Apparently, this arrangement disintegrated in a short time, and Mrs. Z was left alone looking for other men who would deliver "packages."

Mr. Z found companionship with a marvelous lady in town. He had his vasectomy reversed, and subsequently sired several more children with his new wife.

Afterward, the new Mrs. Z had her tubes tied.

Rocky Mountain Oysters

Lars Jensen and his wife had four children, and Lars decided that he should be "fixed" before they had any more "youngins." Lars, his wife, and I met for the first time when I discussed the vasectomy procedure with them.

The Jensens operated a large farm and ranch operation about 50 miles from town that took a substantial commitment of their time. He and his wife managed sections (square miles) of grazing land, thousands of cattle, and multiple employees. Consequently, finding a suitable time for the vasectomy required some planning. After reviewing their pocket calendar, they chose a date on a Friday between branding their cows and their being at the auction yards.

As usual, the vasectomy procedure was scheduled as my last appointment on Friday.

The day of surgery arrived. After the customary greetings and a time to answer any last minute questions from Lars, I prepared to get to the task at hand.

As I started to clean the surgical area, Lars leaned upward on his elbows and asked if he could watch. My surgical room was not equipped with mirrors for the patients to observe, and I was not sure how things would work out with the patient sitting up. Nonetheless, I said, "Sure. Let's see what we can do."

As I carefully administered the local anesthetic to his scrotum, Lars winced a bit, but he continued to watch me quite intently. He wanted me to explain everything I did so he would better understand the procedure. He wanted to see the suture and how I tied knots. He was interested in observing the piece of the vas deferens that I removed. He was particularly interested in knowing how I controlled any bleeding with a fine clamp and a cautery unit.

After I had completed one side of the vasectomy, Lars laid back on the surgical table.

I asked if he was O.K.

He said he was fine. He had seen enough. He just wanted me to keep talking while I completed the other side.

Just as I was placing the final suture in the skin, Lars sat up to examine the results of my efforts. He said, "Damn fine job Doc."

My curiosity got to me. I asked Lars why he was so interested in watching.

He said, "Well, this morning I made 50 steers outa 50 bulls. I just wanted to see if you were neater than I was."

I replied, "Well, how did I do?"

Lars countered with, "Well, we don't clean the sac with anything.

Bleeding is stopped with a paste the Vet gave us. We just slop it on the sac. You didn't have to contend with flying shit for sure. After we're done ripping out his testicles, the critter gets a shot of Teramycin in the ass before we let him loose out in the dusty corral."

After a pause to think, Lars continued with "Doc, I'd have to say that you're a darn sight neater than me. I can say that for sure!"

I started to laugh. Lars was definitely a character, a most wealthy character.

Lars then asked, "Do ya know what we do with all those testicles? We eatum while they're fresh. How'd you and the Mrs. like to come out to the ranch tomorrow for our yearly feast of Rocky Mountain Oysters?"

I thanked Lars for his kind invitation, but I told him I had to be on call at the hospital that weekend.

On Saturday night, I was called to the ER. There was Lars with my share of his Rocky Mountain Oysters.

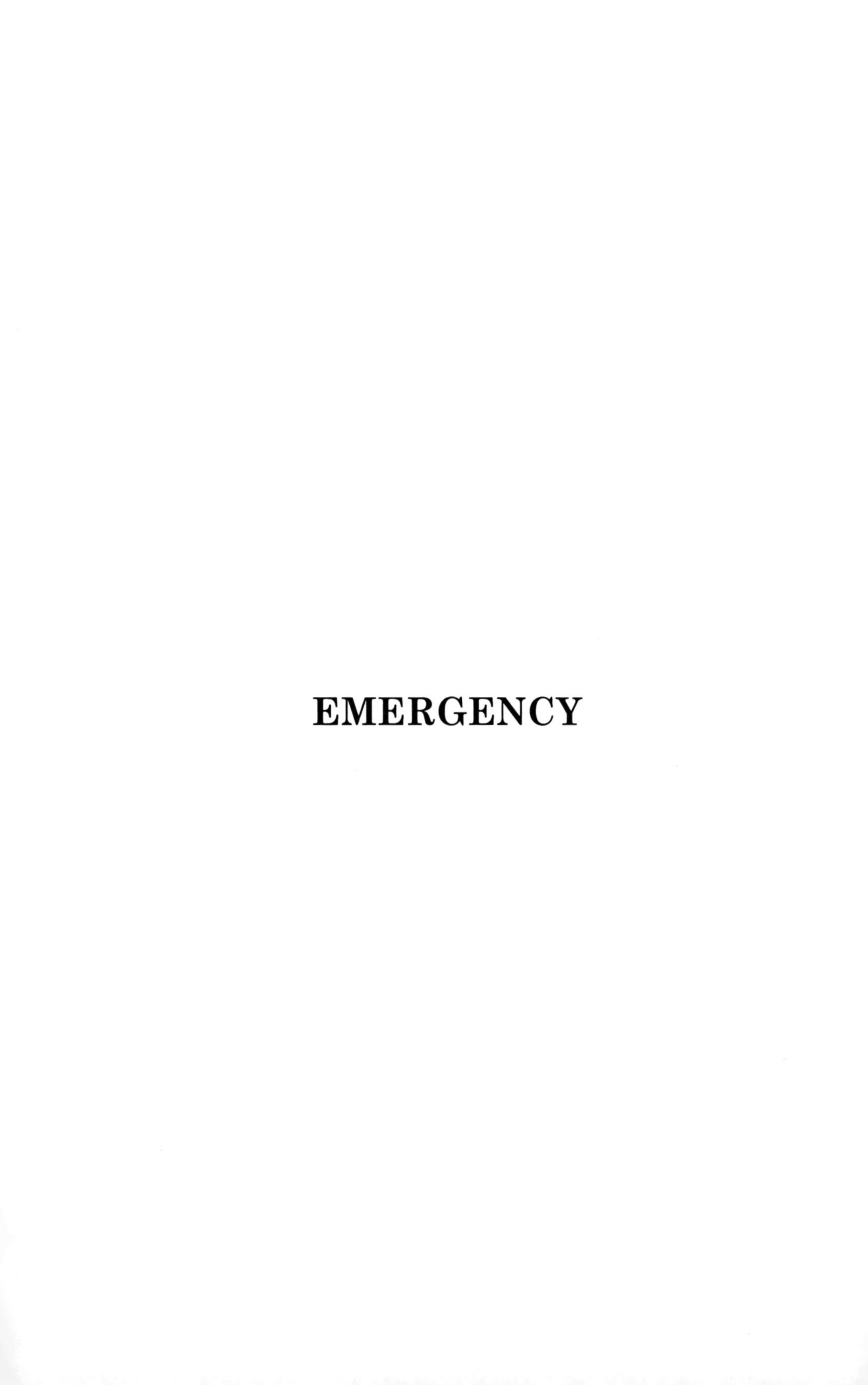

EMERGENCY

"The aim of medicine is to prevent disease and prolong life,
the ideal of medicine is to eliminate the need of a physician."

William J. Mayo, M.D.

"The good physician treats the disease;
the great physician treats the patient who has the disease"

Sir William Osler

The Brass Ring

One evening about suppertime I received a phone call from the nurse in the emergency room. After I determined to whom I was talking, I said something like, “What’s up?”

She replied, “Dr. A, we need you in the ER.”

I asked, “What’s the problem?”

Her response was, “Just come in now, please.”

All the way into town my mind was overflowing with possibilities. Was it a bad wreck? Was someone having a heart attack? Did someone die?

Upon arriving in the ER I found no patients in the usual triage places; the cardiac beds were empty; the trauma area was quiet; and the obstetrics room was vacant. I thought, “What the heck is going on?”

About then the nurse came down the corridor and said, “Dr. A, It’s in here. You’ve got to see this!” She then took me down the hall to a larger room that was usually used for orthopedic procedures. There I saw *the problem.*

There in the middle of the room leaning against an exam table was a man about 60 I guessed with his pants and underwear down around his ankles. His penis was engorged, erect, about 12 inches long, and BLACK! At the base of the penis was a one-inch diameter threaded brass bushing obstructing blood flow and causing the erection. As one would expect, the man was in considerable pain. While I was asking a few questions, the man blurted out, “Whatever you do, don’t call my wife!”

I determined that the fellow was out in his shop and for some reason wanted to know if his “unit” would fit into the bushing; it did. However, the metal ring soon obstructed the blood flow to his penis and made the penis erect. The threads on the bushing prevented our pulling it off the man’s engorged penis. The man apparently tried for several hours to remove the brass plumbing fitting, but alas to no avail. Pain is what finally brought him to the hospital.

I could not readily think of a tool that could cut the metal piece safely. Our attempts using lubricants and force were useless since the tissue of the penis was now covering about half of the width of the fitting. I decided to call someone from engineering, because they had all the tools. Besides, engineering seldom had the opportunity to participate in medical urgencies.

About 10 minutes later, Stan Fisher from engineering arrived. I met him outside the exam room to try to explain our situation. Like a trooper he said, “Let’s take a look and see what I can do for you.”

Stan got a look at this fella’s black penis, his eyes opened wide, and his jaw dropped in awe. I said to Stan, “See our dilemma?”

Stan said the bushing was too big for a little tool. He said he had a **reciprocating saw** or a **blowtorch**.

Now our patient's eyes got REALLY big.

About then I remembered we had just received some new heavy-duty cast saw blades that were used for the new Fiberglas casting material. I thought that the stronger blade just might be tough enough to cut through the brass object. Stan and I decided it wouldn't hurt to try using it; using the blade would not hurt ***us*** anyway.

I got out the cast saw and started to cut the bushing. It worked pretty well until the man said the metal was getting "pretty damn hot!" We also had to deal with all the swollen tissue that by now was totally engulfing the bushing.

Finally, we worked out a procedure where Stan forced a small tongue depressor between the brass fitting and the skin while putting traction on the penis. The nurse dripped ice water onto the metal while I sawed away with the cast saw. After about five minutes of cutting, and allowing time out for our patient to calm down a few times, the brass bushing was removed.

I was most concerned because the penis did not deflate right away, and it stayed black! I figured that I needed a surgical consult.

When I telephoned our general surgeon, Dr. Barrigan, his response to my story was, "You're shitting me, aren't you?"

After he understood the authenticity of my dilemma, he came up to see the man, or rather his penis.

We decided to admit the man to the hospital for observation.

I worried about this guy all night. To my delight, when I came into the hospital the following morning, Dr. Barrigan had already seen the patient and his traumatized organ, declared it functional and out of danger, and sent the man home to explain things to his most embarrassed spouse.

I kept the brass fitting as a souvenir and a conversation piece.

Skin Doc

Poplar, Montana is a small community on an Indian reservation in northeastern Montana. Most physicians in Poplar are repaying the government for school loans by being members of the Indian Health Service Corps (IHS). IHS physicians comprise all specialties by training. However, while in Poplar, all the physicians are GMOs (general medical officers) who are expected to care for the majority of their patients' problems.

Since the physicians in Poplar had minimal medical backup, it was commonplace for the physicians working in our emergency department to receive requests for consultations from Poplar.

On a February weekend in 1978 I was in the emergency room caring for a young man who had been injured in basketball practice that evening. The ER nurse summoned me to the telephone; she did not say why.

When I took the phone, a female voice said, "This is the Poplar Hospital requesting the physician on call for Dr. Phillips."

I replied, "This is Dr. Ashcraft. How may I help you?"

In the background I could hear a male voice yelling, "Get me some god damn help!"

A male, who identified himself as Dr. Phillips, then screamed into the phone. He sounded somewhat frantic, almost hysterical, on the phone. Dr. Phillips was the IHS "Doctor of the Day", which meant that he was covering the town for emergencies. He asked if I delivered babies. When I confirmed that I did deliver babies, he related that he needed some help, NOW!

Apparently, the winter weather was bad and it was preventing travel on the highways. This physician said a pregnant woman came to his hospital's emergency room in labor and ready to deliver.

I asked, "How may I help you? Are you having some problems?"

The physician exclaimed, "Hell yes I'm in trouble! This woman is about to have a baby! I'm a god damned DERMATOLOGIST! I don't deliver babies!"

I had to chuckle to myself after hearing the panic in this man's voice. He was obviously out of his element and scared to his wits end. I asked Dr. Phillips if he had ever delivered a baby.

He forcefully replied, "I'm a GOD DAMN DERMATOLOGIST. What do you think?"

I sensed increasing panic in the physician's voice.

I asked him if there were any nurses around that could help him with the birth. He acknowledged that nurses were present. He handed the phone to the awaiting nurse.

I asked the nurse to describe the situation.

She explained that the patient was an Indian female ready to deliver her third child. The woman's previous births were not eventful as far as the nurse could determine. The nurse then blurted out, "This doctor is a basket case."

I then conversed with Dr. Phillips again. I reminded him that babies were born, not delivered. Women had been doing it successfully without doctors for a million years or so. Firemen and EMTs assist mothers with having babies all the time.

Dr. Phillips was not comforted. He responded, "Then get me an ambulance driver for God's sake!"

Finally, the nurse and I were able to console the anxious Dr. Phillips. Over the phone, with the help of the nurse, the mom, and Mother Nature, we talked the dermatologist through a routine vaginal delivery.

A few weeks later, one of the Poplar ambulance crewmembers informed me that the mother and child were doing fine.

The dermatologist, however, apparently decided that being a general medical officer on an Indian reservation was not his cup of tea. He left Poplar a short time later seeking greener, more comfortable, medical pastures.

Child Down

During the time of the oil boom in Sidney, our medical team spent a lot of time dealing with emergencies. Our spacious new emergency room complex was completed in 1981 just as our oil boom was dying out. However, the new emergency room was well thought out for handling routine emergency traffic as well as the severe catastrophic emergencies that we had become accustomed to managing.

During the late 1970's and early 1980s our community seemed to have a significant number of children who apparently had died from SIDS (Sudden Infant Death Syndrome). The nursing staff in the emergency room had become somewhat sensitized to having very sick infants come to the hospital. Consequently, usually little time was spent in calling a physician to the emergency department for a sick child. The nurses knew that when a child came to the ER unresponsive and required resuscitation, the outcome was invariably grim.

On one nice sunny day I wished I could be outside. Instead, I was in surgery with Dr. Barrigan most of the morning for an emergency procedure. Because of the emergency surgery, my morning office patients had been diverted to the afternoon hours. When I got to my office at about 1:00 in the afternoon, I found the reception area to be standing-room-only with patients.

I had just seen my first afternoon patient when my nurse told me that they needed me in the emergency room STAT for a sick baby. I dropped everything and ran to the emergency room.

As I entered the general emergency area I became aware of a generalized chaos. There appeared to be a mother who was crying and screaming that her baby was dead. The nurses were trying to get things squared away for a resuscitation. In the center of this commotion was a cyanotic child about six months old by my estimation.

I ascertained from the comments being made that the child was found blue and unresponsive at home. The family lived just a very short distance from the hospital. The mother brought her baby girl promptly to the hospital without attempting any type of resuscitation.

As I came upon the youngster, I noticed that the cardiac monitor displayed a regular heart rhythm. Therefore, I knew this baby, obviously, was not dead. It appeared to me that the child may be having a breath holding spell, or it may have had a near SIDS episode.

I thought that if I stimulated the child quickly, its natural reflexes might start it to breathe spontaneously. Therefore, I placed my hands near the left ear and clapped them as loud as I could. I got no response from the child. I then grabbed the child's hands, lifted up the arms, and then dropped the child's arms. I thought that this maneuver might stimulate a Moro or startle reflex.

Fortunately, after this quick maneuver, the youngster performed a magnificent Moro response and started to scream vigorously.

I watched the youngster for about another minute or so to make sure she was doing fine. I then asked the nurse to watch the patient for an hour or so and to let me know if the baby had any more problems.

I then returned to my office to begin sorting through the remaining collection of patients. My total time in the emergency room could not have been more than ten minutes.

Since all went well with the child, I had no further feedback about the child except that she was discharged from the ER in stable condition.

About 17 years later, I was in the emergency room caring for a patient. A middle-aged lady, who was with a family member being treated, came up to me and asked if she could talk to me privately. Since my patient in the emergency room was stable, I escorted the lady to a place we called the green room (because everything was green). This was the room outside the emergency area where we frequently had family consultations.

This lady introduced herself to me and said, "I'm sure you don't remember me." (I was sure also.)

She said to me, " You're the doctor who saved my daughter's life 17 years ago." She went on to say, " I thought that day that you must walk on water because when you came into that emergency room everyone stepped aside. When you clapped your hands and my baby girl woke up, I knew that you did walk on water."

This lady was so emotional and poignant about what I supposedly had done years ago; I was at a loss for words.

She continued to explain that she was quite distraught that day (as I would surmise) and did not have time to thank me personally.

The family moved from Sidney soon after the incident, and she never took the time to thank me by card or by letter. She and her family were now visiting relatives in Sidney.

The mother went on to tell me that her child was a very pretty honor student in high school. The lady asked me if she could give me a long delayed, but well deserved, hug.

What could I say but yes.

She then gave me a long hard hug and a kiss on my left cheek.

I felt embarrassed—and honored.

The lady then summoned her daughter and told her that I was the one who saved her when she was a baby. I then got yet another hug. (I do like hugs.)

I thought to myself that an act that seemed so insignificant to me at the time of the original incident had made a tremendous impact on this mother and her family who will be grateful to me forever.

Little events like this one made all the years of effort and all the study seem worth it.

I thought to myself that something that had become so second nature to me and, apparently so easy for me to forget, was actually a most precious, memorable, and life changing event for this mother and daughter.

These events were now precious to me as well.

Hydrogen Sulfide

The oil drilling business has a multitude of hazards. Not only are there the expected number of injuries associated with operating powerful equipment, but also injuries occur because of cold weather, drug use by the workers, illness, errors in judgment, and exposure to the oil, its contaminants, and the chemicals used to extract it.

Hydrogen sulfide gas (H2S) is a toxic gas that is present in a lot of the crude oil extracted in our area. It smells like rotten eggs. In large concentrations, the gas can be lethal by binding to red blood cells and thereby not allowing oxygen to be delivered to cells; the victim then suffocates.

Drilling companies put forth substantial effort to train employees about the hazards of H2S. Gas masks and ventilation devices are at all well sites and in vehicles. Windsocks fly at each well site so people can stay upwind from the gas. Employees with respiratory problems are cautioned away from H2S wells.

Late one fall afternoon in 1979 an all-employee alert was sent out by the hospital for a major trauma. Apparently, some workers were cleaning out a truck's oil tanker that had been carrying H2S laden oil. One of the employees either jumped or fell into the tank and became unresponsive in short order. A second employee jumped into the tank in a rescue attempt but was soon overcome by fumes. Other employees managed to extract the two victims, but the toxic fumes subdued several more people. Multiple ambulances transported the worst six victims. Many others came in by private vehicle.

The first patient to arrive in our emergency room was a male who was covered with oil and wreaked like a rotten egg. He was dead and was placed in another room out of the way.

The second, third, and fourth victims were having profound respiratory difficulties, but they were alive so far. A team of four was assigned to each victim, and full resuscitative efforts were started on all of them. All the victims had to be intubated and ventilated. Soiled, smelly clothing was removed. Intravenous catheters were started. Bladder catheters were inserted. Blood was drawn for testing. CPR was needed for two patients. The anesthesiologist took charge of the emergent airway issues.

Dr. Berryman and I were the overseers of this pandemonium.

As far as we knew, the only known possible treatment for H2S poisoning was sodium nitrite, a chemical that was packaged in cyanide overdose kits. However, we had never used it.

While Dr. Berryman looked up the treatments for H2S intoxication in our toxicology text, I consulted with the poison control center in Denver.

As we started our fact finding, I noticed I was having a little trouble concentrating. The air was thick with the smell of H2S gas, oil, and dirt. We had about 20 people smelling this stuff in a room no bigger than 14 x 20 feet, the size of our emergency room at the time. I told the nurse we needed to get some fans in the emergency area STAT!

She called engineering STAT for some fans.

Someone from engineering arrived promptly with a fan, *a 12-inch oscillating fan*, dropped it off, and left.

I thought, "My God, we were all in trouble." I called the hospital administrator, told him about our dilemma, and said we needed some ventilation NOW before his employees started dying!

Within minutes, engineering arrived with several 24inch high volume exhaust fans and opened the appropriate building doors and windows. These efforts allowed the stale air to be sucked outside. They also found several air compressors that pumped fresh air directly into the ER.

I now had time to call the Poison Control Center in Denver. The toxicologist on duty told me no one at their facility had any extensive experience with H2S gas. His experience was that of finding bums in the sewers of Denver—dead. He had no experience with the after effects of H2S poisoning. He did recommend using sodium nitrite, but he was not terribly convincing about the prospects of it working. The toxicologist then gave me the name of another physician who had written papers on H2S gas intoxication.

The next consultant was located in Minnesota, not exactly an oil-producing hot bed. This fellow told me his experience was that of patients who had been exposed and *walked into his office*! He had no acute experience. As far as he knew, no one had any acute experience that had been reported where the patient survived. He told me we were breaking new ground and that, whatever the outcomes, he would like to know the results. Finally, he proclaimed, "YOU ARE NOW THE HYDROGEN SULFIDE EXPERTS OF THE UNITED STATES."

I related my conversations to Dr. Bill who was not terribly reassured at being thought of as an expert. He didn't know squat! I didn't know squat! But WE were the only show in town.

Sodium Nitrite was given intravenously to all of the severely ill patients once - twice - three times. It didn't seem to do a darn thing to reverse the effects of the H2S. "So much for poison control!" we thought.

By now, the three patients were being manually ventilated with ambu bags by the emergency personnel and were as stable as they were going to be. Dr. Bill arranged for the victims to be transferred to the Intensive Care Unit (ICU) where they were placed on mechanical ventilators.

Our timing for moving the victims was good because, by now, all the workers were experiencing nausea, headaches, some respiratory distress, and fatigue. A lot of fresh air and time were the cures for non-fatal H2S gas exposure.

Dr. Berryman took control of the ICU victims and left the emergency room.

A nurse touched my shoulder and pointed down a hallway to a long line of people, either standing or sitting in chairs. All of these folks had been part of this toxic exposure. They all needed to be evaluated. I said to the nurse, "I guess that supper is out of the question tonight." I let my wife know I would be home a *lot later* than usual.

Fortunately, except for a couple of people with asthma attacks who were admitted to the hospital, the 20 or so remaining victims were in pretty good shape. All were encouraged to remove their clothes and to shower when they got home. Their contaminated clothes were to be left outside or destroyed. If they had any troubles, they were asked to return.

Additionally, the patients were reassured that they would not die like their fellow employee.

Over the next several weeks, the ICU victims developed a hemorrhagic adult respiratory distress syndrome (ARDS) from the tremendous inflammatory insult to the lungs from the toxins they had inhaled. All had multiple ventilator-associated complications such as collapsed lungs, which required the insertion of chest tubes, and infections. However, all the patients survived and left the hospital, eventually.

Fortunately, the employees who helped with this group of victims did not develop any long lasting problems from H2S gas exposure.

Dr. Bill and I discussed publishing our adventure, but we never did.

The day after the incident, the boss told me that the workers who died and were injured had just finished their H2S training *the day before*!

So much for compliance! The boss told me that the training sessions would be much more intense in the future.

Over time federal government regulatory agencies produced *and enforced* more stringent regulations regarding oilfield safety.

Our community did not have another serious H2S incident during the next 25 years.

The Broken Wrist

Early one evening during a fall hunting season I was manning the ER at the hospital. The place had been crawling with injuries and maladies of all sorts most of the day. During a break in the action, a middle-aged hunter came into the ER with a friend. He was holding his arm that was wrapped up in a coat. The man related that he was up in a tree blind looking for wild game to shoot. Somehow, he fell out of the tree and landed on his arm. He stayed out hunting with his party for the remainder of the day until it became too dark to hunt. He then came to the hospital because his arm was "starting to hurt."

When I examined the man's arm, I noticed an obvious fracture at the wrist with some upward deviation of the radius bone at the wrist. The nerves and blood vessels of the hand seemed intact. The hand was swollen tremendously because it had been hanging and swelling all day! Fortunately, the outside temperature had been about 20 degrees all day, which may have limited the arm swelling a little.

An x-ray revealed a comminuted fracture (many small pieces) of the radius bone at the wrist. With some regional anesthesia, I was able to realign the bone fragments substantially, but not perfectly. However, because of the severe swelling, applying a cast at the time was not a good idea. Therefore, I applied a splint to the arm. I requested to keep the man in the hospital for a day or two until the swelling subsided. A cast could be applied then that would maintain the fracture alignment better. The fellow was further advised that his fracture could be quite troublesome if he did not take care of it.

He refused to stay in the hospital noting that he could keep his arm up at home.

The man was given further instructions by the ER nurse to elevate his arm, a plaster splint was applied to the broken arm, and he was asked to be seen in the office the next day to evaluate the swelling.

The man came to the office three days later. His arm was more swollen than ever. In talking with him, my nurse and I ascertained that the splint put on in the ER relieved a lot of his arm pain. Therefore, he went hunting for two more days and *sort of forgot* about his appointment.

The same information about his arm fracture that had been given to him in the ER was repeated in the office. He declined admission again. Consequently, I elected to have the man agree not to go hunting anymore, keep his arm elevated, and see me in two days. At that time we would re-x-ray the fracture, adjust the alignment as needed, and apply a cast.

He agreed.

He returned *nine days later.* The arm was still swollen from hanging. An x-ray showed calcification from early healing, which one would expect at 12 days after the injury. There was not much I could do at this point.

I consulted Dr. Dan Wallace, an orthopedic specialist, and gave him the case scenario. His comment was, "Tell the guy you're not God. You can't make ice cream outa cowshit!" He suggested that I obtain the best bone reduction I could, apply a heavy long arm cast, and see the guy back in a week.

I followed these instructions (except for the cowshit comment). An appointment was made for one week.

The fellow was seen again *three weeks later.* By now, the wrist was becoming deformed from the healing process. Nothing could be done in terms of bone realignment until the healing had matured, and the kind of function that was left in the hand was determined.

As one might expect, the results of the fracture healing haphazardly was cosmetically unacceptable at six weeks. However, the hand and arm function was pretty good. Therefore, the man was given a slip to see the physical therapist for after-care exercises.

He never showed up.

About six months later I received a notice that the man was suing me for incompetence. He wanted a million dollars because he could not use his arm. He was 45 years old, a mechanic, and could no longer feed his family. He was *entitled* to some compensation.

The Montana Medical-Legal Panel, a group of individuals whose job it was to determine a claim's merits, heard the case first. I prevailed 6 to 0.

The man and his attorney filed a lawsuit anyway.

My insurance company appointed attorney advised me early on that medical liability claims were a far better pay out than the lottery. It was at least 50:50 in Montana at the time.

I suffered through my first depositions. I listened to the litany of lies against me put forth by my accuser and his attorney during his deposition. My attorney prepared me for a trial because I refused to settle the claim.

One evening during this ordeal, one of the nurses came up to me and asked if I was being sued by a certain individual. When I confirmed her query, she advised me that this fellow was playing ill all day, but was repairing auto bodies at night in her neighbor's garage. Also, he was bragging that he was going to hit the "mother load."

I thanked the nurse for her information.

In the morning I talked with my attorney. Soon thereafter our poor, supposedly disabled man was being videotaped.

When the videotape revelation was shown to the patient's lawyer, there was no admission of their guilt. There was a request for a settlement. This is when I learned some of the finer points of the legal profession, the seedier finer points.

The plaintiff's attorney noted that his expenses with the case would not be reimbursed without any insurance money. If they went to trial he would have at least some chance of payment. He also knew that it would cost the insurance company at least $60,000 to go to trial; therefore, the minimum they were going to spend was $60,000 for this case, one-way or the other. Besides, it had been a slow year for his client, and he too could use the money, and *it's just an insurance company's money anyway.*

I thought to myself, "What a crock! How about me?"

The negotiations continued for several weeks between the lawyers - not with me. Finally, they met one morning over coffee at a local restaurant. My insurance company agreed on a payoff of $10,000 (of which the plaintiff's attorney would get 33 percent plus his expenses, or about $9,000), and the plaintiff would receive about $1000 for *his inconvenience*!

The two attorneys then scheduled a social lunch together to take care of some other legal matters.

My attorney's final remarks to me were, "It's done. It's over with. Forget about it. Get on with your life."

The paperwork was done, but ***it*** would never be over. One never forgets about the lies, deceptions, and the process. My life was never the same. I never saw patients in the same light again.

The legal system was not about "right vs. wrong," or "justice vs. injustice," or "good vs. bad," or "malpractice vs. judgment decisions that went bad."

Plain and simple, it was about intimidation and money!

A Missing Link

The fall of 1980 was miserable at best. Everyday seemed to bring a new storm, colder weather, or more traumas from the oil patch. It seemed to me that all these things arrived in Sidney simultaneously.

The Wednesday before Thanksgiving was no exception to my rule. A storm front had moved in earlier in the day making travel treacherous at best. The wind chills were well below zero. People were in a hurry to get away from town for the holidays. I was in the ER, as usual.

About 6 p.m. the hospital received a call from somewhere out in the country that a man had been injured; an ambulance was needed. Fortunately, our EMTs knew the unmarked county roads and farmlands. Somehow, they found the victim inside a semi-truck in the middle of a field way out in the boondocks of Richland County in the dark!

Our first report was, "Heavy set man, confused, covered with mud, no obvious injuries." They were transporting the fellow with oxygen only.

Before arriving at the ER, the EMTs reported deteriorating vital signs. "BP 90. Respirations shallow, but not labored."

When the ambulance arrived and the EMTs had delivered the patient into the ER, I thought to myself, "This guy is not heavy set. He is a whale!" Their patient weighed about 350 pounds and stretched out no more than five-feet eight-inches. He was twice as wide as the stretcher!

The man had a palpable blood pressure, his pulse was rapid, and he was unconscious. He was covered with mud because he and his team of oilfield workers had been out in the farmer's muddy field. I noticed some blood on his right forehead with a small skin tear.

Promptly, I started to look for a vein to insert an IV. I could not find any useable veins because they were covered with layers of fat!

Our orthopedic surgeon happened to come by and offered his help. I asked him to find a site for an IV in the patient's right arm while I looked on the left. After a quick look, he said there were no veins.

I knew that already. I said, "Then put in a cutdown!"

The orthopedist stood up and said, "I'm an orthopedic surgeon. I don't do cutdowns. You need a general surgeon." He then got up and stomped out of the ER.

I wanted to thump that doctor, but I had a bigger problem!

I made a cutdown incision in the left arm, found a suitable vein, and inserted an intravenous catheter.

By now, the anesthetist had arrived and intubated my patient. We now had *some* control of the situation. At least I thought so.

I was wondering if this man had not had a stroke or something similar. I started to ask about any previous medical history, which was unknown. All that was known was that this fellow had attached his semi-truck, using a large chain, to another semi that was stuck in the mud. As he was backing up his truck, the victim had his head outside his window to see because of the poor visibility. The next thing anyone knew was that the chained snapped, and the patient's truck stopped. The workers thought the trucker had stopped to get reconnected. However, when they saw the driver leaning out the window, they knew was wrong.

With this story, I reevaluated the forehead lesion. There was a defect in the skull the size of my little finger. I asked radiology to perform a two view skull series.

The x-rays showed a three quarter inch opened chain link lying in the middle of this man's brain!

Apparently, when the chain broke, the man's face was in the wrong place at the right time to be struck by a single flying chain link. (Talk about bad luck!)

Promptly, I called a neurosurgeon in Billings. Arrangements were made for an airlift despite the terrible weather. The neurosurgeon pointed out that the prognosis was grim at best, and I should inform the family. At that time, however, I had no family information.

The nurses located the family phone number and dialed it for me. The whole clan was congregating in Dickinson, North Dakota for Thanksgiving. They were awaiting the arrival of, a dad, a son, a husband, and my patient at any minute. When I talked to the wife I could visualize her being dumfounded by my comments. At one moment she was thinking about family, friends, and happiness; the next moment she was hearing head trauma, critical condition, poor chance of survival, and sending her husband to Billings by air ambulance from some guy on the phone in an unknown town in Montana.

I tried my best to convey my condolences and best wishes.

I received a call from the neurosurgeon the next day. He complemented the team for our management of the patient. He related that he never saw such extensive brain destruction from a single projectile. The man's intracranial pressures were out of sight and could not be reduced. He said the man's brain was "mush."

The man died soon after his family arrived from North Dakota.

I kept the x-ray and went back to work in the emergency room.

Legs

From 1975 until 1981 Sidney, a town of about 5,000 people was at the epicenter of an American oil boom. The United States was in a recession. The price of crude oil was high. Energy companies were given incentives to explore for new oil, gas, and coal reserves. The Williston Basin, an area extending from above the Canadian Border over western North Dakota and eastern Montana down through Wyoming, had the largest coal and oil reserves in North America. People of all ages flocked to our area in search of high paying jobs. The tremendous influx of people also brought medical problems, day and night.

The Sidney emergency room averaged one airlift a day for over two years at the peak of the boom. I was told that we supplied the Billings hospitals with about a third of their head trauma cases and half of their severe trauma cases over this time frame. Our little ER was the third busiest in patient volume in Montana, being surpassed only by the two hospitals in Billings with their 300 specialty physicians. Our small airport recorded the fourth largest number of takeoffs and landings in the state. Sidney was indeed a busy place!

One very cold Friday evening in the winter of 1978 I received a call from the ER. Someone had been seriously injured on an oilrig, and the ambulance crew thought someone should be available when they arrived.

This type of call was typical. I drove to the hospital expeditiously, but with due caution because of the weather.

I was waiting for the patient when the ambulance arrived. The patient was a 19-year-old man who had suffered extensive leg trauma at the work site. The overalls, or what was left of them, were still covering the patient and his legs. The patient was coherent. His vital signs were excellent. Both legs were deformed, and I could see the end of one thighbone protruding through the remnants of his work clothes. I knew this fellow was going to need some wound debridement and cleansing, so I made arrangements to take the young man promptly to the operating room. Additionally, I called our local general surgeon at the time to come to help.

After our nurse anesthetist had the patient sedated, we removed the teenager's clothes. There was a noticeable absence of significant bleeding. The examination of the boy was unremarkable except both legs had been ripped off at the mid thigh area. The skin looked like it had been crushed. The middle parts of both femurs were mush. The right leg was being held on by a mere slip of skin. The left leg had an intact hamstring muscle complex only. The large blood vessels could be seen pulsating into ends that were also crushed. I knew that there was little we could do for this young man in Sidney.

I tied off the large pulsating arteries just in case they might start to bleed. I cleaned out the dirt and grime as gently and as thoroughly as I could.

The surgeon said, "There is nothing surgical for me to do here, so I am going home." "Clean things up, would you." He then left the hospital.

We had been asked to give a status report to the tool pusher, the boss at the oilrig, after we had evaluated the teen's injuries. When I gave him the bad news, I was told to expect a call from Houston pretty soon. About 15 minutes later, someone from the home office in Houston demanded to talk to the surgeon in charge.

I answered the call because our surgeon went home!

This fellow demanded that I airlift their employee to the nearest LEG TRANSPLANT UNIT!

I wondered, "Where does he think we are?"

I tried to explain to this man that we did not have an air transport in Sidney. For sure, Montana did not have a leg transplant service. If we were to send him to such a place, it would have to be to the Mayo Clinic, Colorado, Utah, or Washington. All of these locations were about 1000 miles away.

His response was, "I don't give a damn where they are! Send him NOW!"

I spent the next several hours trying to find someplace willing to attempt a reimplantation procedure on our patient. In the process I learned that reimplantation was best achieved with clean sharp wounds less than two-hours-old. Our patient had dirty crush injuries now six-hours-old. By the time he got anywhere, the injuries would be at least 10-hours-old.

I was turned down by six medical centers before I called the University of Washington Medical School. A surgery team in Seattle was trying to establish a reimplantation unit and was willing to give it a try if for no other reason than experience.

The home office was notified, the company authorized a jet transport to Seattle, and the young man left Sidney in the early hours of the next morning.

I received a nice letter from the surgeon in Seattle some time later thanking me for considering their services. The letter went on to say that the procedure went well technically, but the patient lost both legs because of the extent of the severe soft tissue crush injury that had destroyed the vascular networks in the legs. The surgeon told me the young man would require extensive and prolonged physical and psychological rehabilitation in Seattle.

After an inquiry of the accident, government investigators determined that drug use by the other floor hands on the drilling rig had been a major contributing factor to the mishap.

A Slippery Ride

The winter of 1982 was miserable! The temperatures were below zero most of the time. The wind chills approached 80 degrees below zero at times. The ER saw a lot of cold trauma in the oil patch workers, especially those workers who came from the southern states and had never experienced freezing weather.

One very cold morning I was in the emergency room about 7 a.m. when three oil field workers dragged in a fellow worker who had been injured at the site. They dropped their fellow worker in a heap in the middle of the floor, and left saying, "He's yours!" The men then left the ER without giving any more details about the accident.

The injured worker was complaining of substantial pain in his low back, legs, and buttocks. His thought processes and behavior suggested to the nurse and me that this man had been taking something other than aspirin while he was working. As soon as possible, we obtained a urine sample for drugs.

Except for the man's pain complaints and his curious behavior, I was unable to find much in terms of physical abnormalities. The patient was in no state of mind to give us anything resembling a reliable history. All he recalled was that he went to work, it was colder than hell, and now he was here, wherever *"here"* was!

Since the man was complaining bitterly of back pain, he was sent to radiology for x-rays.

All pictures of his pelvis, lumbar spine, and hips were unremarkable.

I admitted this fellow into the hospital for observation. I hoped that when his head cleared, we could find out what happened at the oilrig.

The next day the man still had no recall of the previous day's events. Now, he did not recall even going to work. "Great!" I thought

My examination of him on this day, however, was most revealing. This fellow had some bruising on his low back, and his buttocks were black, swollen, and tense. The man could not tolerate even the weight of a sheet on his backside. There he was with his bruised bare butt sticking up between two sheets, one covering his top and one covering his legs.

I ordered some Tylenol for his pain since I figured he had had enough *good stuff* before he came to see us. I asked physical therapy to see the fellow regarding any therapy that their department may have to offer.

The Tool Pusher, the supervisor of the drilling rig, came in about suppertime to talk with me so he could complete his accident reports. This burly fellow was visibly upset. Actually, he was really ticked off! He wanted nothing to do with this employee!

I asked the boss if he could tell me anything about how this fellow got hurt.

He said, "You're god damn right, I can!"

The night was very cold, about 20 degrees below zero and breezy, so who knows what the wind chill factor was. His employee was assigned to work on the "Crow's Nest," the top of the drilling tower.

When the shift is over, the man in the "Crow's Nest" is supposed to make his way down to the main floor of the drilling platform by climbing down a ladder. If there is ever an emergency in the tower, the employee working in the tower has access to an escape cable, which goes from the tower to the ground.

Apparently, my patient, who had been using some unknown substance to keep comfortable in the cold, decided to go off shift the easy way, down the escape cable!

He reportedly grabbed the cable with his frozen gloves, which also was 20 degrees below zero and covered with ice, and slid down. According to his tool pusher, he *raced* down the cable. My patient made it from the 80-foot platform to the frozen ground in no time. The boss estimated that his man hit the frozen ground going about 40 miles per hour and landed squarely on his butt.

The tool pusher told me that his rig had to achieve just one more day without an accident to win an "Injury Free Year" award which would have been accompanied by a $5,000 cash bonus for all hands, and a new car for him.

He then said, "Then this guy pulls this lame-brained stunt for no good reason!"

I could see why the other workers literally "dropped him off" at the hospital. My patient was lucky his "friends" didn't leave him in a field somewhere to freeze to death.

The man's butt improved slowly. He left the hospital about a week later only to go directly to jail. My patient apparently had some "*extra medicinals*" in his clothing toward which the police took offense. Not only did he use his drugs but also he was caught selling them to our junior high school kids. This kind of activity was not a good idea in a small conservative town in eastern Montana.

The last I heard, this fellow was going to stay in jail for a long time.

Alive AGAIN

The hospital emergency room was notified that a man had collapsed on the lawn outside his home. Neighbors had started CPR. The ambulance was needed.

The EMS system was mobilized, and the ambulance was on its way within minutes. Additionally, an EMT who lived nearby heard the call on his scanner and raced to the scene to lend assistance. When the ambulance arrived, the EMTs noted no pulses or breathing and started CPR. They then "packaged" the patient for transport.

The ambulance notified the hospital of their patient's status with CPR in progress. Their estimated arrival time was a few minutes.

Meanwhile, the ER nurse mobilized personnel to the hospital to assist with the resuscitation efforts. This team was in place when the ambulance arrived.

In resuscitation "event," different individuals do multiple tasks essentially simultaneously. The nurse anesthetist, who was Hank Brickle in this case, secured the patient's airway with an endotracheal tube and started to manually ventilate the patient. The EMTs and others continued cardiac compressions. The ER nurse inserted an intravenous catheter. The respiratory therapy aide applied a cardiac monitor. A lab technician was available to obtain blood and fluid samples. This time, I orchestrated this controlled pandemonium we medical people call a CODE.

The man's heart was noted to be in a ventricular fibrillation rhythm (V-FIB), which is not compatible with life. He promptly received electrical direct current (DC) countershocks at 300 joules three times in succession. No change!

He was then given epinephrine through his IV.

After 30 seconds of cardiac compressions, there was no change!

He was shocked three more times. He remained in V-fib.

An anti-arrhythmic drug was given intravenously. No change!

Three more shocks were given. No response!

About now, the ER nurse asked if I could talk to the family briefly. I asked Hank to take over for a few minutes while I met with the family to advise them that things were not looking too good. The family members were advised to "expect the worse," but we would give their dad our best effort.

Two more antiarrhythmic drugs were tried followed by three shocks after each medication to no avail.

As I was contemplating what to do next, the rhythm changed to a flat line.

The man was shocked again three times. No change!

Epinephrine was given again. No change!

With CPR continuing, the same sequence of medications and shocks was repeated. No change. The rhythm remained a flat line. No cardiac activity was discernable!

I looked at Hank for help making "the call." We had been here many times before. Hank verbalized his mental checklist: "Pupils are not reacting; no spontaneous respirations; flat line for about 10 minutes; no real response for 20 minutes." Hank said, "Doc, I think he's gone."

I looked at the clock to record the actual time resuscitation was discontinued. Then I said, "Let's call it."

I asked the others to clean up the patient while I went to speak with the family again. I then turned around to exit the ER trauma room.

I had taken only a few steps when I heard Hank say, "I'll be damned! Doc, come back." Hank said the man made a gasping effort when he pulled out the endotracheal tube.

I looked at the monitor. He had a rhythm.

Did he have a pulse?

I checked his groin for a femoral pulse. He had a pulse.

This guy was alive AGAIN!

Over the next few minutes this old fella put on quite a show for us. He started to breathe on his own. His blood pressure normalized. He started to move his legs. His eyes opened.

I had been a part of literally hundreds of resuscitations. Not once had I seen a patient return from the situation this man was in.

Hank confirmed he had never seen anything like this!

The team continued to watch this man with awe as he progressively, and rapidly, improved.

Once again I asked the team to clean him up to make him presentable to the family.

I then turned to exit the emergency room to give the family a whole new story, one I would not have believed if I had not witnessed it.

Hank and I chatted about this case for a long time. And I do mean a long time.

Our patient sustained a stroke and a heart attack, but I could not determine when.

He recovered, left the hospital, and lived for several more years.

The Stroke

One Saturday morning in late July, I was in the emergency room when an ambulance call came in that stated the EMTs were bringing in a man from a farm who appeared to have had a stroke. His vital signs were stable, but he was not coherent and one side of his body was limp.

A few minutes later the ambulance arrived with their patient. I expected to see an old man. To my surprise, the patient was a 24-year-old man who looked as strong as a horse.

The man's name was Ryan, and he was the son of one of the local farming families. Apparently, Ryan was out in the field swathing grain when a family member noticed that the swather stopped abruptly. Soon thereafter Ryan tried to climb off the machine, but he fell to the ground and failed to get up. That is when the ambulance was summoned.

My examination showed that Ryan was unable to communicate. His airway, breathing, and circulation were without problems. His vital signs were stable. His mental status was confused. Ryan would respond only to pain. The entire left side of Ryan's body was non-functional. His eye examination revealed what I perceived as papilladema, a swelling of the back of the eye caused by an increased intracranial pressure. (These findings suggested to me that something potentially very bad, like bleeding, was happening inside this young man's head.) However, with stable vital signs, I thought perhaps some neurological function could be restored if I acted quickly.

I called a referral neurologist in Billings and related my predicament. This was before the era of the computerized brain scans. Therefore, a more intensive evaluation required a transfer to Billings. The neurologist stated he would make all the arrangements for the transfer on his end at the hospital; he would send out the air transport team within a half hour; the flight team should arrive in about 90 minutes.

In the mean time, he asked me NOT to perform a spinal tap (sticking a needle into the spinal canal for fluid) because of the risk of brain herniation and death associated with the possibility of increased spinal fluid pressure. He also requested certain maneuvers to be done by our team before the transport, such as inserting an intravenous line, obtaining certain lab tests, and so on.

The air transport team arrived as scheduled. Ryan's condition had not changed. He remained stuporous with a non-functional left side. My patient was transferred into the ambulance and then into the airplane for his trip to Billings.

I assumed that it would be the better part of the day or more before I received any communication from Billings, so I planned to leave the hospital after I had completed some paperwork. As it turned out, more patients came into the emergency department afterward, and I did not have an opportunity to leave.

About three hours after Ryan left our hospital, the hospital operator paged me to receive a long distance call. On the telephone was the neurologist from Billings. After such a short period of time I expected the news was not good. My mind was racing with the fact that perhaps Ryan had died in flight.

The physician asked, "Hey, Jim, just what did you say was wrong with this kid?"

I was a bit bewildered, but I explained to him what I had observed in the emergency room. Ryan presented like he had experienced a stroke.

He replied, "What would you say if I told you he *walked off the airplane*?"

I responded with, "I wouldn't believe it."

The neurologist replied, as he was laughing, "Well, he sure did!" He went on to tell me that the transport team had observed the same findings that I had. Just as the airplane was about to land, Ryan awoke with a severe headache.

Again laughing, he said, "He had an atypical migraine! Is that a hoot?"

This physician said he had given Ryan some medication for pain, and he was "perfectly fine." "He was up walking in their emergency room just wondering what had happened to him."

The doctor said Ryan would be observed in the ER only until his family members arrived by car. Then he would instruct the family to have some supper and head back home. The neurologist gave Ryan some literature on migraines. For now, however, he would not start Ryan on any long term medication since this appeared to be his first "headache," even though he had no pain. Ryan would follow up with the neurologist in the near future during an outreach visit to our community.

This physician then retorted, "Isn't this fun? This was the best laugh I've had in a long time. The guy got better, and I didn't have to do a thing! That's my kind of medicine!"

Between patients in the emergency room, I went to the medical records director and asked her to obtain for me the most recent articles on atypical migraines. Then, once again, I hit the books in our medical library.

I saw Ryan, his new wife, and their children many times over the years. As far as I know, he never had another headache.

Barbie

The winter infection season had been busy. The hospital was full of children with croup (a viral disease that causes upper airway inflammation), influenza, and RSV (a viral infection that infects the lungs). Many of the hospital employees were sick as well. The nursing home was closed to all visitors because of the number of elderly patient deaths from influenza.

On a Saturday morning a mother brought in her 12 month old child to the emergency room explaining that her baby had been sick with a "cold" for several days. Her three older kids had been sick too. That morning her infant daughter developed a harsh cough, and it seemed to the mother that she could not catch her breath. Since her child had gotten worse and since the mother had heard about all the sick people in the hospital, she decided to bring the child to be evaluated.

In the emergency room, the child had a fever of 101 degrees. She had a congested nose and was drooling (which I attributed to her teething). The infant had a harsh cough and an inspiratory stridor like one would see with croup. Listening with my stethoscope, I determined that the lungs seemed free of significant funny noises. I was able to localize the noise to the front of the neck.

"Aha! Croup!" I thought.

To be safe, however, I had an x-ray taken of the child's neck to rule out epiglottitis, an infection of the piece of throat tissue that protects the airway. (On a lateral view x-ray, the epiglottis will appear to be a ball of tissue.) In the radiology department the child's respiratory distress increased. The x-ray revealed what appeared to me to be a swollen epiglottis.

"Darn, she had epiglottitis." I diagnosed to myself. I knew that epiglottitis *could* be a life threatening disease because the swollen tissue *could* plug up the trachea (the wind pipe) and produce respiratory compromise. With the child having worsening respiratory issues, I knew she had to be intubated soon!

I tried an intubation, but I was unable to see the airway structures. I asked our anesthetist to try. She too was not successful. She related that all she could see was red, bloody tissue in the throat. She recommended sending the child to a place with specialized pediatric care before it was too late.

Because of the urgency, I arranged for a local pilot to transport the baby, the mom, and a nurse to Billings, about an hour away by airplane. I then called the Billings hospital emergency room to alert them. The ER physician promised to have an ambulance waiting for them at the airport.

Several hours later I received a call from the pediatrician on duty in the Billings emergency room. He informed me that the baby had arrived in stable condition with some respiratory distress. He and an anesthesiologist had reviewed the x-rays and agreed with my diagnosis of epiglottitis. However, they had decided to start antibiotics and observe the child before they attempted an intubation. Soon thereafter, the child developed severe coughing and respiratory distress in the emergency room.

The pediatrician then said, "Just as I was about to try an intubatation, the little girl had a severe coughing fit, and out popped a *small plastic star*! It was the darndest thing! She started to breathe just fine after that." He then said, "We took another x-ray, and the "swollen epiglottis" had disappeared! Isn't that something?"

The mother told the doctors her older kids had been playing with Barbie dolls that morning. Apparently, the baby sister had swallowed a stray Barbie accessory from the floor.

The child was observed in the emergency room for a short time and did just fine. Everyone was able to fly back home with the hometown pilot.

The final diagnoses were: upper respiratory illness, teething, and aspiration of a Barbie doll star with respiratory distress and spontaneous resolution.

EMS:

THE FIRST LINE OF OFFENSE

"Never tell people how to do things.
Tell them what to do
and they will surprise you with their ingenuity."

General George S. Patton

"Its amazing what you can accomplish if you don't care who gets the credit."

Harry S. Truman

"If things go well there is enough credit to go around;
If things go poorly, there is more than enough
blame for everyone."

Earle Lock Neff

The Emergency Team

My family and I arrived in Sidney in April 1976. Soon after my arrival, I was asked by Earl Neff to assist in the training of EMTs (emergency medical technicians) for the local ambulance service. As part of the deal, I would serve *temporarily* as the medical advisor for the ambulance program.

I agreed.

Earl was a hydrology engineer at the local soil research center with a keen interest in emergency medical services (EMS). Later on, many knew him with affection as the "Father of EMS in eastern Montana" and "Mr. EMT." In 1979, through Earl's efforts, our hospital became equipped with the **first** ambulance in the State of Montana to meet federal guidelines. What a coup! (Eat your hearts out Billings, Missoula, and Great Falls.) Earl spread the EMS gospel everywhere he went. In eastern Montana he arranged EMS training from "Opheim (in the Northeast) to Ekalaka (in the Southeast)."

Earl's wife, Ruth, also was an EMT and became an integral part of the EMS team. She assumed the responsibilities for teaching BLS (basic life support) and CPR to hospital employees, teachers, civic groups, youth groups, and *doctors*. When Ruth went on a trauma run, she was known to have the fastest scissors in the west. She could get a trauma patient's clothes off in a heartbeat!

When Earl and I started this collaborative journey in 1976, the ambulance service consisted of three or four hearty souls, a big white ambulance (I called it "The Blunderbus"), and a strong desire to develop a quality first-response team for Richland County. Our second ambulance, by the way, was the local funeral home's backup hearse!

As time passed, we assisted in the training of several hundred dedicated people to serve as EMTs in our EMS program and in emergency programs throughout eastern Montana. Our program was one of the first to have a full team of EMT-Ds. (D signified special training in defibrillation.) Our EMT-Ds could interpret basic electrocardiograms better than many of the physicians on our medical staff! Learning defibrillation eventually became a standard part of EMT training nationwide.

When Earl retired after 20 years or so, others filled his position admirably. Through the years the names of our EMTs changed, but the faces were the same. People, young and not so young, with bright eyes, a desire to learn, and, more importantly, a desire to help their community joined this volunteer effort. At the turn of the new century, the program had about 40 EMTs, two state-of-the-art ambulances at the Sidney Health Center, and quick-response ambulance units in

Fairview, Savage, and Lambert, all small communities within 20 miles of Sidney.

There is a sign over the ambulance door in the emergency department that says, *"Through these doors walk the finest EMTs in Montana."* This was reaffirmed time and time again. Many folks are alive today because of the unselfish efforts of our EMS team. The ambulance program at the Sidney Health Center became the envy of many in Montana, even those in the bigger cities.

Our ambulance service was the only one awarded the Outstanding EMS Program in Montana on two occasions. This attested to the continued dedication, hard work, and community spirit of the many members of our EMS team.

On two occasions, actual accidents handled by our EMTs became scenarios of *"how to do things right"* in the Advanced Trauma Life Support Program (ATLS) presented by the Montana Chapter of the American College of Surgeons.

Those surgeons have a unique, but nice, way of saying "*Thanks*."

Because our EMTs became the de facto "medical experts" in their respective communities, I thought it was appropriate for them to have some experience with obstetrics. I was allowed by our hospital (after some politicking) to allow EMTs to assist with routine deliveries. Of course, I always got the approval of the parents-to-be. Sometimes, the EMT and the parents were friends. I was always concerned about husbands getting upset when the neighbor was looking at and possibly touching his wife's behind. *I actually dreamed of fights in the delivery room.* The problem never arose, however, thank goodness. I think these experiences helped solidify our community's good impression of, and faith in, our ambulance crew.

Ruth and Earl Neff took their turn at a delivery in the mid 1980s. The mom-to-be just happened to be their daughter. They watched and participated in the labor process. Ruth then got to deliver her own beautiful grandchild. What a marvelous experience that was for me. I believe Earl and Ruth treasured the experience too!

When I was teaching classes, I always wondered if what we were doing really made a difference. In retrospect, it was Earl and Ruth Neff and all the EMTs who made such a big difference not only with our patients and neighbors but also with me as a physician. I could never thank all the EMTs enough for giving me the opportunity to be a small part of such a noble and worthwhile endeavor. My experiences with the Richland EMS team will be treasured always. I am glad they allowed me to come along for the ride.

Did we make a difference? I guess the statewide EMS awards and the accolades from their peers throughout Montana speak for themselves.

I retired as "temporary" medical director after 25 years. I would later find out that I was the only physician in the history of Montana

Emergency Services to serve as an ambulance medical director for a *quarter century.*

The old adage that "*Time flies when you are having fun*" certainly applied.

Disconnect

Whenever Earl Neff forecasted a shortage of EMTs for the ambulance program, a new training course would be given. This usually occurred annually as people retired, moved away, or quit for whatever reason. In the early years of the Sidney EMS program, I taught most of the medical anatomy and physiology classes. Earl Neff taught the majority of the technical skills such as extrication, splinting, and operations of the vehicles. Experienced EMTs gave additional instruction to the trainees about procedures and protocols during actual ambulance runs.

Each new program enticed people from all walks of life. From homemakers to teachers, from retired professionals to mechanics, they all volunteered to be punished. (Or they were just plain goofy!) As a rule, the new students had been out of school for some time. Therefore, studying topics such as anatomy, cardiovascular physiology, trauma care, and physical examination was a daunting task indeed. Couple this with the fact that the course required about four months to complete and that the applicants had to pass a detailed exam at its completion to be certified displayed their fortitude and community spirit. After the applicants passed the certifying exam, they served as the "extra man" on a few ambulance runs before being upgraded to the regular rotation for the crews. At some point in time all the EMTs had to get their "feet wet" with their first real ambulance run. This was when the instructors could see how well they had prepared the rookie EMT.

One blustery winter day I was on call in the ER when a call came in from the sheriff's office about an MVA (motor vehicle accident) just south of the four corners junction five miles south of town. The hospital ambulance was dispatched with two new EMTs in command. The ambulance crew called the hospital ER nurse when they had reached the highway to report icy conditions and snow.

The next report was at the scene of the accident. There had been a single vehicle roll over with a single occupant in a small car. The driver had not used seat belts. They would report again when the victim was extricated from the car.

The next communication was, "We are coming in with ... Click." The radio signal was lost.

The nurse replied, "Ambulance One, can you tell us something about the victim? Over."

The ambulance comeback was, "Yes ... Click." The signal was lost again.

Since we wanted to get ready in the ER for a major trauma, if needed, the charge nurse responded, "Ambulance One, can you give us some vital signs for the patient? Over."

The EMTs responded, "Just a moment ... Click."

The team in the ER was beginning to get anxious. In medicine we are taught to fear the worst and plan for it. Since the EMTs were unable to respond appropriately, speculation arose that they were too busy to communicate. Therefore, we had better set up for something serious. With this impulse, the folks in the ER started to check equipment and expose materials and supplies that may be needed in a major trauma.

The nurse called again, "Ambulance One, can you relay the patient's vital signs? Over."

The ambulance acknowledged, "Yes ... Click."

The ER team was now perplexed. "What the heck is going on out there?" asked a curious nurse awaiting some action in the ER.

I asked the nurse to ask for their position. Maybe they needed some help.

She complied with, "Ambulance One, what is your location and your ETA? (Estimated time of arrival)"

The radio cracked, "We're here. Open the door."

I was anxious, miffed, and glad all at once. The crew came in with the male patient in great shape. He was "packaged" on the spine board in textbook fashion with his neck supported by an extrication collar. Oxygen was being administered by mask. A complete printout of the patient's vital signs was available for us to evaluate.

These people had done a fantastic job.

I wondered to myself, "But what about the communication problems? Was the radio faulty or what?"

It seemed that the rookie EMT in charge of relaying information had "missed" the short sessions on "*Using the radio in the ambulance*" and "*Communication with the hospital.*"

He did not know that the radio operator *had to keep the button depressed* on the hand receiver unit the entire time he was talking.

The ER nurse and I unveiled a potentially serious kink in our training program that would be corrected at the next general EMT meeting.

I gave both the EMTs a pat on the back for a job well done.

Crash in the Country

Springtime in eastern Montana is always an emotionally uplifting time of the year. The longer days and increasing temperatures provide escapes from the winter's long freeze. Community activity flourishes as the farmers prepare to plant corn, various grains, and sugar beets. The ranchers deliver newborns into their herds. The local businesses gear up to support the agricultural economy. School and family activities extended outdoors for the first time in months.

The new millennium spring of 2000 was exceptional. The winter had been mild and by late April the temperatures were in the 80s. I too was enjoying the nice weather with some QTT (quality tractor time) on my trusty John Deere 2510. There was always some piece of our 21 acres that was just begging to be cultivated or weeded.

I had just started with some garden tilling when the emergency room nurse called. Apparently, there had been an automobile wreck outside of Lambert, a small community about 20 miles away. Four victims had been identified, all teenagers. Their conditions were unknown. A major trauma alert had been called for all hospital employees.

By the time I arrived at the hospital trauma area, the place was nearly full of medical personnel with more on the way. Extra EMTs came in just in case to lend helping hands. Hank Brickle from anesthesia was making ready his equipment. Nurses were checking the supplies and the electronic units. Dr. Barrigan, the general surgeon, and I made decisions on the mode of triage of the victims and delineated two trauma teams. Radiology was placed on alert. Our team was as ready as we could be.

The first messages came from the quick response unit in Lambert. They were transporting the first two victims. Victim #1 was a teen female with stable vitals and complaining of head and chest pains.

Victim #2 was a teen male with head trauma. Vital signs were marginal. The other victims would require extrication from the vehicle and would be brought in by the Sidney ambulance as soon as possible. Transport time was estimated at 30 minutes.

One of the awaiting nurses was chosen as the trauma record keeper. Her job was to keep a current record of the information we received about the patients on our large trauma chalkboard (the "Big Board"). The radio operator was instructed to talk with the record keeper first. The initial data for the first two victims was then transcribed onto the Big Board.

The second ambulance called in to report that victim #3 had head, chest, and leg injuries. This teen male had been thrown out of the vehicle a considerable distance. He was awake, but confused. He was complaining of a lot of pain. His vitals were stable. The left thighbone was broken, but had been splinted in place.

Victim #4 was a teen male who was found under the car. The car had to be lifted up to remove him. He was not complaining. His vital signs were normal. He had no gross injuries.

This information was recorded onto the Big Board.

Ambulance #1 called in to say victim #2 had worsened. CPR was in progress. The ETA (Estimated time of arrival) was five minutes.

While we were waiting, I asked the group around me which patient they were *most concerned about.* One of the nurses chose the CPR patient because he was going to require the most immediate care. Another chose Victim #3 because of potential shock from blood loss from the fractures. A new EMT spoke up and said, "The fourth kid because he is not complaining. We don't know what's wrong with him. Dr. A., you always told us to watch out for the kids who are quiet because kids don't play by the rules."

"You're right!" I said. I then went on to explain that the trauma team was prepared for three of the victims by the histories received from the ambulances. We could not be lulled to sleep by a victim that "has no gross injuries and is not complaining." The boy should be complaining of *something* if he had been trapped under a car!

The first two patients arrived. Dr. Barrigan took the female victim with possible head and chest injuries.

My team took the young man undergoing CPR who had obvious severe head injuries. Having been in this scenario many times, it was obvious that the boy was near death upon arrival. However, part of my jobs was to help train my coworkers. Therefore, I had Hank Brickle intubate the young man and our team continued with the mechanics of resuscitation. I took over the chest compressions duty. When the monitor revealed ventricular fibrillation, I assigned one of the awaiting people to administer DC countershock three times, which she did with confidence and with the correct technique. Since the rhythm did not change, I had Larry, one of our brand new EMTs, continue with CPR on a real person for the first time. He did a great job! After the patient had been given some epinephrine intravenously for his rhythm without improvement, CPR was halted long enough for another EMT to administer countershocks again. The patient "flat lined," and, after a short discussion with Hank, we discontinued the resuscitation.

We moved the victim's into an empty room, covered him with a sheet, and closed the door. We had no time to waste because the second ambulance was about to unload its cargo of injured people.

My team then assumed control of victim #3 with the multiple injuries. The patient's airway, breathing, and circulation (ABC's) were intact. Neurologically, he was confused but responded to pain and verbal commands. The young man had a bruise on his forehead as if he had hit something with his face. Abrasions were noted on his chest, back, and shoulders apparently from being thrown about 70 feet out into a field. His left femur was fractured in the middle with his leg rotated 180 degrees so that his toes were touching his face! The circulation of his foot, however, was good. The young man's blood pressure started to drop along with a rise in his pulse during my evaluation. Consequently, two large bore intravenous catheters were inserted to administer large quantities of fluid to replace the blood volume that had been lost. A bladder catheter was inserted so we could monitor his urine output.

When I was assured that the boy was hemodynamically stable, I reduced his femur fracture with the assistance of the team members and applied a long leg traction splint. We then waited for more x-rays. His foot pulses remained good. A CT scan revealed an additional burst fracture of a lumbar vertebra and a pelvic fracture; injuries that I knew required surgical stabilization. Arrangements were started for an air transport to Billings.

Dr. Barrigan noted that the girl, victim #1, was fine except for a few bumps and bruises.

He noted, however, that victim #4, *the quiet one* who was trapped under the car, had major second and third degree burns on his leg from lying under the muffler of the car. Additionally, he had sustained a substantial brain injury with a large clot in the brain that was revealed by the CT scan. He too would need specialty care in Billings. Indeed, he was the one that I worried about the most.

The aftermath of the tragedy was predictable. The small community of Lambert, which graduates only six to eight students a year, was grief stricken and in shock. It would have to bury one of its children, but the town and its people would return to "normal" with a lot of time.

The girl would soon return to school, but not as the same person. The boy that died was her boyfriend. She had been the driver of the car.

Victim #3 would require surgery on his back and his leg. His convalescence would be long and would occupy his summer. But he returned school in the fall.

Victim #4 is the one I still think about. His brain injury was substantial. He remained in a coma for about two weeks. Upon awakening, his behavior and mental function had been altered noticeably. His long-term prognosis is unknown.

As for the entire trauma team members, many of whom were friends or neighbors of the victims, the hospital had a post event session to analyze what happened and to talk things out. At the session, I conveyed how proud I was of the performance of our EMT crews under such difficult emotional circumstances. They proved that they were indeed our first best line of offense. Without their prompt response, appropriate "packaging," and expeditious transport, two more victims may have died.

As for Larry, the rookie, I could have hugged him for his performance, but I didn't. I figured a "Well Done!" and a pat on the back was more appropriate.

Kitty's Kozy Kitchen

During the 1980's I was involved with a program called the Montana Family Practice Residency Satellite Program. Since Montana did not have a medical school or a post-graduate training program, it was hoped that we could recruit new physicians to Montana by providing a worthwhile training experience for family medicine residents in training elsewhere. During my participation in the program, I was fortunate to have residents from many locations and with diverse backgrounds.

Since I was involved with the training of EMTs in our area, I attempted to have the resident physicians participate as much as possible in our training sessions. These efforts usually proved to be educational endeavors for all involved.

One of my residents named James came to Sidney from a training program in Philadelphia. To him a "small" hospital had *only* 300 beds. Our hospital had 50 beds. This young man had never been out of the big city except to go to a bigger city, like New York. Obviously, coming to rural eastern Montana was a medical, environmental, and cultural shock. He couldn't sleep for several days after arriving because there was NO NOISE! He couldn't believe the smell of the air or how far one could see.

Ah, Montana, the Big Sky Country!

I had arranged to provide a training session for the ambulance personnel in Richey, Montana, a small community of several hundred folks about 50 miles west of Sidney. The session was scheduled to last about five hours starting at 1 p.m. on a Saturday. This way I had plenty of time to get my work done at the hospital before the drive to Richey. Additionally, the EMT students had plenty of time to get their farm chores and other work completed.

James and I left Sidney about 11 a.m. so we could have lunch in Richey prior to the session. I always tried to support the local businesses since they were good at supporting our medical community in Sidney. We took our time on the Montana highway 200 so James could see the countryside, the vast farms, and the BIG John Deere and International tractors with 8 and 12 tires.

When we arrived in Richey about noon, I took James to "the" cafe in town, Kitty's Kozy Kitchen. Kitty's had the feel of a 1950's diner with a seating capacity of about thirty. The entire business was wide open except for a counter separating the customers from the kitchen and the cashier, who was also the waitress, the dishwasher, and the cook. We were the only customers when we arrived.

As we reviewed the menu, James asked what was good.

I told him that he couldn't go wrong with a hamburger in Montana.

When we were asked for our orders, James ordered a hamburger deluxe, fries, and a chocolate milk shake. I was content with a hamburger and a glass of milk. After ordering, I started to talk about the upcoming EMT program, what my new student was expecting from his Montana experience, etc. However, I could see that I had lost his attention. He was watching the cook.

He asked, "What is she doing?"

I replied, "Making your fries."

He said, "No way! I don't think so. I used to work in McDonalds, and I've cooked a lot of fries, but never like that." By now he was at the counter watching the cook do her thing.

The cook was just peeling a large potato by hand. This young doctor from the East had never seen a real potato! He only knew of ones that came frozen in a bag.

I asked, "Why don't you ask if you may watch?"

James did ask and before I knew it he was in the kitchen peeling his own potato. The lady then pulled out a french fry making tool, showed James how to insert the potato, and instructed him to push down on the handle. Amazing, he had just cut his own french fries. He had a smile from ear to ear. The cook then had James place the potato strips into the deep fat fryer and set the cooking timer.

She pulled out a plastic container from the refrigerator, took an ice cream scoop full of ground meat, and taught him about a hamburger press.

Our young doctor queried, "Where did you get this?" meaning the hamburger.

His new mentor politely pointed out the window toward a cow in the pasture.

James had seen hamburger only in pre-made frozen form, and now he had made his own burger from a real cow! He was having a ball.

The chef put the meat patty onto the grill to cook and gave James instructions on how to cook the burger just right. I could see that my young doctor was having quite a learning experience.

Finally, she asked James to pour a metal container half-full of milk, which he did. He then put four scoops of chocolate ice cream into the milk and was shown how to use a milk shake blender. He thought milk shakes just came from paper cartons.

Somewhat in jest, the chef pointed once again to the cow and said, "That's where the milk comes from."

About the time the shake was done, the timer went off for the fries. James removed the fryer basket and drained the oil. Our meat patties were well done by now, so the "deluxe" needed to be added. James made his choices with his head in the refrigerator.

By now, the cook and I were both laughing. What a sight!

When it was time to leave, James left a $10 tip for the $5 meal!

James had to tell all the EMTs at the conference breaks about how he had cooked his lunch at Kitty's Kozy Kitchen.

Incidentally, the EMT class was a successful adventure too.

A Broken Heart

Sugar beet farming and processing remain an important economic engine for our community. The sugar beet harvest in the fall is a busy and hazardous time of the year. Huge trucks laden with beets are everywhere. Massive pieces of harvesting equipment and tractors are moving in all directions. The highways, roads, and fields of our valley become treacherous byways for the unaware.

One day in the fall of 1995 I was at home when I received a telephone call from Dr. Patrick Barrigan, our local general surgeon. He stated abruptly, "I need you right now! Come straight to surgery."

Having worked with Dr. Barrigan for 15 years and having been in many "tight spots" with him, I knew my services were needed NOW! I told Kay that, "Dr. Barrigan called, and I gotta go." Lord knows how many times she had heard those words. I would let her know what was up when I had time at the hospital.

Upon arriving at the hospital, I went directly to the doctor's lounge where I met Dr. Barrigan. He told me that a lady from Williston, North Dakota was on her way home when she ran her car into the back of a loaded beet truck about 20 miles south of Sidney. The Savage ambulance crew had brought her in. She was in shock with blood in her abdomen, and the surgical crew was transporting the patient to the operating room as we spoke. I changed into surgical scrubs ASAP.

When I walked into the surgical area, controlled pandemonium was the rule. Each person was doing his or her job. Hank Brickle, the nurse anesthetist, was stabilizing the lady for anesthesia. The scrub nurse was arranging the instruments. The ER nurse was inserting a bladder catheter. The charge nurse was scrubbing the entire front of the patient with iodine solution. Many others were waiting around to lend a helping hand.

I washed my hands quickly.

After we arrived in the operating room, Dr. Barrigan and I covered the patient with sterile sheets. We were ready to go once again. (At times like this medicine gave me quite a rush!)

Dr. Barrigan made a midline incision in the abdomen to seek out the source of the bleeding that he had discovered in the emergency room. We found hardly any blood, at least, not nearly enough to make the lady go into shock. Where was the problem?

About now, Hank informed us that he could barely get a blood pressure. The pulse was over 160. He was going to administer some ephedrine to see if he could boost the pressure a bit.

Dr. Barrigan palpated the aorta. It was full, not flat! This lady had plenty of vascular volume. What the heck? "Remember physiology," Pat and I must have thought simultaneously.

Thinking out loud, as we often did, we went through a checklist: "Chest and abdomen trauma, BP down, pulse up, plenty of volume, no source of belly bleeding, maybe in the chest, maybe cardiac tamponade." (A condition where the sac around the heart fills with fluid and does not allow the heart to pump properly.)"

At this point, Dr. Barrigan asked for a long needle connected to a syringe. He placed the needle inside the abdominal wound that he had been made and pushed the needle through the diaphragm into the pericardium (the sac around the heart). Pulling back on the syringe plunger produced bright red blood – lots of blood!

He then withdrew a large volume of blood from the pericardium and asked Hank how things looked on his end of the table.

Hank replied, "BP is 100, pulse is coming down, looks like you found the ticket!"

Dr. Barrigan then commented, "Not yet!" After a short pause to think, he asked, "Does anyone remember that sternal saw that I had the hospital get when I came to town? We could use it right now."

A short discussion ensued among the surgical crewmembers. Jannette, our surgical assistant with years of experience, knew exactly where it had been stored. Jannette always knew where things were stored.

Within moments a helper was unwrapping the previously unused saw. The saw was handed to Dr. Barrigan who placed the hook of the saw at the top of the sternum and said, "Well, here we go kids. Let's see what we can find." He then started the saw, which zipped through the breastbone like a Skil saw through butter.

Directly in front of us was the pericardial sac bulging with blood. We knew the blood had to be coming from a hole in the heart, a damaged vessel on the surface of the heart, or a hole in one of the major vessels entering the heart.

Our search began for the injury began. Dr. Barrigan canvassed the heart entire area for injuries. The right atrium had been perforated. The superior vena cava, the large vein draining into the heart, had a hole in it where it entered the heart at the right atrium. The right atrium had a second hole in it.

I thought to myself, "We were in deep doodoo!"

Dr. Barrigan called out, "Get me a heart surgeon at the Billings Clinic on the phone, NOW!"

Someone asked, "What's the number?"

I called out the number I knew by memory. I had used this number many times over the years.

While the call was being made, Dr. Barrigan and I prepared to close the holes. However, since we had released the restraints of the pericardium, the blood was streaming out of the holes so fast that exposure was impossible to obtain. I could see nothing but blood in our surgical area.

Dr. Barrigan said something like, "I need some plugs."

He then grabbed my left hand and placed three of my fingers directly over the holes like the little Dutch boy shoring up the levy. The bleeding slowed to a trickle.

I thought to myself, "Great! Now what do I do?"

About now, the nurse interrupted and said, "Dr. Mulvaney is on the phone." Dr. Samuel Mulvaney was a cardio-thoracic surgeon at the Billings Clinic, and a heck of a nice guy.

Dr. Barrigan tells me, "Stay just as you are. I'll be right back." (Like I was going home and miss all the fun! Besides my left hand was keeping this lady from bleeding to death!)

The nurse put the phone near Dr. Barrigan's ear. He shouted out, "Hey Sam, I am up to my ass in alligators! I've got this lady with three holes in her heart. My sphincters are getting pretty tight!"

I could hear Dr. Mulvaney say laughingly, "Hey Pat, I hear you. I've been there!"

The two surgeons briefly discussed options, closure, sutures, etc. I still had my fingers in the holes, and finger spasms were starting to set in.

Carefully and meticulously Dr. Barrigan used double layers of suture to close each of the holes in the heart while being careful NOT to sew my glove into the wounds.

There was no bleeding. The patient stabilized.

Hank said, "Looking good my way guys and gals!"

About now, someone reported that the air transport from Billings was at the airport. Dr. Barrigan had someone in the operating room notify them of our situation and that the patient would be ready for transport in about an hour.

While Dr. Barrigan closed the pericardium, inserted chest tubes, and sutured the chest wound; I closed the abdominal wound. Dr. Barrigan said somewhat triumphantly in closing, "By God, we just performed open heart surgery in Sidney, Montana! Today, I think we have a save!"

Hank, who once was a member of an open heart team, chimed in, "Hellava job TEAM!"

The patient got off to Billings without incident.

Pat and I gave a sigh of relief. There were plenty of smiles in our hospital this day and for several more. The team and the system that we had worked on for so long showed that it worked well. From the Savage EMTs quick response unit to the ER trauma team and process to the surgical crew, there was plenty of praise to go around for everyone.

The folks in Billings watched our lady for three days and did nothing more to her before sending her home. Dr. Mulvaney told me his team in Billings could not have done a better job. I expressed my thanks to him for such a nice compliment to Dr. Barrigan and our team.

Our EMTs' performance during this episode helped them to receive their second "Ambulance of the Year" award in the State of Montana.

A short time later I was asked by the OR supervisor to come quickly to the OR. They had something special to show me right now.

I walked over from my office to see the surprise. Waiting in the operating room lounge were Dr. Barrigan and the OR crew surrounding our cardiac surgery lady who was smiling and seemed fit as a fiddle. What a treat!

She had come by to personally express her thanks to all of us. She related the praise from the Billings doctors for our good work. We all received a big hug, and, of course, a photo to immortalize the occasion.

Her visit made this a very good day!

The Fall

The ambulance was called to the local sugar refinery to assist a worker who had fallen off a catwalk. The EMS squad mobilized and was at the factory within minutes since it was only a mile or so from the hospital. The EMTs radioed in their status when they arrived. We understood that they were going up into one of the towers and would be calling back when they had reached the victim.

About 10 minutes later, the emergency room received a transmission stating the victim was a middle-aged male who had fallen approximately 30 feet down a shaft. The man was awake. His vital signs were stable. He had no respiratory difficulties. No obvious injuries were appreciated except for various abrasions. The man did complain of pain in his back, legs, and head. They would call again once the man was "packaged" for transport. (This meant that the victim would be secured onto a spine board, the head would be immobilized, and any obvious bleeding would be contained.)

Another 20 minutes or more went by before the next report. The EMTs reported a most difficult time negotiating the small area inside the shaft. Getting the patient packaged was difficult; however, they managed to get it accomplished. The EMTs reported stable vital signs. They would call us when they were outside the building and ready to come to the hospital.

It seemed like an eternity before the hospital received another transmission. The EMTs now reported that the patient was shocky. CPR had been started. They were in route. The estimated time of arrival was two minutes.

The ER team was ready for the patient. We mobilized quickly in the major trauma room.

The ambulance arrived with the EMTs performing CPR.

In the trauma room, an initial EKG tracing showed coarse ventricular fibrillation. Per ACLS (Advanced Cardiac Life Support) protocol, the man received three successive countershocks with 300 joules of electricity. No response. Resuscitation efforts were continued.

The man was intubated promptly by the awaiting anesthetist and given epinephrine through the endotracheal tube. No response.

He received three more shocks with maximum current. No response.

CPR was continued. He received more epinephrine. No response.

CPR was continued.

The team tried to revive this man for a while longer until his rhythm became a "flat line." The anesthetist stated his pupils "were fixed and not reactive." Our resuscitation efforts were discontinued.

We all wondered, "What happened? He was fine at the top of the shaft. He needed CPR at the bottom."

The EMTs and I discussed the extrication procedure from the tower. The man was lowered with some difficulty feet first because of (1) the EMTs concern for head trauma and (2) it was the only way they could get him down the shaft.

Post mortem x-rays revealed a spinal fracture (with a probable spinal cord trauma).

We surmised that the man had spinal cord shock with a profound loss of blood pressure as his blood pooled in his downward positioned legs. This produced an acute global stroke.

This diagnosis was confirmed by an autopsy.

Earl Neff, our EMT director, would often say, "If things go well there is enough credit to go around; if things go poorly, there is more than enough blame for everyone."

My question to the EMTs was, "What do you do when guidelines are followed, you do your best, and the patient dies?"

I told them, "I get a knot in my stomach!"

A Hunting Mishap

I received a call at home one weekend day during the fall. The nurse reported that there had been a "hunting mishap" in the far northwest area of the county. An ambulance was bringing in an injured hunter. The ambulance crew requested a physician in the emergency room when they arrived.

I asked if there was a report of the victim's injuries.

The nurse replied, "They just said a man was hurt, and they were coming in as fast as they could."

I asked if the ambulance relayed any vital signs.

The nurse replied, "No!"

I thought this was an unusual protocol breech unless the ambulance crew was performing resuscitation and did not have time to call us. I gathered up my black bag and headed to the hospital.

The emergency room was empty when I arrived. I asked the nurse if she had heard anything more from the ambulance crew.

She had not.

I asked about the origin of the ambulance.

The nurse told me the ambulance had not identified itself. She and I decided we would just have to wait and see what came in.

We waited ... and waited ... and waited. An hour passed. We called the law enforcement center to see if they had any information about a hunting accident.

The response was "negative."

Two hours passed and still no ambulance. The nurse had been using a universal hailing frequency on the radio without any replies. We were befuddled.

We worried about the worst because that's what medical people do best.

Before three hours of waiting had elapsed, an ambulance from Poplar pulled up to the entry door of our emergency room. Out stepped two Indian men who obviously had been drinking. One of them said with a slurred voice, "Do ya want to see what we got?"

"Duh!" I thought to myself.

The men pulled out the gurney from the ambulance with its passenger. The male victim was obviously dead. I could tell he had been dead for some time because he was cold and stiff. My examination revealed a hole in the center of the man's chest the size of my thumb between the flaps of his hunting vest. The exit wound from the bullet was in the center of his back and was large enough to fit my fist. The bullet had obviously exploded this man's heart and killed him instantly.

I asked the ambulance drivers if they knew their patient was dead.

One of them said, "Yep."

I then asked them why they drove this man all the way to our town if they knew he was already dead. What did they expect me to do?

A crewmember pointed at me and said with a slurred voice, "So *YOU* could pronounce him dead. Only doctors can do that, you know. Our doctor was out of town, so you were the next one down the road."

I pronounced the man dead on arrival from an apparent gunshot wound and called the county coroner. I then called the sheriff to inform him of the death under "interesting" circumstances.

The man's body was taken to the local funeral home.

The drivers were taken to jail and charged with drunk driving.

I went home for supper.

Breaking the Rules

In the early days of emergency care, hospitals had ambulances that were operated by people with minimal, if any, medical training. The sole purpose of the ambulance driver was to get a patient to the hospital as quickly as possible for evaluation and care. Many, perhaps most, ambulance drivers during this time felt their "medical position" gave them the right to drive as fast as possible with "the pedal to the metal" no matter the condition of their patient, the road conditions, or the weather. Every year multiple ambulance accidents occurred which resulted in the deaths of patients, ambulance drivers, and innocent bystanders.

Early in the development of EMTs (emergency medical technicians) for the emergency medical services (EMS) system in our community I tried to impress upon our volunteers that their most important ambulance call would be their NEXT ONE! EMT safety was my number one priority. Therefore, dangerous situations at an emergency site should be approached with caution, and highway speed limits should be obeyed. My speech was repeated enough times over the years that when I asked the EMTs at the conclusion of a meeting, "What is your most important ambulance call?" In unison, the reply would be, "The NEXT ONE!"

On a fall day I was asked by the emergency room nurse to "hang around" the hospital until the Richey ambulance arrived. (Richey was a rural community about 50 miles to the west that housed a quick response EMS ambulance and crew that was trained at our facility.) The nurse related to me that the ambulance was transporting a woman who had given birth in our hospital about 10 weeks before and was now bleeding. The patient had been unable to contact her physician. Our local obstetrician was out hunting. I was the only one left to see her.

Enroute, the EMTs reported that the woman was bleeding "significantly"; her pulse was weak and 140 beats per minute. Her blood pressure was 80 and barely palpable. The team had applied the MAST suit (Medical Anti Shock Trousers), but had not yet inflated it. They relayed the lady's name so her medical records could be available in the emergency room.

I suspected a piece of retained placenta (afterbirth) as the culprit for the bleeding. This condition often produces, usually, a self-limited episode of uterine bleeding; but it can also cause fatal hemorrhaging. After I reviewed the medical records, I had the lab set aside some units of blood that matched the woman's recorded blood type. I also alerted the surgical team.

When the woman reached the emergency room, she was indeed in dire straits. She was barely responsive. She was in shock with a barely audible blood pressure using an electronic stethoscope. I felt the woman's femoral artery in the groin and could barely feel a pulse. I observed blood literally shooting out her vagina. She was covered with blood, and so were the EMTs.

While nurses inserted two intravenous catheters and the lab tech obtained some blood for evaluation, I extracted a clot from the woman that I estimated to be 500 milliliters (about a pint) and sent it to the pathologist for evaluation. I could feel the uterine cervix was wide open when it should have been closed. I knew we had to act quickly to save this lady's life.

One nurse started squeezing the IV bags to administer fluids as fast as she could. Another nurse obtained some type specific blood from the lab and started to push it in as well. The pharmacist obtained some oxytocin, a medication to make the uterus contract, and pushed it into the intravenous line. I notified the surgical team that an emergency uterine curettage was needed.

About this time, the lab tech informed us that the lady's hematocrit was 21 percent. The medical records revealed that her hematocrit after giving birth 10 weeks before was 42 percent. This woman had lost at least one-half of her blood volume. No wonder she was in trouble!

Thankfully, after a short time, which seemed like forever to me, the woman's vaginal bleeding slowed substantially. When her vital signs had improved somewhat and the anesthetist said she was O.K. for surgery, our patient was taken to the operating room where I performed a uterine curettage. (A procedure that scrapes the lining of the uterus with a sharp oval instrument about the size of a teaspoon.)

A piece of gray "stuff" came out with the scrapings along with clots and some normal looking tissue. The bleeding stopped, apparently as quickly as it had started. Afterward, the anesthetist reported the patient was doing fine, and her vital signs had stabilized.

I thought to myself, *"Only after she received 5 units of blood and 3000 milliliters of fluid!"*

The next morning my patient was alert and doing just fine. She had no bleeding. She only vaguely recalled the events of the previous day after the ambulance had arrived at her home.

I thought that was a good thing.

The pathologist reported that the large blood clot and the uterine samples had large pieces of retained placenta.

The lab reported that the hematocrit after the transfusions was 30 percent. If each unit of blood is good for about three hematocrit points, then my patient received 15 points from her transfusions. Therefore, I figured my patient had actually hemorrhaged down to a hematocrit of about *15 percent.* She had lost about 65 percent of her blood volume!

This woman left the hospital the next day doing well, and she continued to do well.

DOCTOR, WE NEED YOU NOW

"He who knows best knows how little he knows."

Thomas Jefferson

"Make a habit of two things: to help;
or at least to do no harm."

Hippocrates

False Alarm

One evening during the winter of 1978, I had left the hospital about 8 p.m. after seeing a patient in the emergency room. The weather had been intermittently blustery all day. By the time I was headed home a full-fledged blizzard was in progress. We lived approximately five miles from the hospital. The visibility going down the highway toward my home was nonexistent.

When I was about halfway home, I received a call on my beeper that said, "Come to obstetrics STAT!"

In the blinding blizzard, I made a prompt U-turn on the highway. I put my vehicle into four-wheel drive, turned on my flashing lights, and sped to the hospital. I parked my vehicle in front of the emergency room door and ran inside. I ran to the obstetrical floor to assist in the emergency.

When I arrived, the lights were out and not a soul was present. I thought to myself, "Where is everybody? Where is the emergency?"

I walked briskly to the area of the operating rooms thinking that an emergency surgery might be taking place. The surgical suites were dark and still.

I was indeed perplexed. I thought to myself, "What the heck is going on?"

Eventually, I made my way to the medical floor to see if there was any activity. Again, this part of the hospital was extremely quiet too. I met one of the nurses and asked where the emergency was. She looked puzzled and said she knew of no emergency in the hospital that evening. I then told her that I had just been beeped and advised to come to obstetrics STAT *through a blizzard*!

Sitting at the reception desk was a young lady who spoke up. She was the new ward clerk and looked scared to death. She confessed that she had paged me. She related that she had been instructed by another physician to let me know *right away* that I was to be available for a C-section in the morning. She was taught that STAT meant *right away*. Therefore, she called me STAT for obstetrics.

By now I was sweating. I know my heart was pounding in anticipation of an emergency, and because I had to speed through a blizzard for no good reason! What I really wanted to do was to strangle this young lady.

Amazingly, my good sense prevailed. I told the young lady that we needed to have a chat.

I took the young lady aside to a quiet area behind the reception desk. The charge nurse joined us as we discussed what STAT meant in terms of the urgency of medical care being needed.

Afterward, I drove home through the worsening blizzard. I tried to sleep but couldn't. My body was pooped, but my mind was racing.

The following morning I had a discussion with the director of nurses regarding this incident. A protocol for beeper communications was developed over the ensuing weeks. My hope was that no one would ever receive another STAT call without a good reason.

Unfortunately (and fortunately, I guess), human beings are fallible. It seemed to me that each new rookie ward clerk had to test some doctor in some manner at least once. Over the years, my colleagues and I were STAT tested many more times.

That's just how it is.

Gunshot

I was finishing my office dictation late one afternoon in 1980 when my telephone rang. The emergency room nurse was on the phone and notified me there had been a shooting downtown. The ambulance was bringing in a female patient with injuries. They were 30 seconds out. She said, "Come NOW!"

I arrived in the ER at the same time as the ambulance. The EMTs were bringing in a female patient on a stretcher who was barely conscious. The entourage included three EMTs, two people from law enforcement, lab techs, several nurses, friends, neighbors, and God knows who else. There was barely room to move around in our small ER trauma room with all those people in there.

"GIVE US SOME ROOM!" I thought to myself.

I always taught the EMTs, "ABCs first." "ABCs first."

As I examined this woman, I thought to myself: "A -airway: The patient's airway is patent. That's good, B -breathing: The patient's breathing is labored, and she is sweaty. I do not hear any breath sounds on the left side of the chest. With supplemental oxygen her blood oxygen saturation is 98 percent. Excellent, for now, C -circulation: The patient's pulse is rapid and weak. The blood pressure is only 80-90 by palpation (feeling the pulse)."

There was so much noise in the room I could barely think, much less use my stethoscope. I yelled out loud, "Quiet please!" (It has always impressed me that most people in emergency situations seem to think everyone else becomes instantly deaf. Therefore, they talk louder and louder. Since everyone wants to be heard over the pandemonium, the combined voices can become deafening.

"The ABC's are good for now. I will check them again in a few moments," I muttered to myself out loud. "Now, let's look for the injury."

The head and neck revealed no obvious injury.

As I opened the woman's blouse, I could see the likely culprit for her problems. Through the central part of the bra was a hole through which I could easily pass my thumb! The bra had gunpowder marks on it. Under the bra was another hole just under the ribs and in the midline. Again, the hole was as big as my thumb! I shouted out, "What did this?"

One of the police officers replied, "A 357 Magnum, Sir."

I thought to myself, "This lady is in DEEP trouble."

A cursory exam of the front of the now disrobed lady revealed no more obvious injuries. However, as I rolled the patient on her side I saw a gaping hole in her left back. Holy Cow!

I knew this lady needed a trauma surgeon, NOW!

At the time our community had two general surgeons. Our "seasoned" surgeon was about 55 years old. He really did not like uncontrolled surgical situations. I remembered the last time I had called him for a trauma; he wouldn't come and told me to ship the patient out. Dr. Patrick Barrigan was new in town direct from New York City via the Mayo Clinic. My choice was clear. I told the nurse, "Call Dr. Barrigan. Tell him we have a gunshot wound to the abdomen and chest, and we need him NOW!"

It seemed like Dr. Barrigan must have been waiting by his phone because he was at my side in the trauma room in no time. We both started to work to get the patient ready for surgery.

Several large bore intravenous lines were placed. Blood was obtained for a type and cross match, blood counts, coagulation studies, chemistries, and anything else we may need or want later on. A chest tube was inserted into the left chest because of the collapsed lung caused by the bullet. A chest x-ray followed this to ensure the lung had re-inflated. A bladder catheter was inserted. The entire front of the patient was splashed with Betadine solution to kill germs. (Lord knows we didn't want any contamination. We already had pieces of this lady's bra *in her chest cavity*!)

Meredith Townsend, the nurse anesthetist, was ready for us. Jannette Jefferson, the surgical assistant, got the instruments ready to go in the operating room. The surgery team and the operating room were waiting for us. We had the patient as prepared for surgery as she was going to be under the circumstances. Dr. Barrigan said to me something like, "Are you ready for this?"

I had no idea, but I replied, "Let's go!"

The operation began about 6 p.m. When he was assured the patient was adequately stabilized with the anesthesia, Dr. Barrigan made a large midline incision in the abdomen. Blood was everywhere! To me, pieces of the internal organs seemed to be everywhere as well.

I kept saying to myself, "Remember the three Rules of Surgery:

(1) hemostasis (control bleeding)

(2) traction and counter-traction (for maximum exposure)

(3) Put things back together like you took them apart" (hopefully!).

Dr. Barrigan and I communicated as we began working away, "Let's stop the bleeding. Where do we start? The spleen was shattered. The left side of the liver had exploded. The stomach was perforated. We identified a hole in the diaphragm with powder burns around it. Through the diaphragm we are able to visualize the pericardium (the sac around the heart) with a hole in it. It too had powder burns!"

The bleeding slowed with the removal of the spleen fragments and the tying off of the large arteries and veins providing its blood supply.

The liver was oozing severely from its multiple wounds. *The liver does not like to be injured!* It likes to be sutured even less. Dr. Barrigan said, "Suturing liver; its like sewing flatus to moonbeams!" After a brief discussion of our options, a decision was made to remove about half of the liver. Dr. Barrigan quipped, "Heck, this is Medical Center stuff. Just like back at the home of the Mayo brothers in Rochester!" He was having a good time. So was I!

Using mostly heat cautery to control bleeding, Dr. Barrigan undertook the tedious task of amputating part of the liver. This took literally hours. Fortunately, with this part of the job completed, the bleeding was essentially stopped.

Meticulously, Dr. Barrigan sought out and repaired or removed all the damaged tissues in the abdomen that we could find.

Because the bullet had penetrated the chest cavity, the chest cavity had to be investigated. The left side of the chest was opened through another external incision. The heart muscle appeared unharmed. The pericardium was injured, but would survive. A second chest tube was inserted in the left side of the chest. Holes in the lung were repaired.

When I looked up at the clock again, it was about 5 a.m. We had been operating for about 11 hours straight. We still had to close all the holes that we, and the bullet, had made.

I looked at Dr. Barrigan about the time we started to close the abdominal wound. His eyelids were sagging. So were mine. I said something like, "We have been at this all night. We don't have enough energy to do the rest of this together. How about if I close the skin, and you sit down to do the dictation and write orders?"

Dr. Barrigan thought this was a good idea.

As I was suturing the wound, I could not help but reflect upon what I had just been an active participant. Dr. Barrigan was a skilled and talented surgeon indeed. As good as my training had been, I had not seen anything quite like this. The surgical skills required for this degree of trauma and surgical exposure was far beyond my skills.

Over the few years I had been in practice, I had witnessed many physicians come and go in our community. Dr. Barrigan was a young, handsome bachelor who could practice medicine anywhere he wanted. I sure hoped he would stay around awhile in our little town.

We were cleaning up in the operating room just as the day shift was coming to work. We had been up all night.

It was now time for me to shower, prepare for the new day, and make morning rounds.

The law enforcement folks informed us that this lady's truck was locked from the inside, and the gun could not have just "gone off" as she claimed. The gun had a rusty trigger that required a police officer to use two hands to make it discharge. The force of the 357 magnum bullet was sufficient to go through the patient, the truck seat, the back of the pickup cab, the front of the pickup box, and finally become impaled into the tailgate. To them, it certainly looked like a suicide attempt.

Our patient gradually recovered from her "accident" and the surgery. Upon leaving the hospital she complained bitterly about a *sore toe*, **which** she insisted we had caused.

Foot Loose

It was a gorgeous warm sunny Thursday in the mid 1980s. I routinely took Thursdays out of the office to finish paperwork at the hospital. By 10 a.m. my hospital work was completed, and I was anticipating a fine day outdoors. I had called my wife earlier to plan a picnic lunch in the park.

I had walked through the first of the double doors at the hospital entrance when I heard a female voice call out from behind me, "Dr. Ashcraft, We need you NOW in the ER!"

I was miffed! I replied, "This is Thursday. I am not on call."

By now the nurse had caught up with me, grabbed my arm, and stated with authority something like, "Somebody needs you right now!" She then pulled me briskly down the hallway toward the emergency room.

I noticed that one area of the ER had quite a commotion. There was a female's voice screaming and crying. I could hear various nurses giving urgent orders for intravenous lines and fluids, blood type and cross match, CBC, and oxygen.

I questioned the nurse, "What is going on?"

She replied, "This lady just showed up! You'll see; she needs your help."

I made my way into the middle of the mass of humanity surrounding a bed. A scared, naked, pregnant girl was on the bed. I could see blood flowing down her legs. The hospital anesthetist was at the patient's side trying to start an intravenous line. The respiratory therapist was applying an oxygen mask and arranging resuscitation equipment. A nurse was shaving the woman's abdomen. Another nurse was getting ready to insert a bladder catheter.

When I got to the end of the bed I saw a tiny leg hanging out between the girl's legs. Someone called out, " The fetal heart rate is about 80 to 90."

I knew this lady needed a C-section now!

I had recently been to an insurance seminar and heard a discussion about taking the appropriate amount of time to obtain "informed consent." I thought, "What kind of adequate informed consent can you get with this kind of predicament?

The legal answer was "none!"

All I could do was lean over to the young woman and make sure I had her attention. Quickly I told her my name, that we were going take care of her, and not to be afraid. (Like I wasn't? I then left to get ready for surgery.

By the time I got into the operating room, about two minutes later, the surgery crew had the woman ready to go.

While the surgical assistant draped the abdomen, I quickly washed my hands with iodine solution (about 10 seconds). When we were all in position, I nodded to the anesthetist. She anesthetized the woman quickly.

Jannette, the surgical assistant, and I delivered a healthy female child through the abdomen about 45 seconds later.

We both took a big deep breath when the baby cried. I thought I was going to cry! My heart was beating so fast and hard I could hear it in my ears. I wondered what would have happened if the nurse had not been so assertive as I was leaving the hospital.

The remainder of the surgery was uneventful. The new mother and her baby left the operating room and the recovery room in fine shape.

Afterward, I felt compelled to apologize to the nurse for being such a poop. I congratulated her and the rest of the team for a job well done. This was one of those times when we, the team, really did make a difference.

I called Kay at home to tell her there had been a *little delay* at the hospital, but the picnic was still on. I would be home soon.

Just The Flu

This year's January and February brought to Sidney a prolonged influenza epidemic. Our nursing home population was devastated with about 20 percent of the clients dying because of the virus and its associated complications. The majority of the hospital employees were ill, but still trying to work. The medical staff was doing its best to keep all but the very worst patients out of the hospital in an attempt to curtail the spread of the malady. Consequently, I was making many home visits daily to see the elderly and children. The local stores were making a mint selling Thera-Flu, Gatorade, and Nyquil. The pharmacies could barely keep up with the demand for cough suppressants and pain remedies.

I was on my way out of the hospital about noon on February 24th when I was called to the ER STAT! The emergency room nurse and some assistants were bringing a young heavy-set female through the doors while performing CPR. The husband said his wife, Valerie, had been ill for several days with the "flu." When she couldn't stop coughing, he brought her up to the hospital. As he was helping her out of the car, Valerie collapsed and had a seizure in the hospital parking lot.

At the time, the hospital parking lot was in the process of being readied for surfacing with asphalt. It was just mud and gravel associated with a winter thaw. This lady apparently had rolled over with her face down in the mud when she seized, thereby aspirating mud and gravel into her airway.

In the emergency room, Valerie was intubated and ventilated by hand with an ambu bag. Her cardiac function was excellent. After chest x-rays were completed, electrocardiograms were done, blood was drawn for tests, and intravenous catheters were inserted. Valerie was placed on a mechanical ventilator and transported to the intensive care unit.

My patient's chest x-ray was a "white out!" The lungs were full of a pulmonary infiltrate, most likely a severe viral pneumonia, along with whatever comes with aspirating rocks and mud!

The lab reported a positive nonspecific test for influenza. Later on, the lab would determine the virus to be influenza B. The patient's pulmonary function was atrocious, and I knew it was going to get worse. I just didn't know how much worse.

Our hospital had the luxury of employing two recently trained internists, Drs. Anderson and Jameson, who worked in our ER. With their expertise on our staff, a decision was made not to transfer our patient for intensive pulmonary care. I had incurred substantial experience managing ventilator patients during the oil boom and during my training. I was optimistically comfortable taking care of Valerie in our hospital. Besides, I knew the experience for our ICU nurses would be outstanding.

Valerie did get worse—much worse! She developed a full-blown ARDS (adult respiratory distress syndrome), which is essentially a non-cardiac lung edema. The lungs swell up like a sprained ankle would with an injury, and all the edema fluid fills the air sacs. The only way for the patient to survive is with prolonged respiratory system support with a ventilator (to maintain blood oxygen and carbon dioxide levels), meticulous pulmonary care to try to prevent infection, and time.

I met with our internists daily to work on our plan of action. As the days wore on, they became less convinced that our patient would leave the hospital alive. After a stressful day during which: our patient developed bilateral collapsed lungs that required chest tubes; our aging ventilator broke down because it could not generate the pressures needed to keep our patient's airways open; Valerie had a cardiac arrest that was rectified after some considerable effort, Dr. Jameson told me he figured her chances of leaving the hospital were 0 percent.

I took exception to this point of view, and advised him that he was just a natural pessimist. I challenged him to a $5 bet that my patient would leave our facility on her own power someday. Dr. Jameson went one step further. He was so sure about my patient's poor prospects that, if Valerie did survive, he would run down the corridor stark naked for all to see.

I said, "You're on!"

After another 10 difficult days in the ICU, Valerie started to improve slowly but surely. For sure, Valerie had a few setbacks, like bed sores on her low back and skin ulcerations on her heals, but she improved. During this time I had been consulting a pulmonologist in Billings who was quite willing to monitor our pulmonary management of Valerie as long as I kept him informed daily, which I did.

After three weeks, Valerie was trying to breathe by herself. She finally got off the ventilator on her 31st hospital day. The entire ICU staff celebrated our accomplishment; it was deserved praise.

Dr. Jameson said, "She isn't out of the hospital yet!"

Another month was needed for physical and pulmonary therapy. We discovered that Valerie had suffered a stroke at sometime during her ordeal with some residual speech and cognitive difficulties. Therefore, other therapy disciplines were engaged in her care.

Finally, after nine weeks in the hospital, Valerie left on her own power. She had some long-term concerns to deal with, but she had survived.

Dr. Jameson never ran down the hall naked. He just happened to be out of the hospital when our patient was discharged. Therefore, he said, "I can't personally confirm that your patient left under her own power."

One of the ICU nurses said, "Who wants to see his skinny little butt anyway?" We all had a good laugh.

Valerie never remembered a thing around the events of her acute illness or of the time before she came to the hospital. She was able to raise her children with some assistance.

Unfortunately, her husband did not stay by her side. He filed for divorce soon after Valerie went home.

Just a Bellyache

This spring day was gorgeous! The sun was out. It was warm outside. It was my day to be out of the office after I finished my morning hospital visits. It was a perfect day for some QTT (quality tractor time).

I had attached my Triple K cultivator to my John Deere 2510, and I was just getting ready to clean up some weeds along the roadside when Kay called out, "Jim, The phone!"

I was not on call! My patients in the hospital were stable. I had no obstetrics patients due. Drat!

The ER charge nurse on the phone said she had a pregnant lady from out of town with a bellyache. The local physician on ER duty did not do obstetrics. The on-call obstetrician could not be located. The nurse thought the patient should be evaluated before she headed back to her home 50 miles away.

I concurred; I told the nurse I would be in soon.

When I arrived in the emergency room, this young lady named Jennifer was having more than a little "belly ache." She was in labor and near her due date.

This was her second baby; according to Jennifer, her first pregnancy was not complicated in any way. Jennifer was receiving obstetrical care from a Dr. Armstrong in Williston, North Dakota.

I asked the nurse to have the folks in Williston fax this lady's prenatal forms to us ASAP. The nurse left the room to transfer my request to a ward clerk.

Jennifer was already connected to a fetal monitor that showed contractions about every 10 minutes. However, she was having pain almost constantly. My internal examination showed her cervix to be about 4 centimeters dilated with a bulging amniotic sac (her "bag of water"). The baby was head first. I told Jennifer I could not send her home yet. She was in labor, and it looked like she would have a baby soon.

I had the nurse get our patient transferred to obstetrics. Meanwhile, I called home to tell my Kay the situation I was in. I would keep her posted. I then asked the ward clerk about Jennifer's medical records. I was informed our message had been received in Williston. The records would be sent to us as soon as possible.

When I went to see Jennifer, her abdominal pains were intensifying *without* more frequent contractions. I thought, "This lady is abrupting her placenta!" (A condition during which the placenta prematurely separates from the uterine wall. This is usually associated with vaginally bleeding and may be fatal to the mom and baby.) "But she had no vaginal bleeding!"

I called radiology to have them bring our hospital's new bedside ultrasound ASAP. This was a really nice machine with a Technicolor display. It could show us where blood was, where it wasn't, and where it was not supposed to be (hopefully).

The ultrasound tech was at the bedside within a couple of minutes. The pictures confirmed my suspicions, a placenta that was abrupting without external bleeding.

I told the Jennifer that we needed to get her baby out *right now*! Her placenta was coming loose. Her baby might die!

She declared, "Not until I talk with Dr. Armstrong!"

I asked, "Don't you believe me?"

She responded, "I think you just want to cut me open and make more money!"

I was dumfounded. Despite what she had said, I asked the ward clerk mobilize the surgical team for a STAT C-section. I had a nurse call Dr. Barrigan, our general surgeon, and tell him, "We have a lady with an abruption. We need you in surgery now."

I inquired again about the records from Williston. They had not yet arrived.

I asked another clerk to call Williston and to stay on the phone until she found this Dr. Armstrong.

I went back to talk with Jennifer again. Her abdominal pains were intensifying. I repeated that her placenta was ripping loose. To save her baby, she needed to have a C-section immediately!

Her response was, "Not until I talk with Dr. Armstrong!"

The wait was like an eternity for me as I was anticipating the very worst of outcomes for this mom and her babe.

The surgery team arrived promptly and had the surgical suite ready in no time. Dr. Barrigan came running down the surgical corridor soon thereafter.

I advised them all that our patient was not going to have an operation until it was ok'd by her Dr. Armstrong. However, if everything was ready, we could get going within 2-3 minutes of "the call."

Once again, I returned to see Jennifer in her room. About then, the ward clerk asked to me to take a telephone call from Williston. I heard a lady's voice, but all I heard was Armstrong. I told this lady the current situation with her patient, and Jennifer's need for a C-section.

She then blurted out, "What are you waiting for? I am just a *lay midwife!*"

I informed Ms. Armstrong that Jennifer was not going anywhere until she received an OK from her "doctor."

The ward clerk transferred the call to Jennifer's room. After a very short conversation, Jennifer started to cry and said, "Its OK now."

We whisked Jennifer down the corridor to the operating room on a dead run. The anesthetist was going to perform a "crash intubation" because of the urgency.

After another minute or so of waiting in the operating room, which seemed forever, I made the abdominal incision.

Within 60 seconds we delivered a kicking, breathing little baby girl.

Hank, the anesthetist, yelled out, "Way to go TEAM!" After evaluating the female infant briefly on the operating table, I handed her to the awaiting nursery personnel.

As I reached my hand into the uterus to detach and extract the placenta, it just fell out. It was no longer attached! Had we waited another few minutes, the baby would not have survived, and the mom could have bled to death.

"God, were we lucky today!" I thought.

I asked Dr. Barrigan if he would mind closing the wounds. He said he would be glad to assist. As he was suturing, he exclaimed, "Man, I love this! You get to drive thru town as fast as you can with your lights flashing, and NOBODY CARES! We need to do this more often!" He then looked me in the eye and said, "Just kidding. We're getting too damn old for this much excitement!"

I agreed.

Jennifer and her baby left the hospital after a few days. I sent her home with a packet of medical records she could give to the medical person who would provide her post surgery care.

I don't think Jennifer ever understood the seriousness of the situation she had been in. I could only hope that "Dr. Armstrong" would - or could - explain it to her.

Dawson

On a Thursday in early June, supposedly my day off, I was summoned at home to come to the emergency room. The ambulance was at the scene of a semi truck - pedestrian accident on the highway just north of town. A severely injured juvenile who was in shock was being transported. The emergency room nurse wanted me there when the ambulance arrived.

The ambulance and I arrived at about the same time. The male victim was taken to the trauma area in our brand new emergency room. This was my first meeting with Dawson.

Dawson was a 13-year-old local daredevil who, on this occasion, tried to make it across a highway intersection on a motorcycle before a semi-truck got there.

He failed.

Dawson sped through the stop sign and hit the truck squarely between its lights. All he was wearing was a pair of swimming trunks and a helmet. Fortunately, the truck was just accelerating up to highway speed. The highway patrolman guessed the truck was traveling about 40 miles per hour. Dawson was going about the same speed.

A highway patrolman informed me that Dawson was tossed onto a gravel road where he bounced several times. He landed some distance away on the side of the highway. Our victim was unconscious when he was evaluated by the EMTs at the accident scene.

My evaluation of our victim's ABC's showed an adequate **a**irway, unlabored **b**reathing, and a rapid pulse with a low blood pressure.

While the lab personnel obtained blood for evaluation, my secondary exam revealed a deformed right thigh with a femur fracture, a deformed left upper arm with a humerus fracture, a deformed lower left arm with a double bone fracture, a large hematoma on the scalp, innumerable skin abrasions imbedded with pieces of gravel, an altered state of consciousness, and a rigid abdomen. A needle tap of his abdomen revealed blood in the abdomen, indicating a ruptured organ.

I knew that Dawson was going to require an emergency operation to contain the bleeding. Fortunately, our EMS response system had called in the surgical team, the surgeon, and radiology. By the time the surgeon and I had intravenous lines and a bladder catheter inserted, the operating room was awaiting us.

At surgery, Dawson had his spleen removed because it had exploded and could not be salvaged. Fortunately, no other organs were severely injured. After the abdominal wound had been closed and Dawson was stable, we decided to x-ray all his pieces and parts while he remained under anesthesia. Afterward, Dawson's extremities were placed into splints. Then, he was awakened and transferred to a room.

I called Dr. Brad Finkle, an orthopedic surgeon, in Billings to arrange Dawson's transfer for orthopedic repairs of his injuries. Dr. Finkle asked about the young man's age, his injuries, and whether or not his growth plates had fused. I explained the situation as best I could, but Brad decided to have a look at the x-rays before any transfer. He reminded me that the life threatening stuff had been resolved by removing the boy's spleen; there was no need for an orthopedic transfer for several days until I made certain Dawson remained stable. I sent the films by overnight express to Dr. Finkle.

The following day, Dr. Finkle called with his recommendations. He said he would not put bolts, plates, pins, screws or rods into Dawson's injuries because his growth plates were not close to fusing. The surgeries would only increase his chances of having arrested growth in the affected limbs. Dr. Finkle said he would put my patient's limbs in prolonged traction and let the bones heal naturally.

I was fortunate to have had some experience with traction devices during my training. After more discussion with Dr. Finkle, we decided that I would connect Dawson to the various traction devices needed, and I would care for him in our hospital near his home. I would provide Dr. Finkle with periodic updates with x-rays and records. Dr. Finkle was encouraging noting that this was nothing more than "baby sitting with a medical degree."

Several days later, after his mental status had cleared, Dawson was taken to the operating room where I inserted traction pins into his femur just above the knee, into his ulna below the elbow, and through both bones of the forearm near the wrist. These pins were then connected to a system of pulleys and weights in various directions to keep the bone fragments aligned.

The physical therapist and the nurses were trained in the meticulous maintenance needs for the various surgical areas in hopes of preventing infection. Our patient was all set; now all I had to do was to be vigilant, attentive, and pray a lot in hopes that Dawson's youth would do the rest.

As time passed, Dawson's body performed very well. Dr. Finkle or one of his partners had only encouraging words for our team. They were pleased that Dawson did so well in our facility. Brad pointed out that had my patient been in his big city center, his chance of becoming infected was about 80 percent.

Except for being amnesic about the accident, Dawson's mental function returned to what his mother considered normal. I did become a bit annoyed when he wanted some books on riding motorcycles, but he got them anyway. (He didn't recall riding a motorcycle in the accident.)

Dawson remained in the hospital through the summer in traction. After four weeks, the forearm pins were removed and strengthening exercises for the hand and forearm were started. By eight weeks, the humerus pin was removed. The femur pin was removed after 10 weeks.

He still had several weeks of physical therapy and rehabilitation to go by the time school started that fall. I arranged with the junior high school principal to have Dawson tutored in the hospital and at home until he could resume going to school on a full time basis.

My young patient left the hospital after about 13 weeks doing just fine.

Besides saving his mother a lot of money for his medical care, keeping Dawson in our hospital near his home gave our young nurses valuable experience in orthopedic and surgical care.

I had the opportunity to see Dawson and his mother for many more years.

Dawson continued to struggle with life throughout his days. He struggled with school, relationships, marriage, and parenthood. Things in life just never fit quite right for him for some reason or another.

I last saw Dawson for an influenza illness when he was about 31 years old. He had been in bed for about a week before he came into the office. He was now divorced and had custody of his child who too was ill at the time. I gave him some symptomatic remedies, asked him to drink a lot of fluids, but advised him that there really was no treatment for the "real flu." He would just have to "ride it out."

That night at a basketball game a policeman came up to me and asked what I knew about Dawson. He had been found dead at home.

Except for his having the flu, I knew of nothing else. I wondered to myself, "Had I missed something obvious?"

I suggested that an autopsy be done.

The following morning, Dawson's relatives were in my office asking for his medical records. They just knew I screwed up, and I was going to pay! One of the relatives asked, "Who's going to care his child now?"

That afternoon, Dr. Lasater, the hospital pathologist, called to tell me about the autopsy. He informed me that my patient had suffered a massive pulmonary embolism that probably resulted from prolonged inactivity and dehydration. The embolism was so large that the victim most likely died instantly. Additionally, he reported that he had called the family members, who also had contacted him, and told them to, "Go to hell! You have no case!"

Dawson's mom came to my office crying a few days later. She wanted to apologize for the recent behavior of the rest of her family. She wanted me to know that *she knew* I would never do anything to harm her son. She also wanted me to know that she remembered, like yesterday, that fateful day almost 19 years before. She knew that our local medical team, and I, had saved her son, and she was grateful.

I Don't Do Babies

My pregnant patient was near her due date with her third child when she came to the hospital in labor. Her labor progressed unremarkably. During the labor process, the nurses had monitored the mom and the baby and had noticed no abnormalities. My patient was taken to the delivery room when her cervix was completely dilated, and she had an urge to push.

The patient was placed on the obstetrical table and positioned for the delivery. After my patient had pushed several times, her bag of water burst spontaneously, and a massive amount of clear amniotic fluid gushed out along with the *umbilical cord!* The baby's head promptly dropped down farther into the birth canal trapping the prolapsed umbilical cord. My delivery suddenly went from "routine" to an obstetrical emergency. (Obstetrics has been defined as 95 percent boredom and 5 percent sheer terror. I was now in the terror part.)

I immediately tried to free up the cord and push it back inside the uterus.

No Luck!

I then took my left hand and tried to push the infant's head out of the pelvis so I could free the umbilical cord.

No luck again!

I asked the nurses to place the patient in Trendelenburg position (a fancy name for head down on an incline) and to call a hospital emergency for obstetrics. Meanwhile, the baby's heart rate was dropping into the 80s. (It should be around 120 -140.)

After the mom was in the head down position, which took only a few seconds, I was able to put enough force with my arm and hand onto the baby's head to disengage it from the mom's pelvis and to relieve the pressure on the umbilical cord.

The baby's heart rate normalized.

I tried several more times to get the umbilical cord back into the uterus without success. I knew an emergency Cesarean section was needed NOW.

With my left arm and hand keeping the baby's head out of the mom's pelvis against the strength of the uterine contractions, (which, by the way, is an awful lot of work) I asked a nurse to mobilize the surgical team STAT and to get the new general surgeon in town to the operating room NOW!

Meanwhile, another nurse was asked to insert another intravenous line. The lab was called to obtain blood samples for coagulation studies and for a type and cross match just in case the patient needed to have some blood replaced.

All the members of the operating team arrived within a few minutes. The anesthetist came in to talk with the patient. Soon thereafter, the mom in labor and I, with my arm stuck up inside her bottom, went to the operating room.

I asked if the surgeon had arrived.

The nurse informed us, “ He had been notified.”

I was hoping the surgeon would be available to orchestrate the activities in the operating room, but he wasn’t. I had enough to do keeping the baby’s head disengaged, and my arm and hand were starting to have cramps, really bad cramps. I asked the surgical assistant to prep the abdomen and then cover the patient and me with sterile drapes.

I asked the whereabouts of the surgeon.

The answer returned, “He has been notified!”

We all waited for what seemed to me, and my cramping hand, like an eternity. I was just about to start the operation alone when we heard whistling outside the operating room. The surgeon had arrived. He said he did not know we were in such a hurry.

I wondered to myself, “Who called him, and what did they say? How fast does NOW imply?”

The surgeon scrubbed quickly and asked where I wanted him at the operating table. I told him to get ready to take the baby out after I let go of its head.

He agreed.

When I was assured the surgeon was ready to go, I released my hold on the baby’s head, put on a clean glove, and positioned myself at the table.

The surgeon said, “Where do you want me to cut? I don’t do these!”

By now my left hand was cramping severely. I motioned for a sidewise cut just above the pubic bone.

He said, “Let’s do it!”

With noticeable skill, he made a skin incision followed by the appropriate maneuvers to extract a healthy, screaming baby within *60 seconds!*

“Pretty darn good for the first time,” I told him.

The surgeon completed the operation while I assisted him. He apologized for his tardiness noting that he would have hurried if he had known I needed him right away and promised it would not happen again.

When the surgeon came to town, he had a tee shirt made that said, *“I Don’t Do Bones or Babies.”* After this day, he had to put a line through “*Babies*.”

MAKING A DIFFERENCE

"Cure sometimes, treat often, comfort always."

Hippocrates

"I believe that every human mind feels pleasure in doing good to another."

Thomas Jefferson

All That Fat

In the 1980s a frenzy of activity developed over cholesterol, fats, and heart disease. (Personally, I believed this to be a contrived "disease" by the media and the pharmaceutical industry.) Subsequently, since the medical community wanted to "improve" the health of our "fat sick" population, it was not a difficult task to sway physicians to join the bandwagon. The American Medical Association started a campaign to lower cholesterol and heart disease in America. Ironically, the kickoff breakfast for the anti-cholesterol campaign served eggs benedict, a fat and cholesterol-rich meal.

Physicians, hospitals, and clinics across the country, under the disguise of "helping Americans stay healthy," but who were actually just promoting their particular business endeavors, set up cholesterol screening venues. Some were at clinics. Others were at hospitals. Still others were the "mobile vans" that went to shopping malls, senior centers, and civic group meetings. Supposedly, if one knew their own cholesterol level, the implication was he or she would know how to *eliminate their risk* of having a heart attack or a stroke.

Unfortunately, the "rest of the story" about risk was seldom, if ever, presented. That is, what was the family history of heart disease (95 percent of risk)? Did the person smoke? What about obesity, exercise, hypertension, stress, diabetes, etc.? Never was there any mention of the fact that dietary cholesterol is NOT the same cholesterol in the blood. (All dietary fats must be digested into small pieces by the body, and the liver manufactures cholesterols and other similar chemicals needed by the body.)

A lady in her 60s presented herself to my clinic about this time. She was anxious. Her voice quivered. After I introduced myself to her, she blurted out, "They said I'm going to have a stroke!" "What can I do?"

First, I asked her to calm down a bit. Then I asked her to tell me more about what had happened.

She related going to the shopping mall in Billings over the weekend with some friends. While at the Mall, she and her companions had their cholesterols checked for free at the "Cholesterol Mobile" provided by a local hospital.

The lady claimed the nurse advised her that, "Your cholesterol is 264. You are about to have a stroke! You had better see someone right away!" (It should be noted that in the 1970s a cholesterol number under about 300 was acceptable, but "the guidelines" for cholesterol levels had been lowered.) She had been worried sick since learning her cholesterol numbers and had not slept well at all.

I advised the patient that cholesterol is not the only factor that *may* predict *premature* heart disease and stroke. I mentioned the other factors including family history, high blood pressure, diabetes, and so on.

I asked her if she took any medicines.

She replied, "No. I don't even take vitamins." She then said, "I feel healthy as a horse."

I told her that her family history was the number one determinant for having a *premature* vascular event. I emphasized "premature" because that is what the data reflected. I informed her that EVERYONE has vascular disease. A majority of people will eventually die from a heart attack or a stroke.

I asked her, "When did your mother die?"

She replied, "Momma isn't dead! She lives with me. She is 82 years-old and doing fine."

Then I asked, "When did her mother die?"

The lady smiled and laughed saying, "Grandma's not dead. She lives in the nursing home."

I asked the lady to be patient with me while I gathered some information. I bid her good morning, asked her to try to relax, and arranged for her to see me at the end of the day.

She agreed.

Subsequently, I called the hospital and the nursing home to get lab results for this lady's mother and grandmother. Additionally, I asked for any evidence of either of them having "any substantial vascular illness or event."

My nurse gathered the information and presented the documents to me for evaluation before my new patient returned that afternoon.

When the lady returned, she remained nervous and tearful. I said, "I have good news and bad news. What would you like first?"

She responded, "The good news."

I said, "The good news is you have no family history of *premature* vascular disease, heart attacks, or strokes."

She noted, "I could have told you that!"

"But wait, I have more," I returned. I informed her that her cholesterol was 264; her mother's was 346; and her grandmother's was 402! The HDL, the good cholesterol, was "sky high" for all of them.

I suggested to her that, "Your chance of dying early from a heart attack or a stroke is less than your getting hit by a tank in Sidney, Montana in the winter!"

I could see a sense of relief on this lady's face. She even developed a small smile. She then queried, "That's the good news. Now what's the bad?"

I replied, "I don't want you to have another cholesterol test for the rest of your life."

We both laughed.

To reinforce my "bad news," I gave the lady a prescription for a pizza at a local restaurant.

A Touch of Asthma

Ned first came to my office when he was about six-years-old. He was the third child in a family whose parents were local teachers. Unlike his siblings, Ned had been "sickly" almost since day one. He was always thin. His weight was at about the fifth percentile for his age while his height was about the 40th percentile. Ned always seemed to have a "cold" when the others in the family were well. Additionally, he had perpetual ear infections.

At some point before I saw Ned, his parents had taken him to see multiple specialists, including an allergist, who found that he had asthma. Additionally, the allergist determined that Ned was essentially allergic to *"all of God's plants and animals."* For these issues, Ned was supposed to take a collection of medications on a regular basis.

Ned's health problems caused additional friction with his older siblings because they wanted to have a pet, but, because of Ned's health issues, no animals were allowed in the home. He seemed to be the odd man out.

Initially, I saw Ned in my office only sporadically for an acute illness. The majority of his care was directed via the allergist's office in Billings about 270 miles away. I was agreeable to refill his medications when needed so the family would not have to make another long trip to the specialist and incur more medical expenses.

When Ned was about 14 years old, the parents decided that they could not keep going so often out of town for him to see a physician. They asked if I would assume his care, and I agreed.

Initially, I instructed Ned and the parents on the management of his asthma. They were shown how to follow his breathing status with a small, hand-held device called a peak flow meter. They were instructed on emergency measures to follow. Finally, they were instructed on the importance of periodic follow-up visits so I could monitor Ned's asthma and make reports to his allergist.

Like many people with a chronic disease, Ned's compliance with his asthma program was erratic at best. Like most teenagers who want to "fit in", he tended to minimize his health issues. He, like most teens, felt *bullet proof and invincible.* If he didn't complain, there was no issue.

My next visit with Ned was almost two years later! Once again he was subjected to my asthma education talk. Once again, we planned on periodic checks to make sure he was doing O.K. Despite his assurances to comply with his maintenance program, I had a feeling that Ned would not. Besides, he was a teenager. He was *invincible and bullet proof!*

Ned was seen in my office in July two years later. He was now 17 years old. He came in because he was having "a little trouble breathing." He had been having "a little trouble" for several days and had been using his inhalers almost constantly. He agreed that he had not followed the rules.

On examination, Ned was blue! I could hear no air movement in his lungs. I gave him a shot of epinephrine (adrenalin), which gave him some relief, but he was still in a dire situation. Immediately, I took him to the hospital in a wheelchair.

After admission to the hospital, Ned's condition continued to deteriorate. He was subsequently transferred to the intensive care unit where vigorous efforts were used to reverse his asthma. However, our efforts were not successful, and my patient continued to worsen.

Laboratory tests confirmed that Ned was in respiratory failure.

The family was notified that their son would require being placed on a ventilator machine if he were to have a chance to survive. About 7:30 that evening, Ned was sedated, intubated and placed on a mechanical ventilator.

His airway spasm was dramatic with regard to its severity. Despite the continuous administration of medications intravenously and directly into the lungs via a nebulizer, Ned's airway spasms persisted. After consultation with an internist, we elected to use isoproterenol (Isuprel), a very potent bronchodilator, but also a very potent cardiac stimulant. (I had used Isuprel extensively in my training, but its use had waned as newer and safer agents replaced it.) I knew this drug is one that I would not use in an old person with heart disease, but it was worth a try in a teenager.

Fortunately, within a few minutes after the Isuprel was started, Ned's airway spasm started to improve as evidenced by the ventilator requiring less pressure to force air into his lungs. His heart rate increased to about 140, but he showed no signs of cardiac issues. Thank goodness he was a teenager!

I thought Ned was "out of the woods." All I had to do was wait and monitor until the airway spasm resolved for good, which is what typically happens.

Soon thereafter the other medications were stopped. Ned was holding his own on Isuprel and fluids for hydration. Things were looking good. However, I decided to spend the night in the intensive care unit "just in case."

In the early morning hours the ventilator rebelled! TOO MUCH PRESSURE! Ned started to fight the machine. My quick chest exam revealed no airflow in the right side of the chest. A chest x-ray confirmed a collapsed right lung. (A collapsed lung is a common complication of ventilator care.)

I inserted a tube into the right chest to expand the lung. A repeat chest x-ray confirmed expansion of the right lung, but also exposed a collapse of the left lung! After I inserted a tube into the left chest, another x-ray showed expansion of the left lung, but revealed the right lung had collapsed again! I inserted a second tube into the right chest cavity. Another x-ray confirmed re-expansion of both lungs. Whew!

It was time to transfer Ned to a pulmonary center, so I consulted with a pulmonologist in Billings. After a brief discussion, the pulmonologist said he would be glad to take Ned as a patient. He said he would make the transfer arrangements. The pulmonologist called back within a short period of time to tell me that all planes were grounded because of the weather. He wanted to know Ned's status, which, by the way, had improved dramatically after our collapsed lung adventure. The pulmonologist's suggestion was to stop the Isuprel (since it was dangerous) and attempt to wean him off the ventilator when his blood gas measurements met certain criteria.

My attempt to wean Ned off the ventilator was a disaster. He promptly "crashed," and I had a "DO OVER" with his asthma. I did not stop the Isuprel, however.

Another call to the pulmonologist the next day ended with a suggestion to try a modality called CPAP (continuous positive airway pressure). This way Ned would be breathing on his own with an assist from the ventilator when or if he needed it.

This modality was started, and Ned rested nicely the remainder of the day.

All was good with Ned on the CPAP until about 8 a.m. He started to have severe paroxysms of coughing that brought up hard chunks of mucous; this finding hinted that he had been ill a long time. Ned developed worsening airway spasms, and he was exhausted. My attempts to break the spasms with more medications were fruitless.

Another call to the pulmonologist was made. His partner on call related that the weather was still not good. Once again, I sedated my young patient, and I placed him back on full ventilator support about 11 a.m. Ned quieted down once again and allowed the machine to do its work.

The weather started to clear about midnight. I received a call from the air transport team to verify Ned's status and was notified that an air ambulance would be dispatched as soon as possible. The flight team arrived in the early hours of the morning.

After getting Ned transferred to their ventilator, the transport nurse promptly stopped the Isuprel! When I questioned that decision and advised the nurse of our problems with the other medications, she replied, "Doctor's orders. We don't use that stuff in Billings. It's too dangerous!"

Ned was off to Billings.

I received a call much later in the day from the Billings pulmonologist. He related that my patient gave the flight team "a scare" about the time their plane landed when he developed severe airway spasms.

The end of a detailed story was that *Ned was placed back on the Isuprel by the pulmonologist!*

Ned would spend the next three weeks on a ventilator. His asthma improved, but Ned was so weak that he could not walk, or sit, or even feed himself. The long-term use of muscle paralyzing agents and high doses of cortisone while he was on the ventilator caused Ned to develop a severe generalized muscle weakness. After three more weeks of intensive physical therapy and time, Ned returned to our hospital for his continued convalescence.

When he arrived back in Sidney, Ned was barely able to transfer himself from a chair to a bed. He weighed 92 pounds. (He weighed 116 pounds when he was transferred.) He fatigued just trying to eat a meal.

Ned remained in our hospital for about three more weeks. Upon his departure, he was walking for more than an hour without fatigue. His weight was up to 106 pounds.

Ned continued to improve to the point that he was in school full time by Halloween, and his physical therapy was done at home. He even played a few holes of golf.

Ned had several more visitations with the pulmonologist that went well. This physician outlined an asthma care program for him that looked very much like mine. This time, however, our young asthmatic seemed to take things more seriously. (I think he learned the hard way that he was NOT *bullet proof and he was NOT invincible.*)

Medically speaking, Ned did well his senior year in school. Best of all, he was alive to graduate.

In the fall after his graduation, I gave my young patient a "final checkup" before he went to college. I arranged for him to see a physician for follow-up while he was in college. I made sure he had his asthma plan and his peak flow meter.

By all reports from his parents, Ned continued to do well, and he still had his peak flow meter and an asthma plan.

In the Genes

Tom came to see me in the clinic one Wednesday morning. My nurse had written on the routing slip, "Wants a heart check."

I had seen this gentleman previously for minor acute illnesses only. I asked how I might help him.

He insisted he needed to get a treadmill test. His brother had just had a heart attack at age 42. Tom wanted to make sure he wasn't going to have a heart attack too; he had a family to worry about.

I proceeded to obtain a more extensive history.

Tom related always being "healthy." He did not smoke or drink or take any drugs. He performed hard physical labor daily without any problems.

Tom was the youngest of six children and had just turned 40. His family had four boys and two girls. His oldest brother died from a heart attack at age 41. His second brother had a heart stent inserted several years before at age 39. His third brother had just suffered a "bad" heart attack in North Dakota. He was still in critical condition in an intensive care unit.

Tom's father died at an early age in a farm accident. However, all his uncles had strokes or heart attacks before 60. Tom said his mother was in her early 70s and was "doing fine." His sisters were "healthy" as far as he knew.

Tom brought in some papers from the recent Health Fair at the hospital. The papers revealed the results of his Health Fair lab tests. Tom had been reassured by the "*heart test*" results: his cholesterol was 146 (a good number); his HDL (the "good cholesterol") was average at 35; his LDL (the "bad cholesterol") was 125 and in the average range. Overall, he had a pretty good profile. In fact, the lab form stated he was in the *low average range* to have a heart attack in the next 10 years.

I knew that the lab results were merely isolated guesses. I knew from experience that this fellow had BAD GENES. Additionally, a treadmill was not the test he needed. In fact, I guessed that if I stressed his heart too much with an exercise treadmill test, *he might have a heart attack.*

I told Tom I would not do a physical examination on him this day. I told Tom that, in my opinion, he did not need a treadmill. He needed a coronary angiogram and soon. I advised him that 90 percent or more of his risk was his family history; his history really stunk! In my view, he was a ticking time bomb.

Then I asked Tom if he would wait while I consulted with a cardiologist.

He agreed.

Tom and I relocated into my office where I telephoned The Billings Clinic cardiology department in Billings, Montana. The cardiologist on call was Dr. Dave Fennerson, a physician to whom I had referred many cases. With Tom listening to the conversation, I repeated our conversation to Dr. Fennerson. Dave agreed with me. He asked if Tom could be at the Billings Deaconess Hospital at 8 a.m. the next morning.

This got Tom's attention in a hurry. He stated he had to make a few arrangements first, but said he and his wife would be there. They would go to Billings that day and spend the night in a motel.

Dr. Fennerson suggested they plan on staying "a few days just in case."

Tom left my office to make plans for his trip to Billings.

My nurse called me out of an exam room about 2 p.m. the next day to take a call from The Billings Clinic.

Dr. Fennerson was on the phone. He said, "You saved this guy's bacon! I found a 95 percent occlusion of the left main coronary lesion (affectionately known as a Widow Maker), an 85 percent LAD lesion, and a 90 percent circumflex lesion. (These are the percentages of obstruction for the major heart vessels.) This guy was running on borrowed time." Dave went on to say that Tom went straight from the cardiac catheterization lab to the operating room where Dr. Sam Mulvaney performed a triple coronary artery bypass.

Dr. Fennerson then said Tom would be in the hospital for 5-7 days before discharge. He asked if I would arrange for cardiac rehabilitation in Sidney afterward.

I agreed.

Dr. Fennerson then said he would keep me posted on our patient's progress.

Later that day I received a call from Dr. Mulvaney, the heart surgeon. His first words were, "Wow, what a pickup! Good job!"

He then told me the patient had "awful" large vessel disease, but his surgery went very well. Barring any unforeseen issues, our patient would be home in a week and back to work in three months. He then said, "With his good labs, who would have thought his arteries would be so bad?"

I told Dr. Mulvaney that all I did was talk to the patient and get a history.

A mentor in medical school taught me that, *"If you let the patient talk long enough, he will tell you what is wrong with him."*

Once again, the cholesterol number was not everything.

I saw Tom and his wife a few weeks later when he was participating in a cardiac rehabilitation session at our hospital. Tom related to me that the doctors in Billings told him "he was essentially a dead man walking" when he arrived and that I had "saved his bacon."

Tom's wife expressed her heartfelt thanks and asked what they could do to repay me.

I said, " You can be good parents and try to raise good kids."

I cared for Tom and his family for many more years.

Headache

On a Friday in April, Brenda was having a regular day. She was 22 years old at the time. Just about 10 weeks before, she had delivered her second child without any problems. Her life as a new mom was busy, as one would expect, but she and her husband were doing quite well with their family.

On Saturday, Brenda developed a "bad headache." This was a REALLY BAD headache. One like she had never had before. She had tried some over the counter pain medicines that did not help very much. Brenda was not a complainer. In fact, she was usually just the opposite. Her husband figured something was amiss and decided to take her to the hospital emergency room during the late afternoon.

While in the hospital emergency room, Brenda was seen and evaluated by an emergency room physician. Her examination was reported as "not remarkable." Her vital signs were stable. She was not febrile. She displayed no outward signs of an acute infection. The physician thought she might be having a migraine headache episode, administered a narcotic pain reliever, and advised the husband to bring her back if she did not improve.

A few hours went by. Unbelievably, Brenda's headache intensified. In fact, the pain became so severe that she became confused and disoriented. She did not recognize her family members. She started to vomit.

A family member called me at home and told me Brenda's recent history and events as they saw them. At the time of the phone call, she reportedly was lying in her bed in their home, holding her head, and being totally incoherent.

I asked the family to take her to the emergency room where I would meet them.

They arrived just minutes before me. The nurse told me, "Brenda is really sick! Her temperature is 105 degrees. She 's breathing rapidly. She is lethargic and barely responsive!"

On first glance, this girl was acutely ill. She was on the ER exam bed in a fetal position holding her head. She did not respond to my verbal commands.

I thought to myself, "First things first. ABCs." The **a**irway was obviously open without any evidence for obstruction. Her **b**reathing was rapid, but not labored. While listening with my stethoscope, her lungs displayed no evidence for an acute infection. The circulation status was good. The pulse was elevated, but one would expect this with a fever of 105 degrees. Her blood pressure was normal.

I thought, "So far so good."

My secondary examination provided more clues. Obviously, Brenda was having severe head pain. By now, she was just mumbling and whimpering while holding her head. I found no evidence for head trauma. However, her eyes were now pointing *outward*! (This is called a divergent strabismus.) Her eyes were not tracking. Her pupils responded to light, but she did not seem to be able to see. Brenda cried out when I moved her head and neck. However, she seemed to be able to move her head slowly by herself without such discomfort.

Soon thereafter, Brenda was responding only to painful stimuli.

I assessed that my patient had an intracranial event occurring. This could be a hemorrhage, a tumor, an infection, or something more unusual. I told the husband and the family that Brenda appeared to be a very sick girl. (Duh, a pretty obvious conclusion to all, but doctors say these things anyway.) I told them I needed to perform a spinal tap to retrieve a sample of her spinal fluid, and I asked for their permission. Actually, this was just a formality because I had asked the ER nurse beforehand to get out the materials necessary for the procedure.

I had done literally hundreds of spinal taps over the years. This one should be no different. However, this was MY PATIENT! I had assisted her with the delivery of her babies. I took care of her family and her parents' family. I knew that if she had a hemorrhage in her brain, then a spinal tap might kill her. Talk about stress!

As soon as I inserted the spinal needle through the dural membrane (the membrane around the spinal cord that holds in the spinal fluid), I could feel a "pop." (I expected this.) Then the spinal fluid literally shot out of the needle and hit me in the chest. I didn't expect this.) The spinal fluid was obviously under a lot of extra pressure.

The spinal fluid is supposed to be clear. This fluid looked like a milk-shake!

I knew Brenda had meningitis.

As soon as I collected specimens for the lab to culture and to evaluate under a microscope, I asked the nurse to insert two intravenous catheters, one for fluids, and one for antibiotics.

Within minutes, the initial microscopic slides of the spinal fluid showed gross pus and many bacteria with an appearance suggestive of a pneumococcal meningitis. We would not know the specific bacteria until the cultures were completed in two or three days. Until then, I gave Brenda two broad-spectrum antibiotics that would kill most everything.

I advised the family that Brenda had an infection around her brain, I did not know how she got it, and I could not make a guess how she would respond to my treatments. I made the family aware that Brenda might have some residual effects from the infection around her brain. However, I knew she was young and physically strong. We could hope for the best.

I stayed with her the rest of the first day, mostly because I was worried, but also to field the innumerable questions being asked by family members. She remained essentially in a coma for two days. On the third day she responded to voices, but she could not see well. She fell over when we tried to get her up, so I presumed the part of her brain that controlled balance had been affected.

I asked Brenda if she knew where she was.

She replied, "Of course!" But then she could not tell me where.

I asked her if she knew my name.

She responded, "Sure, I know you, silly!" But she could not say my name.

I hoped Brenda's thinking problems would not be permanent.

On the third day, the lab reported the bug as "strep pneumonia" (pneumococcus to me), and the two antibiotics were changed to plain penicillin. Brenda would receive this medicine for 10 more days to eradicate the bacteria from her spinal fluid.

After the sixth day, Brenda had improved substantially. She continued to have some balance difficulties that I hoped would resolve. She continued to have trouble with her memory and problem solving.

By the 11th day, Brenda was ready to take care of her baby. Fortunately, she had little recall of the "bad days." She had virtually no residual deficits from the meningitis that I could discern. She went home doing quite well.

I saw Brenda in the office about two weeks later. She looked great. She said her family had explained to her how I took care of her and stayed by her side, "The Whole Time!"

This was not exactly true, but I didn't say anything.

She then said, "Thank you!" and gave me a big hug. (I found out that she was indeed a strong woman!)

Her mom and dad were in the waiting room. They too came back to my office. Dad shook my hand with a tear in his eye and offered his thanks. Mom was already crying and gave me another hug.

I would have the opportunity to care for three generations of this family for many years. But this episode was the one during which I felt I really had made a difference.

Not My Time

Frank was a 42-year-old man with a stressful oilfield-related job in 1978. His usual day was from about 5 a.m. until 7 to 8 p.m. most days. In his "free time," he and his wife enjoyed spending time with their three teenage children, the oldest of whom had recently graduated from high school. Occasionally, the family would have friends over socially. In the summertime, they enjoyed having barbecue gatherings. It was after one such event that Frank developed severe chest pain. He had experienced similar pain before, but nothing like this. He had not told anyone about the discomfort either.

Frank did not want to "bother" his family, so he drove himself to the emergency room at our hospital. By the time he arrived at the emergency room, his chest pain had subsided. Frank assumed he must have eaten too much and just had another bad "gas attack." However, the nurse on duty suggested that he allow her to at least take his blood pressure.

"It isn't going to cost you anything," she told him.

As soon as he sat down for his blood pressure reading, the pains returned with a vengeance. Frank got pale and sweaty. He became dizzy. His blood pressure fell to 80/60, and his pulse was quite rapid. The nurse placed oxygen on his face and gave him an aspirin. (This is a standard protocol for chest pain.) The nurse paged for assistance.

Since I was already in the hospital, I walked briskly to the ER.

Upon my arrival, the nurse had obtained an electrocardiogram that revealed an acute myocardial infarction pattern (heart attack). An intravenous line was inserted for medications, and Frank was whisked away to the intensive care unit. Nowadays, patients with acute heart attacks receive "clot busters" as soon as possible to open up the plugged heart arteries. However, when Frank became ill, aspirin and heparin (an anticoagulant medicine) were the standard of care. He received the aspirin in the emergency room. He received the heparin through an intravenous catheter in the ICU.

In the intensive care unit, the hospital's heart attack protocol was initiated. A chest x-ray was done. Blood was drawn promptly for chemistries and heart attack markers and these tests would be repeated in several hours. The heart was monitored continuously. The patient had one-to-one nursing until he was stable. Frank would remain in bed to minimize any stress on his heart. Physicians, nurses, and therapists would examine him often. The family was notified as soon as possible about Frank's condition and his admission to the hospital.

When I called Frank's home about his hospital admission, his wife assumed he had gone to the grocery store without talking to anyone. She related that they would be at the hospital very soon.

Just as I was getting off the phone with the family, Frank became sweaty and pale. His blood pressure dropped to zero, nada! The heart monitor showed ventricular fibrillation, a life threatening heart rhythm disturbance. I saw the ICU nurse jump off her chair, race to the bedside, and promptly hit Frank in the chest with a really vicious blow (called a precordial thump). Sometimes this blow will stop an acute rhythm problem. This time it did not.

The nurse then grabbed the cardioversion paddles, yelled out, "CLEAR," and administered 300 joules of electricity into Frank. Fortunately, the heart rhythm normalized. The blood pressure returned to an acceptable level. Frank was "stabilized" for now, but actually his overall condition was "unstable."

Frank survived the first night. The team kept his family informed of his critical status. The lab tests confirmed extensive heart damage. I knew that if Frank survived, he would be "out of action" for months.

I called a regional cardiac center to discuss a transfer for possible heart surgery. The cardiologist and the heart surgeon both wanted to wait until he was "more stable." They informed me that the literature did not support prompt cardiac surgery unless it was done within four hours of the event.

I thought to myself, "Heck, our patients would never be candidates for "immediate surgery" because it took at least four hours to get a patient transported!"

Frank and his family were notified that he could recover in our hospital. After several weeks, the cardiologist would visit with him regarding a possible surgery.

Frank's hospital stay was most unremarkable after the first 36 hours. The nurses noticed, however, that he seemed to be worrying about something all the time. Despite their best efforts to engage him, Frank would not talk to the nurses about his concerns.

It became my turn to become the local psychiatrist.

After supper one day, I asked Frank if we could have a chat.

He agreed.

I told him the nurses had noticed that he seemed to be worrying a lot. I asked if I could help. Did he want to talk about "**it**?"

Frank then blurted out, "Its too early! Its not my time!" He started to cry.

I asked him what he meant.

He said he was worried about his kids. He was worried about his job. He worried who was going to pay the bills?

I told him that these worries were all quite normal after an acute episode like his. However, I told him that I sensed there was something else. I asked him, "Is there something I should know that you haven't told me?"

Frank went on to tell me a TOTALLY DIFFERENT family history than the one he had given to the nurses and me before. He related that no male in his family lived to be 50. They all died when they were 47 years old. He knew he had 5 more years to go!

I was stunned. Here was a man with a known family history of premature fatal heart disease who had ignored the signs of heart problems for some time. Besides, he had a most stressful job, he had smoked three packages of cigarettes daily for "as long as he could remember," he did not exercise, and he drank excessively.

I asked him, "What did you expect to happen?"

He didn't know. He just thought he would die when he turned 47.

Frank saw the cardiologist four weeks later and had a coronary artery bypass soon thereafter.

Four months or so after his heart surgery, Frank returned to the stressful job he knew. He started smoking again. He acted as if nothing had happened to him the previous six months.

A few months later Frank was transferred to another job site in North Dakota.

I had forgotten about him until I read his obituary in the paper several years later. He had died of a massive heart attack while on the job. He was 45 years old.

I thought to myself, "It was still two years early. But I guess it was his time to go."

No Energy

I first met Sarah on the Wednesday afternoon following the midpoint of the first semester of the school year. The weather had been cold and miserable for some time already. Sarah's mom brought her to the clinic for me to see if there was something wrong with Sarah medically before, "she beat her to within an inch of her life!"

At the semester midpoint, the previous Friday, Sarah's mom received a report from the junior high school principal that her daughter was, for the most part, failing academically. Sarah had always been an "average" student, but never failing. Additionally, a report from the physical education instructor stated that, "Sarah was poorly motivated in class and was receiving an "incomplete" so far for this semester because of her "lack of effort and participation."

On this day, Sarah's mom received a call from the school's secretary saying that Sarah had been tardy to *each class* for the past two days! This mother was beside herself to say the least.

All the time I let the mother ramble on, Sarah sat quietly and said nothing. When I asked her about her not making it to class on time, Sarah just replied that she was tired.

Sarah's mother then started ranting again, "She is always tired! She doesn't have the energy to clean her room, or take out the garbage, or DO ANYTHING! I am just tired of it!"

It became obvious to me that nothing was going to get accomplished with the mother in the room. Therefore, after some coaxing, I got the mom to vacate the exam room with my assurances that I would keep her informed about what, if anything, I discovered about Sarah.

Initially, Sarah just did not want to talk. Then, once again, she said that she was just tired "all the time" and began to cry quietly.

Once again, I asked Sarah about why she was late getting to her classes.

Again she responded, "I just get tired."

I asked if she EVER thought of running up the stairs.

She just stared at me and stated firmly, "I have to rest half way up the stairs."

I thought to myself, "Had to rest? This girl was only 13 years old. She should be able to run up the stairs like they were not there!"

I asked about her "lack of effort" in P.E. class.

Sarah said the teacher wanted them to run around the gym five times. She made it only one-half a lap before she had to stop. She could only walk afterward. Apparently, the P.E. teacher was not very appreciative of her efforts.

When I asked about her schoolwork, Sarah just replied that she was just too tired to do homework. She usually went to bed right after supper.

I thought to myself, "This is not the way a normal teenager acts."

I wondered about all sorts of things, including child abuse, after I had witnessed her mother's tirades.

My examination of Sarah was pretty unremarkable except that she had dark rings under her eyes. When I inquired about them, Sarah said she always had them. She said her mother told her they came from not getting good sleep.

I, on the other hand, believed them to be "allergic shiners," dark lines under the eyes of people with allergies, especially children. Additionally, Sarah had pale, boggy mucous membranes in her nose, which also suggested, but did not confirm, allergies.

Because of her complaints of generalized fatigue and lack of energy, I wondered if Sarah did not have an unusual presentation of asthma.

Sarah's chest examination was most unremarkable. There were no funny noises. Air seemed to be moving. But, when I asked her to blow out her air as "hard as she could," Sarah started coughing and continued coughing! (Coughing is a very good sign for airway irritation and asthma.)

I then had Sarah perform a "peak flow" test during which she exhaled forcefully into a device that recorded how hard and fast she could blow out air. This number was then compared to statistical norms for her age and height. Sarah scored at the 40th percentile of normal for her age. (Normal would be more than the 80th percentile.)

I was almost sure by now that she had asthma.

Asthma is a disease of inflammation of the lung that produces an airway spasm that can be reversed to near normal with certain medications. Therefore, to make my diagnosis definite, I administered a medicine to Sarah through a nebulized aerosol. Afterward, I had Sarah wait for 15 minutes in the exam room. While she was waiting, I had my nurse escort the mom back to the examination room.

Upon my return, I repeated the peak flow measurement with Sarah. This time she scored at the 95th percentile, normal! The airway obstruction was reversible. By definition, Sarah indeed had asthma.

I showed the mom Sarah's tests, and I discussed with her my thoughts. Then, as I frequently did to confirm asthma therapy, I asked Sarah to go outside into the parking lot with her mom. She was instructed to RUN to the street and back and then come right back into the exam room through the door in the back of the clinic.

Both Sarah and her mom thought I must be nuts. However, I assured them that I had done this maneuver many times before; and she was safe. The pair then left the office for her parking lot run. I informed my nurse of our "experiment," which she knew quite well, and I asked her to fetch me as soon as they returned.

A few minutes later, Sarah came in smiling. She had run to the street and back WITHOUT GETTING TIRED! Her mother seemed perplexed. A repeat peak flow measurement showed no change in airflow, the 95th percentile.

Now that I had a diagnosis, we needed a plan of action to make Sarah better. I knew the medication I gave her in the office would last only a few hours, so I had to get Sarah started on a regimen of daily medication and lung monitoring using a peak flow meter. Sarah and her mother also needed to de-allergenize their home since a part of Sarah's issues may have been, and most probably was, allergies.

The mother wanted to know what all this was going to cost: they lived paycheck to paycheck; they had no insurance; they had no extra money.

I advised the mom that, "There was always a way."

Because Sarah had been ill for so long, I gave her cortisone, our best anti-inflammation drug, which she would take over the next four weeks. She would gradually decrease the dose until she was off the medicine entirely. (Thank goodness for cortisone, and it is dirt-cheap.) Additionally, Sarah was given an inhaler device called Proventil that contained the airway opener medicine. Finally, I gave her an antihistamine to try to control any allergies.

For their part, Sarah and her mom were asked to clean their home three times over the weekend. At least two cleanings had to be done using a Rinse-n-Vac rug cleaner they could obtain from the local hardware store. While they were still in the office, I called Paul Hubert at the local hardware store and discussed with him my patient's dilemma with funds. He agreed to allow the family to use a machine for the weekend as long as they put up a deposit.

The mom seemed pleased, surprised, and awed at his generosity.

The two promised they would do their part.

I asked Sarah and her mom to return to the clinic in one week for a checkup.

That afternoon, I talked with a drug representative whose company made a lot of products for respiratory disease. After he heard of my young lady's plight, he applied her name to their "in need" program. Sarah would be able to receive her medications for little or no cost as long as her family met the income guidelines.

The next morning, I talked to the junior high school principal. I asked him to monitor Sarah's performance for me, and report to me ONLY if she did not improve.

Thankfully, I never received that call.

When Sarah and her mother returned for her checkup, I could see from their body languages that things at home were better. Anything cloth in the house had been cleaned twice either with the Rinse-n-Vac machine or in their washing machine as I had requested. Sarah had taken her medicine as directed. She still had about three weeks supply of cortisone tablets remaining; she reported having no substantial adverse effects from it. Her breathing medicine seemed to be working fine. Her peak flow measurements were remaining above the 80th percentile all day. Sarah said she could walk up the stairs at school without getting tired. She had a better "attitude" in PE class.

Not much later, I met the P.E. teacher at a basketball game who informed me that Sarah was a new person. Her performance was "excellent." The teacher apologized to me for being so hard on Sarah.

I suggested that the apology be given to Sarah, not me.

The teacher said, "It had been. You are number two."

Sarah returned to being an "average" student. She was no longer late for class. Except for an occasional flare-up of her asthma, she did quite well physically the remainder of her 7th year in school.

The next year, the P.E. teacher noted some "promise" in Sarah's physical talents. She was encouraged to try out for some sporting events, like basketball and track.

She did try out fro sports. She performed well, in fact, very well. B the time of her senior year, Sarah had received conference honors in basketball and track and field. She was a runner-up in the sprint races at the state track meet.

At graduation, it was announced that Sarah had received both an athletic scholarship and an academic scholarship to attend a small liberal arts college.

Bruises

Tom, a 49-year-old farmer, had just come in from doing his daily fall fieldwork. When he took off his clothes to shower, he noticed some big bruises on his thighs and on a calf muscle. He had been pushing around some heavy pieces of equipment during the week, but nothing that he figured should have produced such large bruises. He could not recall anything occurring that day that was out of the ordinary. But again, he was a farmer. He was getting "banged up" all the time.

Tom called my home after supper to ask if he should drive the 40 miles into the emergency room that night or could it wait until the morning. Tom said he had been feeling "poorly" for five or six days. However, he had no specific complaints to speak of. He didn't have sweats, or chills, or body aches, or a cough. His appetite was good. He just wasn't quite right.

Since he did not act acutely ill and since he had been feeling "poorly" for about a week, I asked him to come to my office first thing in the morning.

He agreed.

The following morning Tom arrived as I had requested. Now, however, he had bruises everywhere. With a large bruise under his left eye, Tom appeared to me as though he had been in a fight. According to Tom, the bruises on his thighs and left calf had grown substantially overnight and now covered most of these areas. Additionally, he now had a large bruised area on his buttocks.

Tom also related that, "My urine was "plum red" this morning!"

Again, he denied any constitutional symptoms like nausea, chills, sweats, fever, vomiting, pain, etc.

In addition to Tim's observations of his skin, I appreciated many petechiae (small areas of bleeding) under the mucous lining of his mouth. His urine was essentially blood.

Thinking my patient had developed a clotting problem for some reason, I had him go to the lab for a complete blood count and blood clotting studies.

Dr. Joe Lasater, our local pathologist, summoned me to the lab. Joe told me, "This guy's got something real bad. What's the story?"

I gave Joe as much history as I knew.

Tom's platelets were critically low. His blood was not clotting. His white count was twice normal with 80 percent of the cells appearing malignant. Dr. Joe then asked me to look at Tom's slides with him. The slides were full of immature, nonfunctional white cells and NO PLATELETS (the cells needed for clotting)!

Before I talked to Tom and his wife, I called the hematology department at the Billings Clinic. The hematologist suggested that Tom come to Billings ASAP for platelets and an evaluation. Thereafter, I discussed with Tom and his wife my examination, his labs, and my discussion with the hematologist. They decided to leave as soon as they gathered some clothes and found someone to care children.

Afterward, I talked with Dr. Lasater. His comments for even a short-term survival for this patient were not encouraging. He knew Tom had an acute leukemia, but the specific type required some special testing of the blood.

Tom spent the next month in a Billings hospital with an acute leukemia episode. The hematologists were able to "slow down" his disease with the latest cocktail of anti-cancer poisons. Unfortunately, Tom had a multitude of severe adverse events occur during his treatment.

First, he developed what is called DIC, disseminated intravascular coagulation. (A disorder during which the body bleeds everywhere because it cannot make blood clots.) During this time, Tom suffered a brain hemorrhage resulting in a small stroke. He bled into one eye resulting in blindness in that eye. He had bleeding into his lungs that resulted in respiratory compromise and infections.

Second, he had a reaction to the chemotherapy medications that required immense doses of cortisone to try to control the side effects.

Finally, his heart electrical system stopped working, and he started to have fainting spells (potentially a bad problem when you can't make clots). He received a pacemaker to keep his heart beating.

Tom was sent home "in remission" with the hopes of better things to come. He would be receiving three more courses of "therapy" before he was done, *if he survived.*

The next course of therapy in a month went fine with no unexpected adverse events.

The third course of therapy produced more nausea and fatigue, but Tom's blood counts remained reassuring to the hematologist.

Eight months after his initial visit in my office, the oncologist told the family that Tom was "stable." However, he was depressed, he had minimal vision in one eye, and he had a pacemaker. In an effort to be positive, I suggested to Tom that "all was looking up."

His reply was, "I'm not so sure Doc."

About a week later, I saw Tom for what appeared to be a prostate infection. His blood studies were normal, and he had only a few pus cells in his urine. After consultation with the hematologist, I started Tom on antibiotics.

About five days later, Tom returned with resolution of his urinary symptoms, but now he had severe pain in his back. His urine was full of infection fighting cells, bacteria, and blood. This time, however, his platelet count had dropped off the map again. He had a relapse.

The hematologist wanted him to return to Billings immediately.

Once again, the hematology doctors attempted to control his leukemia flare. This time, however, their efforts were not successful. After 14 days of chemotherapy, Tom had another episode of DIC. This time he sustained a massive hemorrhage into his brain that produced profound and irreversible damage. He died the next day when Tom's wife had the ventilator turned off.

I thought afterwards that we physicians do a lot of awful things (therapy) to our patients knowing with reasonable certainty that the eventual short-term outcomes are poor to nonexistent. Yet we continue to perform these tasks with a "hope and a prayer," thinking that some of these patients, a rare few, might do well.

When our treatment efforts fail, we doctors hope others may benefit somehow from our efforts and our patients' suffering.

Tom's survivors were left with medical expenses over $300,000. Over his last eight months, Tom had about 30 "good" days. He clearly suffered for the other 200 days. Were our medical efforts valiant or just a waste of time and money? I guess it depends upon one's point of view.

Did I make a difference with Tom?

I wish I knew.

Leave Me Alone

Virgil was a man in his 70s who had spent his entire life on a farm in northeastern Montana. For several years before my first meeting with Virgil, his health and quality of life had been deteriorating. Physically he had suffered miserably the previous winter. His family brought him in during the early spring to be evaluated for nursing home care.

I admitted Virgil to our hospital for evaluation. He was a man of few words and obtaining information from him was at best challenging. However, Virgil was adamant that he DID NOT want to go to a nursing home. He noted that, "Everyone knows you just go to one of those places to rot and die! He would rather just die on the farm when his time came."

Besides having multiple infirmities associated with aging and a lifetime of hard labor, Virgil was diagnosed with depression, anxiety, and Parkinson's Disease, a disorder that added to his poor mobility and considerable joint stiffness. Additionally, he had vague intestinal complaints that probably were related to an irritable bowel disorder. His heart, lung, and kidney functions all appeared to be good for his age.

After Virgil had been in the hospital for several days and after I had discussed my evaluation of him with his family, the family members decided that he could not return with them to the farm. They made arrangements for him to become a resident at the local nursing home.

Despite our best efforts to assist Virgil in becoming adjusted to nursing home life, we failed. Over the next three months Virgil was readmitted to the hospital for vague abdominal pains and intermittent diarrhea. After a multitude of tests, my conclusions remained anxiety, depression, and an irritable bowel disorder.

After a rocky first few months, Virgil seemed to show some interest in his new way of life. His family members did not visit often, so he found new "family" and friends among the residents of the nursing home. Unfortunately, it seemed that whenever Virgil started to become close to another resident, that resident would die. Virgil would again become more depressed for a period of time. Virgil often noted that, "He should just die and be done with it all."

For about 18 months Virgil "just got by" at the nursing home. He did not say much unless he was having a lot of pain. He did what he was asked to do by the staff. From a nursing point of view, Virgil was a "good resident."

Just after lunch on a Thursday in late October, a nurse at the nursing home called me at home. She advised me that Virgil was lethargic, he had been having some belly pains all night, and it looked like he had vomited some blood after breakfast.

I asked the nurse to transport Virgil to the emergency room where I would meet him as soon as possible. When I arrived at the hospital, Virgil had not yet arrived. I thought to myself, "I drove five miles in to town faster than he came across the parking lot! What's wrong with this picture?"

When Virgil finally made it to the emergency room, he was in shock with a rapid pulse, a low blood pressure, and a poor mental status. He had dried blood around his mouth and on his shirt. It was obvious to me that Virgil was experiencing an acute gastrointestinal hemorrhage, most likely from an ulcer. I did not have much time to lose to get him stabilized.

The lab personnel were asked to obtain blood for a complete blood count, coagulation studies, chemistries, and blood typing with a cross match for eight units of blood.

While the lab techs were working, the nurse and I started two large bore intravenous catheters and gave saline as fast as we could to try to stabilize his vascular system.

After a short period of time, Virgil had received two liters of fluid. His blood pressure and pulse normalized. His sensorium improved somewhat. Further examination revealed a tender, firm abdomen with pain just below the right rib cage. A rectal exam revealed black stool that was positive for blood. These signs confirmed my initial diagnosis. I knew Virgil needed surgery to survive.

However, I also knew that Virgil did not want to live any longer. He had been miserable at the nursing home for a year and a half and wanted it all to end. I asked for the nurse to bring me his previous hospital records to look for his resuscitation requests. That is, was he DNR (do not resuscitate)?

Unfortunately, the family members had filled out the form with the nurses and wanted everything done.

I then asked for the nursing home records, which would have his DNR status as a routine part of his admission.

The chart came, but the form had never been completed. I was stuck. Legally, I felt I had to do everything I could to save this man.

It was now about 4 p.m. Our local surgeon was out of town. I knew that I did not want to dive into this man's abdomen alone, but he needed an operation. I did not believe he was stable enough to transport to another town. Therefore, I phoned Dr. Leonard Mark, the general surgeon in Wolf Point, Montana, a town about 100 miles away. I explained my dilemma to Leonard. He then asked me to hold on for a moment. After a very short time, he returned and said he could be on the road in 15 minutes. He would be in Sidney about 90 minutes later.

I told Dr. Mark to remember that it was 100 miles on a two-lane road.

He replied, "Don't worry. I'll be taking a nap. Jonathan will be driving." (Jonathan was a friend who frequently drove Dr. Mark.)

By the time Dr. Mark arrived, Virgil had been transferred from the emergency room to the intensive care unit. In addition to the intravenous saline, Virgil had received two units of blood. The operating room was setup; the surgical team was standing.

When Dr. Mark went in to meet and examine Virgil, he noted that the blood pressure was still a bit low. Leonard agreed with my diagnosis of an acute abdomen with a gastrointestinal hemorrhage. He said, "Let's try to stabilize him a bit more before we proceed."

Just as we turned away from the bed, Virgil vomited about two quarts of blood! Leonard then calmly remarked, "I guess he's stable enough. Let's get to it."

While Dr. Mark went to dress into surgical attire, I helped transfer Virgil to the surgical suite. Along the way, Virgil threw up blood again, but not as much as the first time.

The anesthetist asked us to hurry before Virgil lost the rest of his blood!

We complied.

Upon opening Virgil's abdomen, we encountered a massive amount of clotted blood. After most of this blood had been removed, Dr. Mark located a hole in the small bowel just past the stomach. At the base of the perforation was the end of a small artery pumping away. Leonard quietly stated, "I believe we have solved this mystery."

As Dr. Mark was suturing the vessel to control the bleeding, the anesthetist noted that the blood pressure was pretty low.

Leonard calmly said, "Be patient. Give him some more fluids, and he should be better soon."

By the time the small bowel perforation had been closed, the abdomen had been cleaned out with a lot of saline, and the abdominal wound had been closed, Virgil's vital signs stabilized.

Dr. Mark stated, "I guess we're done here. Another life saved! I'm hungry. I'll spring for dinner for the whole team."

After a very late dinner, Jonathan drove Dr. Mark home that night.

I assumed the postoperative care, but I gave Dr. Mark a daily progress report.

When Virgil became more alert, he questioned me why I just did not let him die. I tried to convince him that I felt legally bound to do my best because he had not filled out the appropriate forms.

After about a week, Virgil went back to the nursing home. This time his nursing home chart stated "DNR."

About three months later, Virgil was admitted to the hospital with intestinal complaints of pain and intermittent diarrhea. He and I agreed that there would be no heroic efforts on his behalf. Despite a difficult time in the hospital, Virgil got better once again without much treatment.

He wanted to know why we wouldn't just let him die.

A short time later, I was called to the nursing home after breakfast. The nurse told me that Virgil had died during the night from a gunshot wound.

I asked incredulously, “Are you sure?”

She reaffirmed with, “I’m positive Dr. Jimmie.”

I promptly drove into town and walked directly to the nursing home adjacent to my office. Virgil’s room was at the end of the corridor, and the room farthest away from the nurse’s station. The nurse and a police officer met me at the door to the room.

Virgil was lying peacefully in his bed with his face up, eyes closed, and a bullet hole in the center of his forehead. A .22 caliber pistol was lying on his bed by his right hand.

The nurse remembered that the previous night Virgil was watching his favorite movie, *Shane*, on the television. The nurse related that Virgil seemed to be in very good spirits that last evening. By the nursing report, Virgil told the night nurse that he would go to sleep after Shane rode off into the sunset one last time. The night nurse figured that Virgil would be fine for the night. She denied hearing anything unusual coming from his room. But again, what is the sound of a small pistol compared the noises of a nursing home?

I guess Virgil figured I was never going to help him to die, so he found a way to help himself.

How he got the gun nobody knew.

For the rest of my career, I made sure that my patients’ end of life wishes, not their relatives’ wishes, were recorded promptly in their charts.

Appendicitis

About 10 o'clock one morning a woman brought her 10-year-old son into the clinic because, "He said he had a sore belly." The mother stated that her son was known to "tell stories" so he would not have to go to school. This morning, however, he seemed different. She figured he was faking again but wanted to make sure.

The mother related that her son had been vomiting for two days and had been eating poorly. She did not know if he had a fever. She then told me the family had no extra money for doctor bills.

The boy was obviously ill. He was in his clothes curled up in a ball on the exam table holding his abdomen, but not complaining. His vital signs included a temperature of 101 degrees and a rapid pulse. My examination of the boy's head and neck area revealed only a dry mouth. Except for a rapid heart rate, his heart and lung exams were unremarkable. When I pushed on the right lower part of his abdomen, the boy groaned. I was unable to straighten his legs because of increased right-sided abdominal pain. The boy displayed the classic signs for acute appendicitis.

I advised the mother of my diagnosis and recommended that her son have an operation as soon as possible to remove his appendix. I reassured her that he was not faking this ailment.

After a short discussion, the mother acquiesced, and I made arrangements for the boy to be admitted to the hospital. I then called the operating room. The operating room supervisor told me they were having a slow morning, and I could perform the surgery over the noon break.

I told her I would be there as soon as I could after my morning clinic.

The supervisor said they would have my patient ready.

I started the surgery about 12:30 and had no difficulty removing the boy's inflamed, gangrenous appendix. As I was closing the abdomen, I felt pretty proud of myself. I had saved a life this day.

It was my practice after an operation to sit at a nearby desk to dictate operation notes and to compose post-operation orders while the surgical team performed their duties getting the patient ready for transfer to the recovery area. It was my practice to assist the team with the patient transfer from the surgery table to the recovery gurney.

While I was writing my notes, the surgical tech summoned me to the operating room by waving her arm. Without speaking, she pointed to the young boy's backside.

There were numerous linear welts, open sores, and scars of various ages on his back, buttocks, and legs.

My jaw dropped open.

"How did I miss those?" I said to myself.

In response, I said, "Because you examined him with his clothes on you dummy!"

The surgical tech and I cleaned the wounds and bandaged the open areas before the boy was allowed to go to the recovery area.

After the surgery, I told the mother that the surgery went well, and her son should do just fine. I did not mention the back lesions. Because I had to be back in my clinic soon, I figured I would discuss the subject later. In the interim, I had an obligation to inform the authorities of my suspicion for child abuse, which I did.

That evening I told the mother that I suspected physical abuse of her son and showed her the wounds that had been uncovered. I informed her that the police had been informed and would be talking with her and her husband in the morning. Additionally, I told her that her son was under the legal custody of Child Protection Services and could not leave the hospital without their consent.

The boy left the hospital several days later recuperating just fine from his appendectomy. He was discharged to the care of an anonymous court-appointed guardian where he would remain until the legal issues surrounding his abuse were completed.

I never saw the boy or his parents again.

OH THOSE MOMS

"With what price we pay for the glory of motherhood."

Isadora Duncan

"The moment a child is born, the mother is also born.
She never existed before. The woman existed,
but the mother, never.
A mother is something absolutely new."

Rajneesh

Bonus

Anne came to the hospital near her due date in the mid 1970s after her bag of water ruptured at home. This was her fourth pregnancy. Her previous three pregnancies had been unremarkable by all accounts. By the time Anne and her husband had made the 30-mile trip to town, she was in a good labor pattern.

Anne labored uneventfully and was taken to the delivery area when she felt like pushing.

Without much difficulty, Anne pushed out a healthy female infant.

Afterward I noticed her abdomen had not gotten much smaller.

I checked the vagina and sure enough there was a butt! There was a bonus baby! Anne was going to deliver twins!

I asked if any of the nurses had heard two heart tones while Anne was laboring. The answer was, "No."

I recalled marking Anne's obstetric record with two heart tones early on in her pregnancy, but I had not heard them since. Since Anne's abdomen had not gotten unusually large during the pregnancy, I assumed that I was mistaken. (This was in the era before ultrasounds and fetal monitors were available at our hospital.)

I had delivered breech babies before. In fact, my very first delivery was in a migrant tent years before where I helped a Mexican migrant lady deliver a 9-pound breech baby with the skillful hands of a veteran obstetrician guiding my way.

I opened the second bag of water with an instrument and carefully extracted the legs one at a time. After some gentle manipulation and proper positioning of the baby's arms, shoulders, and head and with some gentle, but firm, pressure on the mom's abdomen provided by the attending nurse, a baby boy was born a few minutes later.

The baby came out a bit stunned, but after I gave him a few puffs of mouth-to-mouth ventilation, he was crying just like his older sister.

After the two placentas (afterbirths) extruded spontaneously, and a small laceration at the outlet of the birth canal had been repaired, Anne was returned to her room. Her babies were taken to the nursery.

Our nursery, like all nurseries, has a viewing area with a large window. When babies are born, it seemed that all the hospital staff, the visitors, and the hospital patients who were able made a pilgrimage to this area to see nature's new creations on display.

While I was in the nursery writing notes in the new babies' charts, I overheard someone say, "Ah, twins, a boy AND a girl! **I wonder if they are *identical*?"**

In a serious tone, another voice chimed in, "Can't tell yet. They have to wait until the lab checks the afterbirths!"

AWOL Mom

The day was a Thursday. I remember this because it was my usual day out of the office, and I was supposed to be irrigating my fields. It was about 5 o'clock in the afternoon. I had just completed helping a lady deliver her baby, and I was at the obstetric floor nursing station completing the usual post-delivery paperwork and dictation. The nurse said to me, "Dr. A. I have a phone call for you from the Poplar ER."

Poplar is a small community located about 70 miles northwest of our town. It is part of an Indian reservation. The Indian Health Service usually employs the physicians working there.

On the phone was a male who identified himself as a physician who had the "duty" for the day. He said he had a female Native American patient in his ER who was in early labor. She had no prenatal records. He informed me that he was an internist. This doctor told me that he was willing to attempt a "natural" birth, but this baby was backwards! He was definitely not comfortable trying to assist this lady with a breech birth. He went on to say he had no backup, either from anesthesia or a physician. He wanted to send the lady out before HE got into trouble.

I agreed to the transfer.

I asked the nurse to keep me posted about when the ambulance left Poplar and their estimated time of arrival. I figured that the ambulance would arrive in about 90 minutes. Therefore, instead of driving the five miles to my home, I went to the medical records department to complete some more paperwork.

An hour passed. I had completed my records so I went back to the obstetrics wing to ask the nurse for an update. She related that the hospital had not yet received any communication from the Poplar ambulance.

"That's odd," I muttered to myself.

I asked the nurse to call the Poplar hospital and find out when the ambulance left their facility.

She complied and soon reported, "They left about 5:15. The hospital said we should have received a call from them by now."

The nurse and I started wondering what happened to the ambulance. I asked the charge nurse to call the Poplar ambulance directly since our EMS system had their ambulance radio frequency.

The nurse made the call. There was no reply.

She called again. There was no reply.

The nurse and I started to think something was amiss. We notified the sheriff and the highway patrol of the ambulance that may be missing. Since it was time for the nursing shifts to change, the oncoming staff was informed of our missing ambulance and patient.

About 10 o'clock, the hospital received a call from the Law Enforcement Center. They advised us that all the law enforcement personnel between the two towns had been searching for the ambulance, and it WAS NOT along the highway. They were going to expand the search to off highway roads, but this was going to take quite a while.

Since I wanted to be available when the ambulance arrived, I decided to stay at the hospital for the night. I called home to let my wife, Kay, know of my plans.

Around midnight, the emergency room received another call from the law enforcement center. They were calling off the search for the night; they would start the search again before sunrise.

I thanked them for their efforts and wished them a "good night."

Soon thereafter the ER nurse called me. She said, "Dr. A. The Poplar ambulance just called. It will be here in 5 minutes."

I thought, "What the...?"

The ambulance finally arrived, and the patient was "deposited" onto a hospital bed by the Poplar EMTs. They were all drunk, including the patient! One EMT told us they stopped off at a bar near Brockton, a small town about 50 miles away, to "have one for the road."

That was seven hours ago!

The ambulance driver told us they were going to "catch a few winks" before they drove home.

I asked the nurse to notify law enforcement pronto.

My patient was indeed pregnant. My best guess was that she was about 38 weeks by her size. She was somnolent from the booze, and barely arousable. The fetal monitor showed no uterine activity! My pelvic exam revealed A HEAD!

I said to myself, "This baby is not breech, and probably never was!"

Since the patient came with no prenatal records, I asked the lab to draw prenatal labs *and* a blood alcohol level.

The woman's labs were fine except the blood alcohol level was0.34 percent. 0.1 percent was legally drunk and 0.37 percent was supposedly coma and death.

If this lady had been in labor, the alcohol had stopped it. If she had been drinking like this her entire pregnancy, I knew the baby had a good chance of having fetal alcohol syndrome.

For now, I decided to let the patient "sleep off" the booze and to let Mother Nature take its course afterward.

I went home to sleep.

The patient's labor started about 6 a.m. By 10 a.m., she pushed out a screaming baby boy head first weighing about eight pounds.

The mom told us that this was her fourth baby, each one by a different father. The other three kids had been taken away from her by Child Protection Services and were in foster care.

After the delivery, I called the Poplar hospital to talk with the referring physician who thought this lady was having a breech baby.

I was informed that he went off duty at 6 p.m. the night before, right after he had transferred the patient, and he was on vacation!

Child Protection Services was notified of the circumstances surrounding this delivery.

This mom went home the next morning with her family, but without her baby.

Stella

I was called to the hospital late in the evening in July to see a lady from Glendive, Montana who was in labor. Her name was Stella.

I had seen Stella on one previous occasion as an obstetrics patient. She had a C-section with her first child and wanted to attempt a VBAC (vaginal birth after C-section). The physicians in Glendive were unwilling to allow her this option. They believed in the old adage of, "Once a C-section, always a C-section."

About this time, VBACs had become popular in America in an effort to decrease the number of operative deliveries in America. However, there were certain restrictions and boundaries under which a VBAC was considered to be a safe option for selected patients. I supported and had attended VBAC births. My success rate was about 85 percent.

I always presented the patient with my list of "automatic stops," those situations for which a VBAC was not considered safe. I gave Stella this list at our first visit. She agreed with them and wished to proceed with a potential VBAC delivery.

When I arrived at the hospital, the front desk personnel were gone for the day. Therefore, I made my way to obstetrics instead of the emergency room. Stella was in bed having what appeared to be vigorous labor with its attendant discomfort. The nurses had obtained her vitals signs. The baby's heart tones seemed fine. She was contracting about every three minutes.

My internal examination revealed a male child who was breech! Stella's cervix was almost completely dilated. She was ready to deliver this baby!

A breech was "way out of bounds" for a VBAC. Stella and I both knew the "rules.

Almost immediately I went to the nurses' station and had the staff call for a STAT C-section. I meant NOW!

I went back to see Stella to advise her of OUR predicament. Having a breech presentation was one of the automatic stops, and I thought she should have a C-section as soon as possible.

Emphatically, she said, "No!"

I implored her to change her mind.

The answer was still, "No." She said, "I am not having an operation."

I asked the nurse to talk with her.

Stella's reply remained the same.

By now, the anesthetist and the surgical team had the operating room prepared for surgery and were waiting. I informed them about the patient's decision. I asked them to be ready in case I needed them.

Our time was very short. Again, I advised Stella that I thought she should have a C-section.

Again, she said, "No!"

Stella was taken down the surgical corridor. Instead of turning right into the operating suites, we turned her bed left into the delivery area. As we passed by, I asked the OR team to come with us "just in case."

As Stella was being placed onto the delivery table, the baby's heart tones dropped. Fortunately, the baby's butt was ready to come out. With assistance rendered by Dr. Wilson, who had come in to assist, a baby boy was delivered without much difficulty for a breech. The baby was floppy, not breathing, and did not have a detectable heart rate.

Dr. Wilson said, "Oh, damn!"

I asked the nurse to care for the mom while Dr. Wilson, the anesthetist and I took care of the baby. I started to ventilate the baby, but this was not producing a heartbeat.

The nurse called out, "First Apgar is zero!" (The Apgar scoring system to evaluate newborns at birth was developed Dr. Virginia Apgar in 1952.)

While Dr. Wilson continued with chest compressions and the anesthetist assumed the ventilation duties, I asked the nurse for some cardiac epinephrine.

The chest compressions were halted temporarily, and I injected epinephrine directly into the baby's heart. Dr. Wilson restarted the chest compressions.

Within moments the baby had a pulse. Chest compressions were continued until the heart rate was above 80 beats per minute. Ventilation was maintained, however. The nurse called out, "Apgar at five minutes is three!"

The baby was floppy, but alive. While the resuscitation efforts continued next to me, I directed my attention to Stella. I manually delivered the placenta, checked for lacerations both externally and inside the uterus, and decided that Stella could safely return to her room.

By now the nurse called out, "Apgar at 10 minutes is 6!" This meant that the baby had a heart rate above 100 (2 points), some spontaneous respiratory effort (1 point), some color other than pale blue (1 point), some limb motion (1 point) and some reflexes (1 point). It became apparent that the resuscitation was going to take some time, and the baby was going to require newborn intensive care.

The regional newborn ICU in Billings was notified, and they mobilized their flight team. I inserted an endotracheal tube into the baby's windpipe since I anticipated his requiring long-term ventilation. We continued to assist the baby's ventilation while we waited for the transport team. Additionally, an intravenous catheter line was inserted through the umbilical vein.

I went back to Stella's room to update her on her baby boy's status. I found her sitting up in bed smoking a cigarette and apparently doing just fine. I told her that her son would soon be transported to Billings for special care, which she appeared to understand.

The transport team arrived, "packaged" the baby for transport by putting him on their mechanical ventilator, and took off to Billings.

I received a telephone call from Billings after the team had arrived. Except for some issues with the ventilator, which required a nurse to hand ventilate the child, the trip went well.

Stella left our hospital the next day to be with her newborn in Billings. She was given my usual post partum instructions and was asked to return to see me in three to six weeks. She never returned.

I did not receive a discharge note from the Billings ICU. I assumed all had gone well with the baby's care. I soon forgot about Stella and her baby.

I received a notice three to four years later from an attorney in Great Falls, Montana; Stella was suing me for a "failure to perform a C-section!" I was shocked, astonished, and dismayed all at once.

I reported this letter to my liability insurance company, and I was assigned to an attorney in Billings for my defense.

After all the records had been obtained and the attorney and I had several meetings, we went before the Montana Medical-Legal Panel. I prevailed 6 to 0. Before we left the building, however, my attorney was advised that Stella and her attorney were going to proceed with litigation. They were not interested in a settlement. They wanted a trial.

My attorney continued to reassure me about the positive points of the case. In fact, he did not think they had a case. "But," he said, "You can never tell what a jury will do!" These words stuck with me and haunted me daily.

I reviewed the records many times. Each time I came up with the same conclusion: I would not have done anything differently.

Initially, the trial was to be held in Sidney, the town of the reported injury. However, my attorney called me one day to inform me that the case would now be tried in Federal Court in Billings. Apparently, Stella's attorneys had advised her to move out of the state to improve her chances in a Federal jurisdiction. She moved her family to Bismarck, North Dakota from Great Falls. Her son continued to receive care by pediatricians in Bismarck.

Over the next year or so, legal documents and medical records seemed to be coming from all directions. One of the court documents stated that Stella wanted 64 million dollars! I panicked. After I talked with my attorney, I was assured that sum would never be allowed in Montana. However, if I did lose and if that was the amount I had to give them, I would be bankrupt forever!

Not long afterward, my attorney called to say he had received the records for Aaron, the child, from the Q&R Clinic in Bismarck. Those records specifically stated that Aaron had brain damage directly related to *meningitis* that he had suffered as an infant while in Great Falls. We knew that we needed to obtain those documents.

The Great Falls records noted that Aaron was doing well until he had bacterial meningitis. *Afterward*, he developed substantial neurological problems.

I thought I was home free. The case could be dismissed with this new information, I assumed. The attorneys "discussed" the two sets of records indicating meningitis was the culprit for Aaron's issues. Stella's attorney just re-filed the complaint with a requested monetary settlement of 16 million dollars.

The days and weeks and months passed as my attorney and I prepared for my day in court. I gave my depositions. I was present at all the other depositions, and there were plenty of them. These activities took me away from providing care to other patients. My court date was now only several months away.

My attorney called one morning and said brusquely, "Your insurance company just fired me. They're bringing in a high profile guy from Idaho. His name is Quinn. I don't know anything about him. They will contact you." He then hung up.

I was just dazed. This was yet another twist to an incredible legal mess.

The next day I was called by Mr. Quinn's office. He wanted to meet me in two days to go over my case. He attempted to change the court date to give him more time, but the judge said no. Their team would have to work quickly.

I met with Mr. Quinn's team of attorneys in Sidney. This time I had a team of three on my side. We had meetings on three successive days. At night, the team was pouring over the records while my anxiety levels mounted. I tried anything to get my mind off this "adventure," but nothing really helped.

My team reported to me that they had to find medical experts on my side. They had to find and interview a lot of people as witnesses who included Dr. Wilson, who had since moved back to Canada, the surgical team, the nurses, and anyone else they could find who had contact with Stella during her stay at the Sidney hospital. They would keep me updated on their progress with intermittent phone calls and meetings.

Out of the blue, I received a call one morning from an unknown male. He asked, "Is this Dr. Ashcraft?"

I replied, "Yes it is. How may I help you?"

He responded, "Are you the one in a lawsuit with Barnhard as an expert?" Dr. Barnhard was a "pediatric neurologist" at the Q&R Clinic in Bismarck who was the "expert" for the plaintiffs.

I said, "Yes."

The man asserted, "Barnhard did not pass his Boards! Just tell your attorney that Barnhard did not pass his Boards. He will know what to do." He then hung up.

I promptly called Mr. Quinn's office and talked to one of the team members. I was thanked and told that they would "look into it."

Stella's attorneys wanted two weeks to present their case. Judge James Battin allowed 10 days for the entire trial. My team told me it was going to be a "stretch" to get everything done.

My wife, Kay, and I went to Billings several days before the trial was to begin. I went over the records again, and again, with the team. They informed me of the witnesses they had brought in for my defense. Also, they needed to "prepare" me to give my testimony.

I was told our case was strong, "BUT YOU CAN NEVER TELL WHAT A JURY WILL DO!"

The trial proceedings started with the selection of a jury and alternates, which took the first day. That night the legal team and I reviewed more documents. Mr. Quinn pointed his finger at me and said, "Tomorrow, YOU put on your game face!"

The trial started with each side offering comments. Stella's attorneys called as an "expert" an administrative nurse from Great Falls. There was an immediate objection from my team. After a behind doors consultation with the Judge, this lady was not allowed to testify. My attorney informed me that in her deposition, this lady stated she had no obstetrics experience and that she was better than any doctor. The Judge decreed that she was not a peer of a family physician and not an expert of any kind!

Stella took the witness stand next. During her testimony, she admitted that she and her husband had arrived from Glendive about 6 p.m. They drove around town until she had "pushing" pains before they went to the hospital. She had planned all along not to have a C-section.

The next day, we heard from a physical therapist economist who detailed the potential future costs of the care and equipment the damaged child would require. Additionally, we heard from a host of therapists that explained in laborious detail Aaron's physical and mental deficits.

The next day, Dr. Barnhard took the stand. He described to the jury in graphic detail how awful I had taken care of Aaron. He stated that, "It is malpractice *not* to intubate a baby *before* it has a chance to breathe!"

I assured my lawyer that was impossible.

Mr. Quinn started by asking Dr. Barnhard about his training and certification as a pediatric neurologist. Dr. Barnhard said he practiced pediatrics and neurology in Bismarck, North Dakota. He was asked if he was Board Certified. Dr. Barnhard stated he "had not yet obtained the requisite test scores."

Mr. Quinn then said, "What you are telling this Court is that you FLUNKED your Boards!"

Dr. Barnhard responded, "I have not obtained the requisite test scores yet."

Mr. Quinn pressed on asking, "How many tests have you passed?"

The reply was, "There are five parts to the Boards. I have attained the requisite score on two."

Mr. Quinn responded, "You have received the "requisite scores" on two of five tests. You flunked the tests in my book!"

After a few incidental queries of the doctor, Mr. Quinn asked Dr. Barnhard to review his notes regarding Aaron. Specifically, he wanted the court and the jury to know what his notes stated about Aaron after his examination on a specific date.

Dr. Barnhard read his dictated notes to the court. Essentially, he noted that Aaron's deficits were a direct result of a failure to perform a C-section at the time of birth.

Mr. Quinn asked the date of that notation. When Dr. Barnhard responded, Mr. Quinn pointed out that our set of records and those that went to the Medical-Legal Panel showed that HE, Dr. Barnhard, had recorded in the medical records on the very same day that Aaron's neurological deficits were a direct result of *bacterial meningitis*, not birth trauma! Mr. Quinn wanted the good doctor to explain the "apparent" discrepancy to the court.

The doctor could not. *He had been caught falsifying his records.*

Judge Battin interrupted by telling the two attorneys that the proceedings would be halted until the matter was clarified in his mind. He then ordered the records from the Q&R Clinic be obtained that day.

After a several hour delay, Stella's attorneys explained to the Court that, "The records can not be found. They are missing from the medical records department."

Before he was allowed to vacate the witness stand, Mr. Quinn reminded the Court that Dr. Barnhard had FLUNKED his Boards, AND his own records appeared to have been altered, AND the original records could not be found!

The plaintiff's final "expert" was an 82-year-old obstetrician who, when questioned, admitted that I had done everything by the book. However, he said, even if the woman refused a C-section, "He would have held her down and cut the kid out!"

Mr. Quinn asked the obstetrician about informed consent, and the patient's right of choice.

The doctor said it was not relevant in this case.

My defense consisted of a neonatologist from Boise, Idaho and a family physician from Choteau, Montana. Both stated that I had performed quite well and appropriately under extreme circumstances.

I then took the witness stand. Over the next two days I relived over and over again the events that occurred during the 45 minutes before Aaron's birth and the subsequent resuscitation efforts. I spent about 10 hours testifying, and my story never changed.

On the final day of defense, Mr. Quinn called Evelyn T. Lawrence to the stand. E.T. was the nursing aide who was assigned to Stella after her delivery. She described in vivid detail how she remembered that Stella was not upset. Indeed, she recalled that the lady was quite proud of herself for delivering her baby naturally, even though the baby was seriously ill.

I wanted to jump on the stand and give her a hug.

The next day the court and the jury heard the closing arguments. About 11 a.m. Judge Battin excused the jury to deliberate.

Mr. Quinn said we should go out to lunch, so we did.

Gary, one of the attorneys on my legal team said, "Well, it will be about two hours or two days."

By 12:30 we were called back into the courtroom.

After all the parties were assembled, Judge Battin asked, "Has the jury reached a verdict?"

The response was, "We have Your Honor."

As we stood up, Nancy, one of my attorneys, grabbed my hand tightly.

The jury foreman handed a slip of paper to the court clerk who read, "Not guilty!"

One cannot believe the rush of relief that came over me. I had to sit down to compose myself.

Judge Battin thanked the jury members and then dismissed them.

The trial was over.

Mr. Quinn invited Kay and me to a celebration dinner that evening. He ordered a bottle of Dom Perignon champagne that came in its own box. The bottle of beverage was consumed that evening; Kay and I kept the bottle and box as keepsakes.

Before the trial had started, I learned from my attorneys that the St. Vincent Hospital had already given the family $600,000 for the in-flight "ventilator mishap." Dr. Wilson was not implicated because he lived in Canada. The Sidney hospital had put in an additional $200,000 for reasons I would never understand.

The child had been receiving Medicaid payments for his medical bills for a long time. I learned that all the money the family received from litigation had to be used to repay Medicaid. Consequently, I believe they may have ended up worse off than when they started.

When I returned home, I phoned Dr. Bryan Salvino, the neonatologist in Bismarck. I told him about what I had learned about his backup pediatrician, Dr. Barnhard, and what he had said in court under oath.

Within a week, Dr. Barnhard was no longer practicing in North Dakota.

I have been told winning this case cost me "nothing."

But, I did pay a price. The income lost from multiple weeks not working plus my office expenses, the cost of paying for a replacement physician, and the mental stress of almost four years of legal activity. And, perhaps the worst of all, my liability insurance premium doubled.

I won, but I lost.

However, I could have lost more, much more.

I would not, I could not, view my patients, my colleagues and hospitals with the same trust ever again.

Rosa

I met Rosa when she arrived at our emergency room in labor. She was a 17-year-old Mexican girl who migrated with her family yearly from Eagle Pass, Texas to perform various tasks in the local sugar beet fields. She, like most other migrant workers I encountered, had received no prenatal care in Texas. Upon arriving in Montana, she qualified immediately for Medicaid funds to pay for her medical care.

Rosa was admitted to our obstetrical area in active labor. Since she spoke no English, the hospital staff had retained a middle-aged female family member to act as an interpreter.

Rosa performed admirably during her first labor experience. Our interpreter seemed adept at keeping Rosa informed about what was occurring and maintaining her composure. Rosa was transferred to our delivery room at an appropriate time. Without any analgesia and in total control of her emotions, Rosa pushed out a baby like she had done it before.

The nursing staff and I were impressed.

After I had made sure the newborn was stable and doing well, I checked to see if Rosa had incurred any lacerations during the delivery. She had not; all was going well.

After a few minutes, Rosa had some abdominal cramping as the placenta, or afterbirth, was being expulsed. All of a sudden, she started to kick and flail and screamed to high heaven. The interpreter tried to console her, but was not successful. The nurse attempted to keep Rosa from kicking, but she was tossed aside with ease by an out of control leg. I just attempted to avoid being kicked in the head.

The placenta extruded from the birth canal, and Rosa became uncontrollably hysterical.

We were all wondering what in the world was going on. Our interpreter was no longer useful.

The nurse told me that the patient's vitals were stable. I saw no excessive bleeding. All was good, I thought. Rosa started crying uncontrollably and screaming profanities at me between sobs, *in English!* I had not a clue what she was experiencing—or why?

The nurse and I cleaned up our patient and prepared to transfer her back to her room. When we attempted to place the new child in Rosa's arms, the screaming and the crying intensified.

Rosa's emotional tirade continued all the way down the hallway enroute toward her room. As we passed the nurses' station, our Hispanic ward clerk politely asked, "What did you do to her? She's saying that she can't have any more babies!"

I told her I did not have a clue. Everything was textbook. I thought the delivery had gone well.

The ward clerk advised me that our interpreter was not very good. Apparently, she spoke a different dialect and was making mistakes.

On the spot I recruited the ward clerk as our new interpreter.

The ward clerk patiently spent about 10 minutes conversing with our patient in her hospital room. Afterward, she came out smiling and almost ready to laugh.

At least Rosa was no longer raising the dead with her screams. I was curious to know what had happened in the delivery room.

The ward clerk said the interpreter had told Rosa that she could no longer become pregnant when the afterbirth came out. Rosa thought the placenta had to stay inside so her next baby could have a spot to latch on to. When the placenta came out, Rosa thought I had sterilized her!

Using pictures that were available from my office, the ward clerk was kind enough to explain to Rosa the "facts of pregnancy" that same day.

Thereafter, Rosa wanted her newborn. And all was good once again.

I assisted Rosa with three more births over the next four years when she returned to work in the sugar beet fields of Richland County.

Simple as ABC

On the day before the Independence Day holiday in 1987 I was covering patients for the other physician who shared office space with me. One of the patients I saw that day was a delightful lady named Denise who was about 10 days past her "due date" with her second child. Except for being "overdue," Denise was doing just fine.

Many physicians become quite anxious when a lady goes past her estimated delivery date and want to "take control." However, "officially," according to the literature, being "overdue" means being at least 42 weeks gestation by good measurements or dates. I was always a "foot dragger" when it came to pregnant ladies until they had reached 42 weeks gestation unless there was a darn good reason to hasten a delivery. Then I would become more aggressive in trying to get the baby delivered. Over 30 plus years in practice, I *had* to induce a patient's labor for post dates only once.

I was once told by what I considered a wise and experienced obstetrician that, *"The best place for an obstetrician during labor is locked in a closet so he can't mess with Mother Nature."* I took this pearl to heart over the years.

Since I had just met Denise, I discussed my philosophy regarding post-dates pregnancies with her. Apparently, she came to our office because of our "hands off" type of obstetrical care. An obstetrician who wanted to induce her labor early had managed her first pregnancy. She prevailed and delivered her first child at 41+ weeks. She did not want to see that obstetrician again.

Denise went into labor several days after our visit and gave birth to a gorgeous female infant weighing almost eight pounds. The hospital staff and I always found it rewarding to attend a birth where everything went well, the parents loved their new baby, and the mom did a great job. Denise did a great job!

Denise's usual physician had returned by her first post delivery visit, so he resumed her care.

I did not have the opportunity to see her again for more than two years. By then, her previous physician had moved on, and I was in my office once again as a solo practitioner.

Just after Labor Day in 1989, Denise came to my office for an obstetrical visit. She had always had regular menstrual cycles and "knew" when she had gotten pregnant. She figured that she was about "three months along." She had given birth to two children previously without incident. She was healthy, she took no drugs, and her home life, though hectic, was stable.

My examination of Denise on this day, however, was not that of a "normal" pregnancy at 12 weeks gestation; her uterus was far too large.

Under these circumstances, only a few things can be amiss: the mother's dates are off for some reason, the uterus has a tumor of some sort, or there is a multiple pregnancy in the uterus. Before the days of the ultrasound, physicians had to wait until the baby's bones had enough calcium to show on x-rays or just wait until the mom delivered her infants. Obstetrical ultrasound allowed us to delve into pregnancies and fetal growth like never before. I requested an ultrasound to determine the gestational age of Denise's pregnancy.

About five days later I received a call from the radiology department. The ultrasound technician asked me to come over to see "something interesting" on Denise's ultrasound. Since I was always interested in learning, I promptly made my way to the hospital for my educational experience for this day. (The hospital was part of our medical complex and not far away.)

The ultrasound tech sported a smile from ear to ear; Denise had a glassy eyed stare.

I asked, "What ya got?"

"TRIPLETS!" was the reply. "TRIPLETS!"

I looked at the ultrasound monitor with bemusement. There they were, three little ones about 14 weeks by size and all doing well. Anxiety then attacked me. I thought to myself, "Now what do we do?" Denise and I had to have a long discussion about this pregnancy. I knew I needed to talk to a perinatologist, a specialist in complicated pregnancies.

Denise was to take her news home, digest it with her husband, family, and friends, and return to see me in a short time. I, in the meantime, had my homework to do.

When Denise and her husband came to see me about two weeks later, they were still in disbelief. Despite viewing the ultrasound several times, they remained "shocked." They had wanted a third child. They did not expect three at once.

I lead a discussion about multiple baby pregnancies. The more babies you carry, the more complications you anticipate. It is that simple. If a singlet pregnancy produces 10 complications, then twins may have 10 x 10 or 100 complications and triplets can expect 10 x 10 x 10 or 1000 complications! Obviously, with a potential for a marked increase in problems, closer surveillance would be needed with this pregnancy. This would mean more clinic visits, more tests, and more expense.

I told the pair that I delivered babies, but I was a family physician, not an obstetrician. His office was across the hall, and he may be the better physician to provide her care.

Denise was quick to reply that she did not want to see him, nor did she want him to touch her! They would place their faith and trust in my staff and me.

Denise was advised that I had contacted a specialist in Great Falls, Montana about her. He thought that as long as she was doing well, Denise could continue her visits near home. At the first sign of trouble, however, the specialist would be like to see her. I agreed to talk with him after each visit to compare notes.

The pair was advised that the theoretical chances of her having her babies in our hospital were at best 50:50, but more realistically they were 20:1 against. I suggested to Denise that she should discuss her situation with her employer because she would probably require more breaks, more time off for rest, etc. I suggested that the pair become familiar with support groups and literature about multiple births. (I always figured the more the patient knew, the easier my job became and the better things went.)

Denise and her husband seemed to understand what I had said and were willing to go along with "the plan." However, because of family issues, Denise requested to be sent to Bismarck, North Dakota if a transfer became necessary. This certainly was a reasonable request. All I had to do was find a perinatologist in Bismarck.

Bismarck, North Dakota did not have a perinatologist. However, there was a local obstetrician who cared for most of the high-risk moms. I contacted him, related Denise's story to that point in time, and asked for his suggestions. His response was, "You're doing just fine. Just keep me posted." He agreed with everything the perinatologist had told me. I now had two consultants.

Initially, I saw Denise about every two weeks. When she was about 30 weeks pregnant, I planned to see her every week until she delivered, or more often if she had complications. At each visit, Denise and I discussed "the plan," that is, what would occur if things started to look adverse for her or her babies. At each visit Denise would look at me, smile, and say I worried too much. The fact was that I knew too much, I had experienced many bad things with multiple births, and, as a rule, I was a conscientious "worry wart." Denise knew that we both were in uncharted waters.

Except for a few minor issues, Denise's pregnancy progressed according to the best of all possible plans. She continued to work until near her due date. Except for getting tired easily, Denise never complained. Multiple ultrasound examinations of the babies showed "normal" progression of growth. I even made special trips to Denise's place of work to talk to her coworkers and her supervisor. They always confirmed that except for her enlarging tummy, Denise was always the same, quiet, considerate person and in good spirits.

My consultations with the specialists were always encouraging, but the rules were the same: Transfer at ANY HINT of trouble. This concept was reinforced many times with Denise. As time passed, she became more convinced, at least to me, that she would not have to leave town. Denise would just tell me, "Doctor, You worry too much!"

An x-ray evaluation at 36 weeks showed three babies, all head down and ready to come out. The radiology tech said it looked like "three little soldiers all falling in line."

By now, the entire town was "expecting." Frequently, when I was in town, a fellow citizen who wanted to know how Denise was doing would stop me on the sidewalk or in a store. She had become the talk of all the ladies in the local banks. A local lady, who also had delivered triplets in another town about 30 years before, came in to visit with me about her experience - on several occasions!

At the 36-week mark, I informed the medical staff and the hospital staff about the possible impending delivery. They were advised to be "ready just in case she goes into labor in town." All these folks were given updates after each clinic visit. Multiple nurses canceled vacation plans so they could be available IF something happened. They just wanted to be part of something very special IF it occurred.

On the morning of Friday, March 2nd, Denise came to the hospital after her bag of water had broken at home. She was at 38 weeks gestation, full term for triplets. She was not having severe contractions. The first baby's head was in her pelvis and ready to come out.

I contacted the consultant in Bismarck who was ready to take the mom in transfer. The parents and I reviewed Denise's status and "the plan" one last time. I related to Denise and her husband all I knew at the time. I advised the pair that since Denise was not in active labor, NOW was her last chance to be transported.

Denise just looked at her husband and then to me. She said with a smile, "We've done pretty good so far. I'm staying."

I sent out the word that Denise was in the hospital and that she was not leaving town for her delivery! Each baby would require a team of three *just in case*. In short order, I heard back from the nursing staff that EVERYONE was available. All the available physicians were ready as well, except for the obstetrician. He came in like a mad hatter! Between his expletives, he said he did not know anything of this "nonsense!" He asserted, "No woman with triplets has a RIGHT to deliver in a small hospital like this!" He then stormed off to, "talk to this woman."

We were all taken aback by his actions. The obstetrician returned within a few minutes all sweaty and flushed. All he said was, "When can I do MY surgery?" as he looked at the surgical team members.

They didn't reply right away. Then one of them said firmly, "When we're done here, doctor."

I was asked to go to see Denise immediately afterward. The nurse said she was quite upset. Upon my arrival in her room, I could see that Denise and her husband were really upset. Denise was crying. Apparently, the obstetrician had behaved most unprofessionally with them, and his language was abusive according to the nurses. Denise said, "Don't you let that man near me again!"

I told the pair that the obstetrician was the one with the most experience in these matters, and he should be available if he would. After a few moments of reflection, Denise agreed. But she did not want him to say one more word!

All this commotion had started Denise's labor in earnest. She was transferred to the delivery suite.

In the meantime, someone from the surgery team had a "discussion" with the obstetrician and told him to *"get his head out of his ass and help this woman!"*

He showed up a few minutes later in a scrub suit ready for work.

The delivery room was stuffed with two people from anesthesia, four operating room assistants, three people for each baby, Denise, dad, the obstetrician, my assistant, and three sets of instruments. There was an overflow crowd outside the door of perhaps ten nurses – just in case.

Within a very short time, Denise was completely dilated. The baby's heart tones slowed so mom was placed on her left side. The babys' heart tones normalized.

The first baby came out without any problems. It was a girl. I named her baby "A."

After the umbilical cord had been clamped and cut, baby A was handed to her awaiting team. Her Apgar scores were 7 and 8. Excellent!

The head of the second baby was also pointed downward. The amniotic sac (the sac enclosing the baby) was intact. The obstetrician asked if he could assist. He ruptured the amniotic sac and manually rotated the head for delivery, and then he got out of the way. Unfortunately, the rotation placed the head in a face up position instead of face down. Denise pushed the second baby out without any trouble anyhow. It too was a girl. I named her baby "B."

After the umbilical cord had been clamped and cut, baby B was handed to her team. Her Apgar scores were 7 and 8. Fantastic!

The head of the third infant was down and ready to come out. The bag of water was ruptured, and this time Denise was allowed to do all the work herself. Baby number three came out after a few pushes. It was another girl. I named her baby "C."

Again, after the umbilical cord had been clamped and cut, baby C was handed to her team. Her Apgar scores were 7 and 8. Simply amazing!

The babies' weights were: 6 pounds, 6 ounces, 6 pounds, 4 ounces, and 6 pounds, 3 ounces. That was almost 19 pounds of baby!

The massive placenta was extruded a few minutes after baby "C" was born.

Denise had no extra bleeding and all was good, very good!

I said, "Thanks to you all for your help!"

A round of applause for Denise, her husband, and their three new babies followed.

The obstetrician got up, walked over to the operating room supervisor, and said abruptly, "I'm ready to do MY surgery now."

The reply was, "We're going to take a break." "We'll call you when *we're* ready."

I called the consultants to let them know the outcome. The perinatologist told me, "You just made history. Family docs just don't deliver triplets in this day and age, especially full term ones!"

I told him that mom did all the work, and I did all the worrying.

On the fifth hospital day, Denise and her new family were doing well and went home.

Later on, we found out that the triplets were identical, a rare occurrence indeed.

Denise made sure that my office received picture updates of the threesome as they grew up, which I placed in a display case in my office.

At high school graduation, the girls were all at the top of their class. Baby "C," Chelsea, had a 4.0 average. Baby "A," Allison, and baby "B," Bridget, each received a single "B" grade in high school. They all received scholarships for college.

Over the years I tried to find the odds of a family physician delivering triplets at term naturally. I found that I was the only recorded family physician to deliver triplets in Montana in 30 years. Not one family physician in Montana had since been so fortunate *to even try*.

The odds of my delivering identical triplets at term were estimated to me to be *at least* one chance in a million births!

Impossible

Abigail Knutson was a 34-year-old lady who presented herself to my office in the morning one early-fall day complaining that she just did not feel right. She had been experiencing intermittent nausea with occasional vomiting for about a month "for no good reason." She had no complaints of fevers, chills, diarrhea, body aches, or respiratory symptoms that would suggest an infectious problem. She denied food intolerances and abdominal pains.

During our interview Abigail interjected spontaneously that her female cycles had always been painful and erratic, and "*I can't get pregnant!*" She added that she and her husband had tried for 10 years to have a baby, but were not successful. She had undergone three operations and many tests to find a reason for her infertility. Apparently, she and her husband had been told by a fertility gynecologist in Billings no more than three months before that they should consider adoption if they wanted children. Abigail related that this physician had informed them that "her tubes were scarred shut," and her husband "did not have enough sperm to get her pregnant anyway."

To me, Abigail's symptoms sounded like the classic signs of early pregnancy. I inquired if her breasts were "different" in any way.

She replied that her nipples were more tender than usual.

I asked if I could do a few tests to help me sort things out.

She agreed.

Before obtaining a blood sample, I asked my nurse to perform a urine pregnancy test. As I suspected, the test was positive.

When I gave Abigail the "good news" that she appeared to be pregnant, her response was, "That's impossible!"

I offered for her to repeat the test for herself.

She said she would like that.

Therefore, I asked my nurse to facilitate Abigail's performance of her own urine pregnancy test. The result was the same, POSITIVE.

Abigail sat in the exam room in disbelief. She kept saying, "How can this be? How can this be?" I didn't know if she was happy, sad, or just plain shocked.

Because Abigail's last menstrual cycle was unknown, I had no exact clinical way to find out how far along her pregnancy was. Also, with her history of "scarred tubes," I knew the chance of her having an ectopic pregnancy (a pregnancy outside the uterus) was increased. Therefore, I suggested that she obtain an ultrasound of her uterus to see "what, if anything, was going on down there."

She agreed, but first she had to tell her husband, Dale. Abigail wanted her husband to be at her side when the test was done.

An obstetrical ultrasound was completed over the lunch hour. Abigail, escorted by her husband with the ultrasound pictures in his hand, returned to my office in the early afternoon. The pictures revealed an intrauterine pregnancy at about eight weeks gestation. I explained the ultrasound pictures to the pair; I estimated Abigail's due date and asked what they wanted to do next.

They had no idea. They were stunned!

I explained in entry-level detail how I usually provided obstetrical care, but I remarked to the pair that the specialist in Billings certainly could follow them. They related that they just needed some time to digest the events of the day. They would get back to me after they made a decision.

Several days later, the pair returned to my office. They had overcome the initial shock of the pregnancy. Dale informed me that they had become resigned to the fact that adoption was their only option to have a family. Now everything had changed essentially overnight. They were overjoyed.

Abigail stated that it would be silly to go back and forth to Billings for care.

Dale asked if I would be his wife's obstetrician.

I agreed.

I had a more extensive discussion with the pair about the potential pitfalls and hazards of pregnancy in general; with her gynecologic history, Abigail might have a more risky pregnancy. I asked my nurse to start a new obstetrical record, to obtain the usual prenatal blood tests, and to arrange for another visit in about a month.

I asked Abigail if she wanted me to inform her fertility doctor about her pregnancy.

She said, "That would be a nice thing to do."

The next day I called the obstetrician in Billings to give him the "good news." After I spoke, he retorted firmly, "That's impossible!" and hung up the phone.

I surmised that I must have called him at a bad time.

As the time passed, my concerns about Abigail having a complicated pregnancy proved ill founded. She breezed through the pregnancy without a single abnormal event. Abigail gave birth to a healthy female child near her due date the "natural way," without any drugs or assistance.

In the delivery area, I took Polaroid pictures of the newborn girl, the mom and new baby, and the new family together.

Afterward, I sent one of the pictures and a short note to the obstetrician to let him know that all had gone well.

Within a few days, I received an envelope from the obstetrician. He had the picture returned. On the back was written in bold capital letters "JACKASS!"

I figured that he thought I was trying to upstage the "expert," or he just didn't appreciate being reminded of his mistakes. Either way, I decided this man was just a real "poop." He must have forgotten that "Mother Nature always wins!" or "You can't fool with Mother Nature!"

About 11 months had passed when Abigail came to my office feeling "funny" again. The "infertile" woman was pregnant again. Abigail and Dale were ecstatic beyond belief. Now they would be blessed with two children.

Another seven months went by quickly, and Abigail delivered another healthy female.

Another year passed before Abigail came in bearing her THIRD pregnancy. She was now almost 39 years old. Once again, the pregnancy and the birth went according to Mother Nature's plan. This time a healthy baby boy was the result.

The day after this delivery Dale and Abigail appeared concerned. They were worried that somehow the "infertile woman" and the "infertile man" had become "Fertile Myrtle" and "Fertile Fred." They had decided their family was large enough, and the baby factory "that was not supposed to be" had to be shut down.

I discussed the possible options for temporary and permanent birth control. Together, they agreed they wanted a *permanent solution.*

The next morning I tied Abigail's fallopian tubes, and, over the noon break, I performed Dale's vasectomy.

They said they wanted a permanent solution, and *they meant it!*

Not To Be

In a late summer of the early 1980s I had a young lady come to see me for prenatal care. Her name was Miranda, and she was 26 years old. She came to our community from Georgia with her fiancé who worked for an oil company. Miranda had the gracious personality one would expect from a southern belle, and the delightful accent to match.

At the time of our first visit, Miranda was about 14 weeks pregnant. Miranda was terribly concerned for her pregnancy because she had already experienced six spontaneous miscarriages around six months of gestation. She obviously had no problem getting pregnant, but she certainly had difficulties holding on to the pregnancies. She was what physicians would label as a "habitual aborter."

My examination of Miranda was essentially normal except for an enlarged uterus that verified her pregnancy and its approximate age.

An ultrasound confirmed the pregnancy to be about 14 weeks.

I offered to have Miranda seen by a perinatologist, an obstetrician who specialized in high-risk pregnancies.

She declined because of her limited finances and the distances she would need to travel.

However, I informed her that I would consult a specialist and together we could put together a plan of care for her.

She replied that she would appreciate all we could do for her and her baby.

At the time, newborns were not considered viable until they were born after at least 26 weeks of gestation. Before that gestation, medicine did not have much to offer except drugs to stop premature labor and to fight infections. Miranda appeared well aware of the "rules for premature births" because she had experienced them six times before. Together we hoped for and planned for a term pregnancy.

Miranda came to my office weekly for evaluations as my precautionary measure. My hope was that if some correctable abnormality occurred, then perhaps I could intercede promptly. At least that was my hope. It was *our* hope.

For the next 10 weeks, Miranda managed her pregnancy well. She remained positive. She was gracious and thankful for everything that anyone did for her and her baby. She got plenty of rest. She remained active, but not overly so. She ate well. Her relationship with her fiancé was blossoming by the day.

Just after Christmas Day, Miranda came to the hospital in the middle of the night having mild contractions. She was just 24 weeks pregnant, a borderline gestation for her baby's survival. My examination of her revealed no obvious infection, but I started her on antibiotics anyway. She would remain on the medications until culture reports had been completed after three days. Her pelvic exam also revealed a closed cervix to her uterus despite her contractions. Therefore, I started Miranda on a drug to abort her labor.

Fortunately, the contractions abated promptly, and we just had to monitor her condition thereafter.

Miranda remained in the hospital three days without contractions. Her cultures were negative for an obvious infection, so the antibiotics were stopped. I was cautiously optimistic that with labor control medication at home, Miranda's pregnancy could continue a while longer. And it did.

Miranda resumed her weekly evaluations. Over the next four weeks, she did not have a single problem. Her cervix remained closed. My optimism for having a good outcome for this pregnancy increased with each passing week.

Just 24 hours after our last visit, Miranda came to the hospital in mild labor. The medication to abate her labor either was no longer effective at the current dose, or it was not going to work anymore. When I evaluated Miranda, her cervix was dilated to 3 centimeters. (Full dilatation of the cervix for a term infant is a diameter of about 10 centimeters. However, for a now 28-week baby, 6 or 7 centimeters would be a full dilatation.) I decided to attempt to slow down the labor again, but I knew that Miranda needed to be in a high-risk newborn center if her baby was going to have the best chance for survival.

I contacted Dr. Bryan Salvino, the neonatologist in Bismarck, North Dakota, to arrange for a transport. I had utilized Dr. Salvino's services many times over the years, and we had an excellent working relationship. After our discussion, Dr. Salvino thought it would be better and faster for him to come to the baby because of the late hour of the day and because the February winter weather was not good. He asked that I arrange to take the baby out by Caesarean section to minimize its stress and bruising.

I assured him we would be ready when he arrived.

I discussed my plan of action with Miranda who consented. I knew that this scenario had been rehearsed in the hospital before, but this would be the first time our hospital team would get to put all the pieces together for real.

While Dr. Salvino was making the one-hour flight to our community, I mobilized the surgical team and the nursery team. Miranda was taken to the operating room and prepared for surgery before Dr. Salvino arrived with his neonatal transport team.

About 6 p.m. Dr. Salvino and his assistant arrived without fanfare. He introduced himself to Miranda and told her that he was there to take care of her baby as best he could.

In her normally gracious way, Miranda thanked him for braving the elements to help.

Dr. Salvino asked us to allow him about five minutes to set up his equipment before we started.

I told him I would not start until he gave us the O.K.

When Dr. Salvino affirmed that he was ready, I asked for an O.K. from the anesthetist who reminded me, "Gently, Doctor, Gently!"

Carefully, I opened Miranda's abdomen, then her uterus, and then I carefully extracted a very small female baby.

Dr. Salvino took the baby from me for his resuscitation efforts while I continued with the operation.

Before I had completed closing the abdomen, Dr. Salvino came to the operating table and said, "Jim, the baby is just too bruised. It can't survive."

Mentally kicking myself, I responded, "I was as careful as I know how."

He replied, "I know, I was watching. This baby was bruising BEFORE it came out. She's just too early. She didn't have a chance." He then leaned over to Miranda and said, "I am sorry. We did everything we could."

Miranda's response was, "You people have tried harder to save my baby than anyone ever has. I thank you." Dr. Salvino then handed Miranda her infant daughter. Miranda held her baby until well after death had occurred.

I completed the operation. After Miranda was observed in the recovery area for a short time, she was transported back to her room.

Dr. Salvino left as soon as he knew the mother was fine and after he bid her farewell. Before departing, he complemented our medical team for its efforts, and expressed hope that our next meeting would have a happier outcome.

When a baby dies in a small hospital the mood of the entire staff can be awful for days. Such was the case the following morning when I made rounds on the obstetrics wing. My patient depressed, and so were the nurses. As I reviewed Miranda's chart that morning, I noted that it was her birthday. I decided on the spot it was time for a PARTY! A combined birthday, Valentine's Day, cold winter's day, pick everyone up party! That afternoon and into the night there was an all-comers gathering in Miranda's room with cake, ice cream, treats, and a huge birthday card for all to sign.

If nothing else, the festivities made me feel better!

After recuperating for several more days in the hospital, Miranda was ready to go home. Before discharging her, I asked her to see me in about six weeks for a final post operation checkup. Miranda informed me she would be gone by then. Her fiancé had lost his job as the oil field business was slowing down. They would be heading home to Georgia in about a week.

She thanked the staff and me for all we had done, and had tried to do, for her and her baby, and the PARTY! She promised to see a doctor as soon as they got home.

As she departed, I wished her my very best.

I learned a few weeks later that Miranda and her fiancé did not make it home to Georgia. They were killed in an automobile accident while driving during a winter storm somewhere in the Midwest.

After some reflection, it appeared to me that the worst things in my job seemed to happen to the best people.

An Experiment

Soon after starting my medical practice, I developed an expanding obstetrical practice. This happened for several reasons. First, the physicians in my community and in the surrounding communities were aging and eliminating obstetrics from the services they provided. Second, the regional oil boom brought in a lot of younger workers and their families who were having children. Third, the new employees for the hospital were mostly right out of training and of childbearing age. As these employees settled in the area, they too were starting families.

I met Mary for the first time in the summer of 1977. She came to see me because "I was the new guy in town," and because she did not want to go to her local doctor in a nearby community for fears of "small town gossip." Mary had already experienced three early miscarriages in the past two years that had been attended by her local physician. Despite supposed medical confidentiality, "her whole life story was known by every Tom, Dick, and Harry in the town."

She was pregnant again and afraid of having another miscarriage. If that were to occur, Mary did not want anyone, except her husband, to know. She thought that her current pregnancy was about "six weeks along."

Mary voiced additional pressures from her husband and his family to produce a son to maintain the family lineage. Apparently, this social pressure was far more than subtle nudging. Her husband's friends, their spouses, and even neighbors were apparently questioning her about, "When she was going to have "that boy!" When she had a miscarriage, instead of condolences, she was confronted with "You blew it again." or "What's the matter with you?" or "Looks like you're one heifer he'll have to put out to pasture!" Mary said she truly loved her husband. She thought that if she could have a baby boy then all would be as it used to be between them.

I knew that if Mary had already experienced three early miscarriages, then she might be one of those women who had difficulty maintaining a pregnancy past 12 weeks of gestation. Unfortunately, medical wisdom at the time suggested that nothing could be done to prevent this phenomenon. Some doctors called this problem "perpetual blighted ovum syndrome." However, I knew that some research was being done with hormone manipulation in the early part of pregnancies in women like Mary.

I confirmed a positive pregnancy test. I confirmed the estimated duration of the pregnancy by taking a history and performing a gynecologic exam. I then asked Mary to return in a few days after I had an opportunity to talk with some of the physicians doing the research regarding frequent miscarriages.

She agreed.

Over the next couple of days, I had our medical records librarian obtain as many articles for me as she could, and I spoke with fertility specialists at three medical schools. The field of hormone supplementation in early pregnancy was in its infancy and there were no concrete studies to guide them or me. However, there was a suspicion that early miscarriages may be caused by a failure of the ovaries to produce enough hormones. Specifically, it was thought that the lack of the hormone called progesterone was the culprit. The specialists did not know how much, how often, or how long the hormone supplements should or could be used. But they all thought that progesterone hormone supplementation *should work.*

Essentially, this meant that I was on my own.

Mary returned a day early because she started to have some spotting, just like before. After another positive pregnancy test was confirmed, I talked with Mary about my investigation. She wanted to try the hormone because "she had to do something."

Soon thereafter, I gave Mary an injection of progesterone. A recommended dose was unknown, so I gave what I considered a substantial amount. Additionally, I gave her a prescription for the hormone in pill form to take daily. I asked Mary to call me daily to report her status.

Mary called the next day and reported her bleeding had stopped. She still felt pregnant too. She called the next day, and the next, and daily for a month and reported no adverse symptoms or signs, except those of pregnancy.

I saw Mary again when she was about 12 weeks pregnant by her dates. Her examination was normal and her uterus was the appropriate size for a three-month pregnancy. Using my unicorn fetoscope, I heard heart tones. Unfortunately, this apparatus did not allow Mary to hear the sounds. However, I asked my nurse to confirm my findings, and she did.

Mary wanted to know how long she should take the pills. I told her I did not know. However, I knew that the placenta took over the hormone production for the pregnancy between 12 and 14 weeks. I rationalized that taking the hormone supplements up to 16 weeks should give us a "buffer." After I explained my thinking, I asked Mary to continue the pills for another month.

Another month went by and Mary still had no problems, so she stopped the hormone pills as I had requested. Nothing happened. She had no cramps, no bleeding, nothing!

We were both pleased to say the least.

Mary's pregnancy continued to term with the delivery of a viable, 8-pound 11-ounce baby boy. Mary was overcome with joy. The father and the relatives seemed pretty pleased too.

A little over a year later, Mary returned again with an early pregnancy. She had some mild spotting, and wanted to use the hormone therapy again.

I concurred.

Once again this maneuver worked. The hormones were stopped at four months just like before. This time, Mary presented her husband with a healthy female child delivered at term as an early Christmas present. It seemed to me that all was good in Mary's world once again.

Unfortunately, just a few days later which was the day after New Year's, I saw Mary in the emergency room. She reported being beaten by her husband after she walked in on him and her best friend together *in her bed in her home.* She said her children were "safe" with a neighbor who worked for Child Protective Services.

She filed a complaint against her husband, and he had been put into jail.

The husband's family was literally "up in arms" against HER. (Apparently, they thought their daughter-in-law *deserved* a beating or worse.)

Mary felt forced to obtain a legal restraining order against her husband and his relatives to protect herself and her children.

Soon after he was released from jail, Mary's husband filed for divorce for "irreconcilable differences." He apparently had been working on a divorce with an attorney for months before the last baby was born.

Mary's *best friend* filed for a divorce from her husband at about the same time.

The divorce was finalized a few months later; Mary's ex-husband left town with his latest new lady friend – who, by the way, was NOT Mary's ex-best friend!

For the next two years, Mary struggled financially and emotionally while trying to raise her two kids by herself. She refused to have any contact with her ex-husband's clan. Since her parents had died, she was alone except for a few friends.

Then one day in a local park, she met a former high school classmate who had returned to the area to manage the family farm. As Mary put it, "He just fell in love with my two kids; and ME TOO!" Soon the pair married and moved out to his farm.

Together they would have one more child.

I had the opportunity to see all of Mary's kids grow up and graduate from high school.

Terror

About an hour after Julia had an unremarkable delivery of a large healthy baby she started to bleed from her uterus. Postpartum (after delivery) bleeding is not uncommon, and the obstetrics unit nurses are acutely watchful for this problem. Usually, massaging the uterus from the outside along with some medication easily controls the bleeding.

When Julia started to bleed, the nurse on duty administered intravenous oxytocin (a drug that makes the uterus muscle contract) and massaged her uterus. The bleeding abated a short time, but soon resumed with a vengeance. That was when the nurse summoned me to the bedside.

When I arrived the nurse had already expressed about 500 cc (about a pint) of clot from Julia's uterus. I expulsed an additional 1000 cc of clot, and the bleeding persisted. The uterus would not clamp down to control the bleeding despite more medication and my *vigorous crushing massage!*

Having been in this situation before I anticipated more problems. While Julia's vital signs were stable, I was able to insert a second intravenous line for fluids and medications.

Julia then had multiple profound uterine and abdominal contractions that literally shot blood out of her vagina. Some of the blood hit the bathroom wall some eight feet away, and a lot of it hit me. Her blood pressure dropped to below 60 systolic (120 is normal) and her pulse became barely perceptible. She had gone into shock! I estimated that she had lost about 6 units of blood already, and the bleeding had not stopped! (A human body usually has only 12 to 15 units of blood.)

I told the nurse we needed some blood NOW!

She asked, "What type?"

I knew my patient did not have the one-hour time frame for the lab to make sure the blood was totally compatible. I also knew that the hospital did not stock 10 units of blood of any one type. I had to make a quick decision. I yelled out, "RED!"

The nurse responded, "What doctor?"

I repeated, "RED! If its blood, I want it all NOW!" I knew if my patient survived I would have to deal with the consequences of my giving incompatible blood later, but at least she would be alive.

I asked the nurse to call the obstetrician to come to obstetrics STAT for a possible emergency hysterectomy.

The nurse returned after paging the doctor. She announced that he was 50 miles away at an outreach clinic, and he could be here in about an hour.

I did not have an hour. I feared my patient might be dead by then.

The lab tech arrived with the blood and said, "You will have to sign some forms for extraordinary circumstances."

I said, "Later. Now, I want the blood."

My patient was now unconscious with a blood pressure of 50. I could not feel her pulse. I was afraid she was going to die before my eyes!

I remembered that the pharmacist had been making some prostaglandin (a chemical that produces uterine contractions) suppositories for the obstetrician so he could induce labor. I asked the nurse to have two suppositories brought now to the room.

As I continued to vigorously massage Julia's uterus, two nurses were squeezing blood bags to get blood into her veins as fast as possible and a third was monitoring the intravenous line with saline fluid with medication. A fourth nurse was taking vital signs while a fifth was recording the events.

Within a few minutes the suppositories arrived. I inserted one into the rectum and one into the uterus. We all continued our tasks and hoped for the bleeding to quit.

After another 5 to 10 minutes, the bleeding stopped as abruptly as it had started. Julia's blood pressure gradually increased to 60, then to 80, then to 100. She had stabilized. She was arousable but not coherent.

The obstetrician arrived about 20 minutes after Julia stabilized. He noticed five nurses and one doctor covered with blood. He looked around the room to see the blood all over the walls. He said, "Looks like you've had one helluva day. I've been there, and I know how you feel. I'm around if you need me." He then departed.

We observed Julia in her room until an intensive care bed could be mobilized. She was then transferred to the intensive care unit.

I had no idea what was going to happen since I had given Julia blood that was not her type. I knew that the body's reaction to the foreign blood could also kill her, especially if she had received incompatible blood before. But for now she was alive!

I stayed in the ICU that afternoon and night. Julia was intermittently delirious. Her body temperature rose to 107.5 degrees despite being on cooling blankets and being packed with ice. Her vital signs remained stable otherwise. Fortunate, she had no more bleeding.

To my surprise, the fever resolved in the early morning.

The blood count the next morning was satisfactory. The blood smear did not show any anomalies.

During her "60 minute adventure," Julia received eight units of blood, 3000 cc of saline fluid, and a lot of medication. I estimated that Julia lost about 80 percent of her blood volume in about 30 minutes

The subsequent day Julia's body was "even." That is, her blood count and her vital signs were back to where they started. She remained stable thereafter.

I questioned Julia later about her recollections of the resuscitation episode and her time in the intensive care unit.

She had no definite memory of the events. She vaguely recalled being "cold."

All she knew was that when she woke up she got to hold her beautiful baby girl!

GIVING BACK

"From what we get, we can make a living;
what we give, however, makes a life."

Arthur Ashe

"No one has ever become poor by giving."

Anne Frank

"I feel that the greatest reward for doing
is the opportunity to do more."

Jonas Salk

Tickets

Within a few months of moving into our new home in the country in 1976, it became obvious to my wife, Kay, and me that we were definitely "under equipped" to take care of our property. The 18-inch electric lawn mower that we had was no match for the weeds. Besides, it took hours to get the grass mowed just around the house. We still had two more acres that needed our attention.

We had very few extra dollars, but early the next spring Kay and I decided to "bite the bullet" and purchase a lawn and garden tractor sold by Montgomery Wards. Additionally, we bought a blade, a mower, wheel weights, and a heavy-duty tiller. We knew that we were no longer without "the right stuff."

Along with the machinery came an extended warranty, which proved to be a blessing. We beat the dickens out of that mower and tiller while getting our piece of prairie into shape.

After my first mishap with our new tractor/mower, I took it to the Sidney Carburetor and Electric garage to perform the needed repairs. These folks provided the "authorized service" for my warranty. I left the machine and was given instructions to return the next day.

The following day I returned, and I met Harry Ronigen, the owner, who loved to talk. He informed me that my tractor was the first Montgomery Ward mower he had ever worked on. He said it was also the easiest to work on. Harry questioned me about my job, how I liked the town, etc. He also filled my ear about himself, some history of the town, and how nice it was to have new faces in the community.

A month or so later I damaged the tiller again. (That creeping Jenny was tough stuff to kill!) Once again I was at Harry's shop. This time, the repair could be done promptly, so I waited. I was reading Harry's wall materials (to keep my perpetually restless mind entertained) when I came across an advertisement for the Shriners Circus that was coming to town soon. The advertisement was to purchase tickets so kids could go to the circus for free. I never got to go to the circus as a boy, so I thought this was a grand idea.

Harry was one of the local Shriners. When I asked how to buy tickets, he looked puzzled. He wanted to know why.

I thought this was a bit odd since all the Shriners wanted to do was to let kids have some fun. I told him I would buy a book of 10 tickets for $10.

He was response was, "Are you sure?"

Before I could ask him about the problem, Harry informed me that the doctors in town and the hospital administration had made it known to the area businesses and clubs, in no uncertain terms, that there would be "no solicitation to, or anywhere near, them!" According to Harry, their position was, "This town is just lucky to have us. We do enough for the people of this town. Don't bother us!"

I started to laugh. I replied, "You're kidding me, aren't you?"

Harry replied, "No, they are quite serious. The Shriner's received one nasty letter from the medical staff. They did not plan on getting another."

I thought that position was ludicrous, and I told Harry so. To prove my point, I ordered 100 tickets.

I believe I shocked Harry. But, he smiled, retrieved my tickets, and took my check.

I asked him how to distribute the tickets.

He noted that I could give them out to kids in the office, take them to the schools, or leave them with him. The Shriners would make sure they were used.

I decided to let Harry do the work.

I then loaded my repaired tractor onto my pickup and headed home.

I mentioned my ticket purchase to Kay, but I did not give it much thought. I just thought I had done my good deed for the day.

About two weeks later the doctors held their monthly medical staff meeting. These meetings, as a rule, were mundane at best. However, on this day, one of the physicians related he had been to a Kiwanis meeting. He had heard that Dr. Ashcraft had purchased tickets for the circus. Now "they," meaning the local businessmen, wanted all the doctors to "pony up." He was visibly upset. He stared at me and wanted to know what I had to say.

Before I spoke, another physician informed me about the unwritten "*do not participate*" rule in town.

I informed the medical staff and the hospital administrator that part of "my" job was to be part of the community. I could send kids to the circus if I wanted. As far as I knew, America was still a free country!

The first physician responded with, "You just don't know what you've done."

The rest of the meeting was boring as usual. However, the attitude of my "colleagues" made me mad!

The next day I went down to Sidney Carb and Electric. I bought another 100 tickets from Harry Ronigen. This time, however, I gave the tickets out myself!

Kay and I went to the circus with our kids and found Harry handing out his tickets as promised. He mentioned that the hospital administrator bought 100 tickets too!

I invited Harry to come to my office *anytime* to help kids.

Over the ensuing years, Harry and I had a fruitful relationship for the Shriners. Our medical staff supported multiple screening clinics for birth defects. Our local Shriners were instrumental in obtaining orthopedic care for several local children we identified in our clinics.

Kids from various groups started to come to my office for financial assistance through all types of fundraising efforts, and over the years they just kept coming.

My staff knew that if the kids did the soliciting, they were never refused.

A Place to Walk

I had been in practice about a year and a half. There were now just two of us in the clinic after three other physicians had departed for various reasons, and we were profoundly busy! One day in the late fall the weather was horrendous. Winter weather had arrived two months before and stayed. My partner had taken the weekend off to visit his relatives in western Montana; because of an ice storm, he was unable to return home that week. I, therefore, got the "opportunity" to see all of my patients and all of my associate's patients until he was able to return.

My last patient just before lunch had a note on the chart that said, "Heart check." The receptionist told me this fellow was "one of the richest men in town, and he had his hands in everything!"

I was not sure why she told me this, but she did. As I entered the room, I introduced myself and apologized that my partner could not be in the clinic to see him.

He said quietly, "His absence is understandable considering the weather."

This fellow was mild mannered, soft-spoken, and profoundly courteous. Certainly, he was different from the impression of him I had inferred from my receptionist's comments. He went on to say that he had recently suffered a mild heart attack and had a coronary artery bypass done in Billings several months before. He was now following his cardiologist's instructions to get a checkup monthly for six months. This was his first checkup outside of Billings.

I reviewed the man's records from Billings and noted that he was to be in a cardiac rehabilitation program. When I asked him if he had signed up for cardiac rehab at our hospital, he informed me that there was no program locally.

I asked him how much exercise, particularly walking, he was doing daily.

He said he had been walking down the country roads until the weather changed. Since then, he had been walking for an hour twice daily inside the local Safeway store. He then said, "Its kind of embarrassing when you walk all that time and don't buy anything. I feel that people are just watching me because I have been sick. I am really not a public kind of person."

I was intrigued with this gentle man so much that we spent the entire next hour talking about a variety of topics. The topic that he was most interested in, however, was finding a way to have a place that people like him could exercise inside during the cold weather. He was not talking about right away, but some day.

I did not have the opportunity to see this man professionally again. However, I started to think about all my patients who could use a place to walk in the winter: the folks suffering with arthritis; the people who had surgery or heart attacks; patients who had orthopedic problems; my list seemed endless. For whatever reason, I started to investigate the possibilities of finding such a place.

I talked with the local schools, but they were not interested in sharing their facilities with the public except for city league basketball on Sundays.

I asked the County Commissioners if one of the seldom-used buildings at the fairgrounds could be remodeled for a walking facility. There was no discussion. The answer was "No!"

I inquired about using the Army Reserve building since it was used mostly on weekends. I was told "the type of activities I envisioned would not meet the scrutiny of the Department of Defense."

I talked with the powers to be at the hospital who told me "only if insurance would pay for it." I was further admonished with, "This is a hospital, not a health club! We take care of sick people!"

Everywhere I turned someone always had a "good reason" *not to do it*.

My interest in the idea of a winter walking facility waned because of a public lack of interest and because of the increased demands upon my time by the oil boom that was going on at the time.

With the oil boom, however, came a need for more doctors and a larger clinic facility, which meant more useable space indoors. I signed up to be on the committee to build a new clinic because I just knew that a walking area could be put in the basement of the new 14-suite clinic building.

I was shot down yet again. A full basement in the new clinic building was eliminated to cut costs. The new clinic opened in 1980.

In 1979, the hospital's emergency room proved to be too small and inadequate for the volume of trauma patients we were attending. Therefore, a major 20,000 square foot addition to the hospital was planned with a foundation capacity to add four floors on top, if needed. Throughout the planning and building process I continued to inquire about "What goes into the basement?"

The hospital administrator told me that a new dietary section was going there.

However, the dietitian and the architects kept telling me a new kitchen was impossible because *no elevators* were planned.

The hospital addition was completed in 1981. The basement remained empty. There was *no elevator.*

I approached all the hospital board members at their meetings and individually outside of their meetings about making a winter walking place for OUR patients and OUR neighbors in the new, unoccupied basement. My ideas fell upon deaf ears and cold shoulders time and time again.

One day, I asked Pete Orville, the hospital's maintenance supervisor, to allow me to look into the basement to see what could be planned. He warned me that there was only a ladder for entry into the basement and only a single light. I had to promise to be very careful.

I promised.

As we were heading toward the door that would lead us into the basement, Pete said, "You know this basement is classified as a "*crawl space*" by the State of Montana so the hospital can comply with some silly Medicare rules."

After we went through the door, the supervisor lead me to an opening in the floor with a steel ladder leading straight down into a dark abyss. He said, "The ladder is 14 feet tall, so be careful."

Pete and I navigated the ladder to the basement floor. There was a small "security" light a long way away from the ladder. The remainder of the basement was pitch black! Fortunately for me, Pete brought along a large flashlight.

As he allowed me to survey the black basement, I found the area to be massive. I asked Pete, "Do you have any idea how big this place is?"

He replied, "Yes, Sir! It has 15,500 square feet plus or minus with 14 foot sidewalls. The concrete walls are 14 inches thick with steel bar reinforcement every four to six inches." (Pete came to the hospital from the military.)

In amazement at the size of this cavern, I responded, "And they call this a CRAWL SPACE!"

Pete replied with a wry smile, "Yes, Sir! That's the government for you."

Afterward, I asked Pete if I could see the blueprints for the addition. He took me to his office and gave me a spare copy. Later, I took out some graph paper to see just what could be put into this "crawl space."

I continued to inquire about a potential project at the Board level at every opportunity. Finally, in the spring of 1984, after almost five years, the Board told me to, "Get on with your project, and quit bothering us."

I was not sure exactly where I should start, but I knew there had to be a better access into the basement besides the steel ladder. Two of my neighbors just happened to be welders. I took one of them, Kendall, to the hospital that first weekend to look at the possibility of building some stairs. After just a few minutes, Kendall knew exactly what to do and how to do it.

I asked how long it would take him to make and to install a stairway.

He asked me to give him a week.

I then asked what it would cost me.

He said we would discuss it when the job was done.

Kendall asked our other welder neighbor, Barry, to give him a hand. The pair had a set of heavy-duty steel, oilfield grade stairs in place in a week. My cost was only the price of the materials.

Barry said, "Anything for the kids."

Afterward, I was able to have people familiar with construction view the potential project on site. One of them was Kenny Eastwick, a carpenter by trade, but someone with connections in the local industry, and someone who truly wanted to lend a helping hand. He also knew the people and skills needed to put a project like this together; I certainly didn't.

Kenny and I started a committee of two to brainstorm what needed to be done. We thought the project should be tax deductible for donations, so we recruited an attorney who was adept at applying for a corporation license and a 401(c) 3 tax-exempt status.

There would be money to manage, so a banker and an accountant were recruited.

An aerobics instructor joined the group because she and her instructors wanted a consistent place to exercise.

Several other "at large" community members joined in to help the cause.

After our first several meetings, I knew I was over my head. I had a grand idea, but no experience. Fortunately, the committee members each had invaluable expertise and/or connections to get this project off the ground. The banker and the accountant searched for places to obtain grant funding. The attorney performed the necessary legal work for incorporation. Kenny contacted electricians, concrete contractors, ventilation companies, and lumber yards for bids. The aerobics team worked on projects to make money. Another member had a plumbing supply business. His job was to obtain bids for the plumbing, septic, and bathrooms.

By late summer, I thought all systems were a go. But then came a fateful meeting for our committee. Unknown to us was a small "health club" south of town in a person's home. When news around town that our project was gaining momentum, the owner had a fit, and she convinced her clients that the hospital was going to run her out of business with its new fitness club. Her clients and their acquaintances in turn became vindictive against our committee members. The banker reported losing major accounts. The accountant lost some significant clients. The attorney was physically threatened. The contractors lost out on bids that they should have won.

I knew none of this was taking place. I guess no one had the nerve to threaten a doctor. Anyway, I felt awful and responsible. I knew these folks were just trying to do something good for the community, and it was costing them dearly. I disbanded the committee, thanked the members, and told them I would proceed by myself. (By the way, the "health club" lady left town soon after our committee disbanded. She just wanted to create a stink before she left town, and she did!)

I moped around for several weeks wondering what I was going to do, if anything! Then one day in the clinic I had the opportunity to talk with Al Kinsky, one of the valley's life-long residents. He noticed that I was not my usual upbeat self and inquired why.

I gave him my sad tale of the faltering project.

He then said to me, "It has always seemed to me that most people won't get behind a project until they can see something happening. Now I have a front-end loader, and I have a dump truck. When can we start digging?"

In a heartbeat I said, "Are you sure? How about this weekend?"

He replied, "We'll be there at 8 o'clock Saturday morning."

At the agreed hour, Al and his wife, Beth, arrived for work. They dug through 12 feet of dirt and made a ramp down to the basement wall. Making a place to walk in the winter was underway.

I arranged for a company with special saws to make a 12-foot wide hole in the 14-inch thick basement wall.

Gene Patterson at Sidney Red-E-Mix removed the massive concrete block with his "big toys."

I figured that all I ever wanted was a place for people to walk in the winter. With a solid floor and a few lights, I would have accomplished my goal. Kay agreed, and we borrowed $40,000 to install a concrete floor and install some lights.

From a distance, Kenny had been keeping an eye on what I had been doing. He knew that the bids for the concrete work had come in well over my budget. Therefore, he had a concrete contractor friend contact me one day about doing the concrete work for less than half the other bids, *if he could work during his spare time*. Kenny then convinced the electricians to "sharpen their pencils" substantially for a good community project. With the money he saved, two energy-efficient air exchangers were purchased and installed.

After the concrete floor was completed, more people became curious and wanted to become involved. Just like Al Kinsky had said, "Most people won't get behind a project until they can see something happening."

Soon the committee was up and running again. The project received some grants after the corporation and its tax exempt status had been approved. One committee member helped arrange for all the plumbing, septic, and bathrooms to do be done at a greatly reduced cost. The aerobics classes had marathon sessions to raise money for a wooden exercise floor. A local engineering firm plotted out a walking track for the grand sum of a large pizza and a pitcher of beer for the crew. Getting volunteer workers together to build the track and the exercise floor proved not to be a problem. Another committee member found a fitness club going out of business in the Midwest and purchased a full line of used Nautilus exercise equipment for about 80 percent off retail- delivered and installed.

The Center opened officially in the spring of 1985 with a community carnival and a 24-hour walk-a-thon. A lot more people than I could have imagined wanted a place to walk in the winter.

Our Community Health and Fitness Center recorded over 50,000 visits the first year with no employees supervising the facility. The community took care of the place like it was their own, and it was.

As the years went by, the Fitness Center added racquetball courts, a reception area, employees, more machines, a manager, and dedicated exercise programs. Elevators were installed so the hospital's physical therapy and cardiac rehab programs could send patients down to the Center routinely. Area schools sent their athletes to train in the off seasons.

The Hospital started using the Fitness Center regularly as a recruiting tool and an employee benefit.

The Community Health and Fitness Center was the only one of its kind in the country! It truly was a successful community project.

And to think, *all I wanted was a place for people to walk in the winter.*

Building a Road

After I arrived home one spring day in 1989, Kay told me that Larry Charles, our good friend and neighbor, had called during the day. Kay related that he and Randy Dane, the high school track coach, were getting a group together to build an all weather track at the high school. Larry had asked Kay to be part of the group since she had expressed an interest in track and field. Kay added that she informed Larry she was not very good at "that sort of thing." Then she told me, "So I volunteered you. The first meeting is next Tuesday."

Larry and I both were runners in high school and college. We both had children who could benefit from an all-weather track facility at the high school. Our current track was in terrible disarray. Our high school had not hosted a track meet for more than 20 years.

Randy Dane, who had been a champion runner in high school, had a dream to have an all-weather track. I knew that an all-weather track had been proposed before on three separate occasions. Each time the projects fizzled for one reason or another. Randy hoped a renewed effort would be successful this time.

I really did not need another project, but I thought it would not hurt for me to hear what the folks wanted to do.

Tuesday came and Larry picked me up on his way to the high school. Mr. Dane met us outside a classroom and thanked us for attending. Larry and I took our seats and waited while a few more interested people arrived.

At the appointed time, Mr. Dane started the meeting by greeting us. Then he said, "We have to find a way to come up with $100,000, that is the cost to build an all-weather track. I hope we can come up with some ideas to the raise the funds."

Almost immediately came a response from a lady sitting by the windows, "We can have bake sales."

I thought this was going to be a "serious" meeting. Almost as quickly I blurted out, "*That's 100,000 cakes!* With a population of 5,000, every person in town would have to eat 20 cakes! I don't think that is a viable choice!"

Randy Dane could see that the tone of the meeting had become subdued almost immediately. He pointed out that WE would just have to come up with a different way to raise the money.

Larry wanted to know where the construction figures came from. In addition, he wanted to know what kind of time and effort was going to be required of the committee members.

Mr. Dane pointed to a pile of papers when he said the figures came from "there." These were a set of some original plans for a track. As Randy mulled through the papers, he started naming the various parts involved in the construction. These included gravel, asphalt, rubberized coating, and so on. He said the "asphalt surface" had to be put down first. This would be covered by an all-weather surface to be put on by an outfit out of Texas.

I asked to look at the list of materials needed. When I was finished, I asked, "Why can't we do this in parts? Let's first build a road for $50,000. Then, we can put on the rubber surface later. If all we get done is the asphalt road, our track would still be much better than it is now."

Randy Dane and the group agreed.

Randy asked how I proposed to get the money for the road.

I responded by saying I did not have a clue. I was a physician for crying out loud. I thought we should ask some people who built roads for some guidance.

There was a general discussion about who built roads in the area. There was the County, the City, Franz Construction, and several places in Williston, North Dakota. Larry noted that the Richland County Commissioners were to meet in several days and suggested that our efforts begin with them.

Mr. Dane chimed in and asked if Larry and I would be willing to visit with the County Commissioners.

We agreed.

Larry and I were given the list of materials needed and the proposed plans for a track. The committee was scheduled to meet again in two weeks to review any progress and consider more funding ideas.

I arrived at the county courthouse about 8 a.m. to visit with the commissioners. Unfortunately, Larry had an unforeseen obligation at work and could not attend. I was alone and felt a bit intimidated. I did not have an appointment. I had no idea what I was going to say, and what if they didn't want to talk to me?

I asked the secretary for an appointment.

She told me to "walk right in."

Upon entering the room, the three commissioners were sitting at a table looking at some documents. One commissioner promptly said, "I hear you guys want to build a track at the high school, and you're looking for handouts. Well, you're wasting your time. We, meaning Richland County, don't have any money."

John Evers, one of the commissioners, promptly said, "Let's at least hear what this young man has to say."

I thanked them for their time. I informed them of Mr. Dane's track group and that we were investigating ways to build an asphalt road. Since the County made roads, our group was looking for ideas that the commissioners may have that could be of assistance.

Appearing curious, Mr. Evers inquired, "What exactly do you want from us if its not money?"

Without thinking, and while looking at the list of materials, I said, "Gravel. We will need gravel to build a road."

The commissioners each sat up showing a little more interest. John said, "Hell, man, we've got gravel. The County owns mountains of gravel. How much do you need?"

I showed the commissioners the list of needed materials. After looking at the documents, the commissioners huddled for a discussion. Mr. Evers said, "I think you can plan on the County supplying your committee with all the gravel it needs."

I expressed my thanks and was about to exit when another commissioner asked, "How are you going to move this stuff?"

I told them that they were my first stop. Actually, I had not thought that far ahead. They asked for me to give them a minute. Once again, the commissioners huddled and talked among themselves for several minutes. After a short deliberation, John Evers said, "The County will dig the gravel for you. We will transport the gravel to the work site and unload it. And, if you do not have a work crew, we will supply you with the County road crew and County surveyor to make sure the thing gets done right. What do you think?"

What I thought was amazement. These men were truly interested in our project. They offered to me much more than I knew to ask for. I could only express my sincere thanks. I told them the track committee would keep them apprised of our progress.

As I left the county courthouse I could only think to myself, "WOW!"

My stop the next morning was at City Hall to talk with the mayor. When I asked to see the mayor, again without an appointment, the secretary informed me that he was out. She then said, "You may see Mr. Murphy. He's been waiting for you."

I thought, "How can that be? Nobody knew I was coming. Or did they?"

Terry Murphy was the Director of Public Works. As I went into his office and sat down, he said, "I hear you want to build a track. I have to tell you the City doesn't have any extra money."

I presented to Mr. Murphy the same information I had given to the County Commissioners no more than a few hours before. He wanted to know what the commissioners had said.

After I apprised him of the County's commitment to our project, Mr. Murphy said, "The city has no extra money. But, we do have loaders and trucks. We have a place on the river that needs some reinforcement fill, so your committee can count on the city to haul away all the concrete from the old track." He added, "We also have an oil warming facility. When it comes time to build the road, we will keep the road oil hot until you need it."

Mr. Murphy asked if we had any road oil yet. When I replied that we did not, he suggested that I have a chat with Jack Morrison, the new manager of the Cenex facility in town, to see if he could possibly help out.

I thanked him and left once again feeling pretty darn good.

I went from the City Hall directly to the Cenex facility. I was told that Mr. Morrison was gone, but he could see me at 7 a.m. the next day.

I made an appointment.

Jack Morrison had been in our town no more than a month or so. He was just getting settled into his office chair when I saw him the next morning. After introducing myself to him, I made a similar presentation. His response was, "Our charitable dollars are spoken for by December of the previous year. I do not believe there are any funds left. How much are you looking for?"

I told him I was not looking for money. I was looking for road oil.

He seemed most intrigued. He said nobody had ever asked him for *road oil.* He wanted to know what type, how much, and other things I did not have a clue about. I told him I was just a doctor, and that I knew absolutely nothing about road building. However, I suggested that he should speak with the County Road Supervisor for specifics.

Mr. Morrison then said, "I have to go to Corporate in Minnesota in a few days. I won't guarantee anything, but I will see what I can do. I will also talk with the road supervisor. Can you meet me in a week?"

I said yes, and we agreed upon a time.

At our agreed upon time, I met with Mr. Morrison over lunch. He reiterated that he had gone to Corporate and presented our project. He then said, "They turned me down. All the money for the year is gone."

I thanked him for trying, and started to discuss something else when he interrupted with, "They told me there was no extra money, but there was road oil!" Mr. Morrison pronounced, "Cenex Land O' Lakes through the Cenex refinery will provide to your committee, at your request, all the road oil needed to complete your project at NO COST to you."

I thought, "Holy Cow! What generosity!"

I gave a heart-felt "Thank-you" to Mr. Morrison.

I felt so good I could not eat. I had to go for a walk.

The next day was Tuesday, and our second track committee meeting. Larry and I met with the others as planned. A lot of excellent suggestions came to surface about fund raising, including bake sales. I then advised the group about the commitments from the County, the City, and the Cenex refinery. The track committee appeared to be well on our way.

Randy Dane then said, "I guess we should ask the School Board if we can do this."

There was a loud moan of disbelief from the group. This was *a major oversight.* He had not asked permission! Following some vigorous discussion, the group decided to go to the next School Board trustees meeting and overwhelm them with our numbers!

The committee members filled the room at the School Board meeting. Since we did not have time to ask to be placed on the regular agenda, Mr. Dane asked for a procedural exception. Mr. Dane persevered through his stuttering and presented our proposal to the School Board. He pointed to our group as his support. He told the Board of our commitments to date and respectfully requested their approval of our project.

After a short discussion, the Board Chairman stated our group could proceed. The Board, however, expected to be kept "in the loop."

I, for one, was feeling pretty good about now.

Mr. Dane asked to be recognized again. He stated that since the school district would be the ultimate beneficiary of an all-weather track, he thought the Board should commit $10,000 toward the project.

There was a prompt, "No!" expressed by multiple Board members.

After a brief pause, the Board secretary spoke. She said, "I'm not sure, but I believe there are extra funds in the heating budget."

The Chairman called a recess to check into her assertions.

After a few minutes, the Board members returned. The Board Chairman exclaimed, "You have your $10,000. Now get out of here."

Over the coming weeks, the group obtained commitments from many other individuals and companies for goods and services, and very little money.

The biggest surprise came from Franz Construction. Don Franz, the owner, bid about $9,000 for paving our highway, a $35,000 value. He charged us just for the materials he would have to buy.

Kay received a call from Randy Dane soon after the paving bids had come in. Randy was ecstatic about our chances to get the job done (finally!). He had been adding up "some numbers" and announced, "We only need $5,000 more, and it's a go!"

After the telephone call, Kay relayed the message to me, and we talked together about the needed funds. She mentioned, "We've got the money."

I reminded Kay that she managed the books.

Within a few minutes, Kay returned a call to Mr. Dane and declared, "You've got the money."

By now, I too was listening on the phone. Mr. Dane said, "We'll let everyone know."

Kay uttered softly, "Just say you had an anonymous donor."

And so it was.

Over the next few months, the old track was torn up by Sidney Red-E-Mix's monster backhoe for FREE. The city crews and our track group removed the debris for FREE. The County Surveyor surveyed the track, and the County road crew under his direction laid down the gravel base for FREE. Cenex supplied the road oil for FREE. Franz Construction finished the highway almost for free. The County commissioners were seen putting up fence for FREE. Shifts of volunteers from the local banks became the cleanup crews for FREE. Local printers and businesses put up more goods and services for FREE.

Our now growing legion of supporters had all sorts of fundraisers to raise the money needed for the rubber surface of an all-weather track.

The entire volunteer project was conceived, developed, and completed in about eight months!

When the track was finally completed, the last fundraiser was a city wide Walk-Run-A-Thon.

As always, any project has naysayers; that seems to be the American way or just human nature. This project was no exception. However, when the first track meet in 20 years was held at the new facility and the town's people saw the 37 school buses of track kids in town, I think *everyone* had to agree this was a good, and a successful, community project.

And we didn't have to sell 100,000 cakes!

LOOKING AHEAD

"When one door of happiness closes, another opens; but often we look so long at the closed door that we do not see the one which has been opened for us."

Helen Keller

"I am still learning."

Michelangelo

"It is a common saying, and in everybody's mouth, that life is but a sojourn."

Plato

The Next Prescription

Many, if not all, physicians get the impression at some point in their careers that they are indispensable. This may be true on rare occasions, but Mother Nature has a way of letting us all know, often without our realizing, that we are really disposable items in the grand scheme of things. The new must replace the aging. The young physicians must replace their elder colleagues. The "experienced" physician in time must realize that it is time to step aside and allow the younger generation to work, to keep informed, to accept their new social responsibilities, and to educate their successors. That is the way things have been in medicine since the time of Hippocrates (460 BC).

Sometime during my practice years I decided that I would like to try teaching. To be sure, I was teaching in some respects all the time. At any point in time, I had students who were nurses, high school students, EMTs, medical students, physician residents in training, and others. However, I felt it was my duty to continue to help educate physicians toward the end of my career just like others had helped to educate me.

My office nurse once asked me what I wanted to do when my kids grew up.

Without hesitation I answered, "To teach."

An old adage in medical training is, "See one, Do one, Teach one." I spent one third of my life dreaming and training to become a physician. The next third was used up utilizing the skills that I had learned over my years practicing medicine. I figured my final days in medicine should be used helping to train others to take care of me when I get old.

THE END ... AND A BEGINNING

The middle-aged woman approached me after the high school graduation ceremony. She had misty eyes and looked at me as if the words would not or could not come. She came close to me and said quietly while sobbing, “You brought my brother back after his heart attack. You helped my husband and me after his accident. You saved my daughter from bleeding to death after her baby was born. Now you help my granddaughter go to college.”

Before she could continue, I interrupted and said, “Thank-you for allowing me the privilege to help.”

She gave me a hug, and all was good!

LaVergne, TN USA
20 April 2010
179967LV00001B/9/P